FAMILY BUSINESS CASE STUDIES ACROSS THE WORLD

FAMILY BUSINESS CASE STUDIES ACROSS THE WORLD

SUCCESSION AND GOVERNANCE IN A DISRUPTIVE ERA

EDITED BY

JEREMY CHENG
*Researcher, Center for Family Business,
The Chinese University of Hong Kong, China*

LUIS DÍAZ-MATAJIRA
*Assistant Professor,
Universidad de los Andes School of Management, Colombia*

NUPUR PAVAN BANG
*Associate Director, Thomas Schmidheiny Centre for Family Enterprise,
Indian School of Business, India*

RODRIGO BASCO
*Professor and Sheikh Saoud bin Khalid bin Khalid Al-Qassimi Chair in Family
Business, American University of Sharjah, UAE*

ANDREA CALABRÒ
*Professor of Family Business and Entrepreneurship,
IPAG Business School, France*

ALBERT E. JAMES
*Associate Professor, Rowe School of Business,
Dalhousie University, Canada*

GEORGES SAMARA
Assistant Professor, University of Sharjah, UAE

Cheltenham, UK • Northampton, MA, USA

Published by
Edward Elgar Publishing Limited
The Lypiatts
15 Lansdown Road
Cheltenham
Glos GL50 2JA
UK

Edward Elgar Publishing, Inc.
William Pratt House
9 Dewey Court
Northampton
Massachusetts 01060
USA

Paperback edition 2022

A catalogue record for this book
is available from the British Library

Library of Congress Control Number: 2022932632

This book is available electronically in the **Elgar**online
Business subject collection
http://dx.doi.org/10.4337/9781800884250

MIX
Paper | Supporting
responsible forestry
FSC www.fsc.org   FSC® C013604

ISBN 978 1 80088 424 3 (cased)
ISBN 978 1 80088 425 0 (eBook)
ISBN 978 1 0353 0908 5 (paperback)
Printed and bound by CPI Group (UK) Ltd, Croydon, CR0 4YY

CONTENTS

FIGURES

TABLES

CONTRIBUTORS

Daniël Agterhuis studied Finance & Control at Windesheim University of Applied Sciences, the Netherlands. He graduated at the Dutch Centre of Expertise in Family Business on the subject of internationalization of the family firm and started working at the centre in August 2019.

Dalal Alrubaishi, PhD, is an Associate Professor in Entrepreneurship and Family Business at the College of Business Administration in Princess Nourah bint Abdulrahman University (PNU), Riyadh, Saudi Arabia. Coming from a family business herself, Dalal's research focuses on the entrepreneurial behaviour of family businesses, succession planning, culture, and family business innovation.

Kevin Au, PhD, is an Associate Professor at The Chinese University of Hong Kong and serves as Director for its Center for Entrepreneurship and Center for Family Business. He tries to inspire founders, corporations, business families, research organizations, and students to gain a spirit of entrepreneurship, and helps as a mentor or an investor when the opportunity calls for it.

Nunzia Auletta holds a PhD in Political Science from Universidad Simón Bolívar, Venezuela, an MBA from IESA Business School, Venezuela, and is a politologist from Universitá di Roma "La Sapienza". She has been Full Professor of Innovation and Entrepreneurship and Development Director at IESA since 2008 and a visiting professor at Latin American and European schools. She is an editor of books and business journals and author of more than 50 articles, book chapters, and cases published in peer-reviewed publications and research networks.

Ameline Bordas is a Senior Research Analyst at Audencia Business School, France. She works on corporate social responsibility (CSR) strategy and management issues. Since 2017, Ameline has worked on projects related to sustainable development strategy, equal pay for women and men, and family entrepreneurship.

Stephen Browne is a Research Assistant for the National Centre for Family Business in Dublin City University. As an early career researcher his research explores the role of tradition and resilient behaviour in multi-generational family firms.

César Cáceres Dagnino is a Professor in Family Business, Director of the Family Business Center, and has been Director of the Business Administration Program at Universidad de Piura, Peru. He is a STEP researcher, advisor of the Fundación Másfamilia, Spain. He co-founded IFFD Peru and holds a Master's in Business Administration from PAD Business School, Peru.

Myriam Cano-Rubio, PhD, is an Assistant Professor of International Management at the University of Jaén. Her research interests are related to the international strategy of family businesses. She has published several papers related to family business, internationalization strategy, familiness, and corporate governance. Previously, she worked as export manager and R&D technician and accountant.

Kelly Xing Chen obtained her PhD degree from The Chinese University of Hong Kong, specializing in strategy and international business. She is an Assistant Professor in the Lee Shau Kee School of Business and Administration at the Hong Kong Metropolitan University.

Hsi-Mei Chung, PhD, is a Professor in the Department of Business Administration, I-Shou University, Taiwan. She received her PhD from the Department of Business Management, National Sun Yat-sen University. Her research interests include strategic management, corporate governance, family business, family business group, and family governance.

Eric Clinton, PhD, is an Associate Professor in Entrepreneurship at Dublin City University and a visiting professor at Babson College, USA. He serves as Director of the DCU National Centre for Family Business, a leading European family business research centre. In 2021/22, he was awarded the FOBI Scholar in Residence Award at Grand Valley State University, USA.

Alexandre Dias da Cunha is an Assistant Professor (Adjunct) at Nova SBE in Lisbon, Portugal, leading the school's Family Business Initiative. Additionally, Alexandre is Senior Advisor and Associate Partner at Cambridge Advisors to Family Enterprise, an international firm serving family enterprises. He is also a board member of different family firms.

Irmak Erdogan received her PhD in Management from Boğaziçi University, Istanbul. Her research is at the intersection of organizational behaviour and strategy, focusing primarily on family businesses. On these topics, she has published articles in journals including *Entrepreneurship Theory & Practice* and *International Journal of Human Resource Management*.

Steve Gaklis is a Research Fellow of the Institute of Family Entrepreneurship at Babson College, USA, and late-stage PhD researcher in Entrepreneurship and Family Business. His current research interests lie at the intersection of family business and entrepreneurship. The goal of his research is to investigate organizational sponsorship in the context of new business incubation and understand how dynastic family firms use mechanisms associated with sponsorship activities to support new business.

Remedios Hernández-Linares, PhD, is an Associate Professor in the Department of Financial Economic and Accounting at Universidad de Extremadura, Spain. Her research interests include business strategy, entrepreneurship, and family business. Her work has appeared in journals such as *Journal of Small Business Management*, *Family Business Review*, *Journal of Knowledge Management*, and *Scientometrics*.

María Jesús Hernández-Ortiz, PhD, is a Professor in Business Administration at the University of Jaén in Spain with four decades of experience in teaching and research. She led the Chair of Family Business at the University of Jaén between 2001 and 2017, and she continued as a member of the research team.

Marshall Jen, MBA, is a Project Director at Center for Family Business, The Chinese University of Hong Kong, and a Lecturer in Family Business and Entrepreneurship. Marshall is also an advisor to families with a focus on family education, family business leadership and polygamous families.

Peter Klein, PhD, is a Professor of Family Business at the HSBA Hamburg School of Business Administration, Germany, and is responsible for IMF Institute for Mittelstand and Family Firms in Hamburg. He has extensive management experiences in family businesses and is a board member of the Nissen Foundation.

Jolanda D.A. Knobel is a Researcher and Lecturer in Family Business at the Dutch Centre of Expertise in Family Businesses at the Windesheim University of Applied Sciences in the Netherlands. Her research focuses on governance in family firms and family firms' financing.

Brittany Kraus is a PhD candidate in English at Dalhousie University, Canada. Her doctoral research focuses on refugee narratives and representations of immigration/exile in contemporary Canadian literature and drama. Brittany has taught multiple English and creative writing classes at Dalhousie and is currently teaching Communications for the Sobey School of Business at Saint Mary's University.

Yi-Chun Lu received her PhD from the Department of Business Management, National Sun Yat-sen University, Taiwan. She is currently a Visiting Postdoctoral Researcher for the project on "Impact of Family Assets on Corporate Structures and Outcomes", University of Copenhagen, Denmark, and is an Adjunct Assistant Professor at National Chung Cheng University, Taiwan. Her research interests include family business, family business group, and corporate governance.

Antonio Martínez Valdez worked as a Research Assistant at the Universidad de Piura's Business Family Centre for over a year along with the centre's director, César Cáceres Dagnino. He is currently studying Business Administration at the Universidad de Piura and works as a Commercial Banking Trainee at Banco Santander.

Patricia Monteferrante holds a PhD in Management and a Master's degree in Management from Tulane University, USA, and a Master's degree in Public Policies from IESA Business School, Venezuela. She is an Economist from Universidad Católica Andrés Bello, Venezuela. She has been Full Professor of Family Businesses and Human Resources Management at IESA Business School since 2005 and is also Coordinator of the Center for Innovation and Entrepreneurship at IESA.

Carmen Pachas Orihuela, MBA, has 20 years' experience in executive and managerial positions in the financial sector in Peru. She has served as Executive Director, teacher, and investigator at PAD Business School and University of Piura in the past 15 years. She is currently investigating the influence of business families in rural areas for her doctoral thesis in humanities.

Francisca Panadés-Zamora is a PhD student at the University of Jaén. Her research interests include aspects related to the commitment and continuity of family businesses. She has been a member of the Family Business Chair at the University of Jaén, Spain, since 2018.

Stefan Prigge, PhD, is a Professor of Finance and Accounting at HSBA Hamburg School of Business Administration, Germany, and a member of the IMF Institute for Mittelstand and Family Firms in Hamburg. His major fields of interest are governance and finance that he applies to family firms and professional sport.

Miruna Radu-Lefebvre, PhD, is Editor-in-chief of *Entrepreneurship & Regional Development* and Professor of Entrepreneurship and Head of the Chair Family Entrepreneurship & Society at Audencia Business School, France. Drawing on social psychology, entrepreneurship, and family business, she investigates entrepreneurial identity, legacy, and succession through a socio-constructive, relational lens.

Kavil Ramachandran, PhD, is a Professor and Executive Director of the Thomas Schmidheiny Centre for Family Enterprise at the Indian School of Business. He has done extensive research on various aspects of family business and has published in *Journal of Business Venturing, Global Strategy Journal* and *Journal of Business Ethics*. His special areas of interest are strategy, governance, and professionalization. He has been a consultant to family businesses in India and outside. He is a frequent speaker on family business and regularly contributes to the media.

Elena Rozhdestvenskaya, Doctor of Sciences in Sociology, is a Professor in the Faculty of Social Sciences and Leading Research Fellow in the International Laboratory for Social Integration Research at HSE University, Russia, and Leading Research Fellow of the Institute of Sociology, Russian Academy of Sciences. Her main interests include elite research, family business research, and qualitative sociology.

Andrea Santiago, DBA, is a Visiting Researcher at the University of St. La Salle in Bacolod City, Philippines. She previously held the Basant and Sarala Birla Professorial Chair in Asian Family Corporations during the time that she was Professor at the Asian Institute of Management (AIM). Prior to joining AIM, she was Professor at De La Salle University, Manila, Philippines, where she founded the Family Business Studies Center. She is well published and has earned accolades for her research endeavours. Among her current activities, she enjoys most writing teaching cases.

Rosemarie Steenbeek is a Researcher of Family Business at the Dutch Centre of Expertise in Family Businesses at the Windesheim University of Applied Sciences in the Netherlands. Her research focuses on family values and its impact on sustainable entrepreneurship with the family firm.

Elizabeth Tetzlaff is a PhD candidate in Management, in Family Business and Entrepreneurship at the Telfer School of Management, University of Ottawa, Canada. She holds a Bachelor of Arts Honours degree in English Literature from the University of King's College, Canada, and a Master of Arts degree in English Literature from Dalhousie University. Elizabeth's research interest centres around transgenerational entrepreneurship and family business. Specifically, her research explores the impact of mental health not only in terms of the functioning of the business family, but also on the health and vitality of the family business.

Manuel Carlos Vallejo-Martos, PhD, is a Professor in the Management Department and has led the Chair of Family Firm of the University of Jaén in Spain since 2018. He earned his PhD in the Culture of Family Firms in 2003 and is Fellow of the Family Firm Institute, USA.

Julian van den Akker studied Finance & Control at Windesheim University of Applied Sciences in the Netherlands. He graduated at the Dutch Centre of Expertise in Family Business on the subject of shared ownership in agricultural family firms, and started working at the centre in September 2019.

Judith van Helvert, PhD, is a Professor of Family Business at the Dutch Centre of Expertise in Family Businesses at the Windesheim University of Applied Sciences in the Netherlands. Her research focuses on entrepreneurial families and how family dynamics impact business activities.

Stefano Wagner is a third-generation member of the Avila Wagner family. He lives and works for the family business in his hometown of Pasto, in the Southern part of Colombia. He holds a BA in Business Administration from Universidad de los Andes, and was an exchange student in Germany. He is currently working in his family business as Manager Advisor.

You-Fong Wu is a postgraduate student at the Institute of Human Resource Management at National Sun Yat-sen University, Taiwan. His research interests include how individuals can achieve high performance at work while maintaining well-being, and in what corporate contexts this can be sustained or encouraged.

Özlem Yildirim-Öktem, PhD, is a Professor of Management and is currently the Director of the School of Applied Disciplines at Boğaziçi University, Istanbul. Her research interests include family businesses, organizational structures, and strategy. She has publications in *British Journal of Management*, *Journal of Business Research*, *Personnel Review*, and *Journal of Sustainable Tourism*.

ABOUT THE EDITORS

Jeremy Cheng is a Researcher at the Center for Family Business at The Chinese University of Hong Kong. He is a member of the Global Survey/Case Committee of the STEP (Successful Transgenerational Entrepreneurship Practices) Project Global Consortium. He serves the Family Firm Institute (FFI) as Founding Chair of its Asian Circle, faculty member of the FFI Global Education Network, and member of the Research Applied Board of *Family Business Review*. He was granted the FFI Fellow status in 2019 and the Barbara Hollander Award in 2021. His research focuses on governance, family office, transgenerational entrepreneurship, and family advisory practices. To inform his research, Jeremy advises a few ethnic Chinese families in Asia, spanning from local millionaires to Forbes billionaires.

Luis Díaz-Matajira is Assistant Professor at the School of Management Universidad de los Andes, Bogotá, Colombia, where he has served as Director of Management Academic Area and the Undergraduate Program. His learning and research interests are in the fields of family business strategy, leadership, and corporate social responsibility. He holds a BA in Economics, an MSc in Development Studies and a PhD in Management. He was a post-doctoral researcher at Audencia Business School, France. He has been part of the STEP (Successful Transgenerational Entrepreneurship Practices) Project Global Consortium since 2006 and now serves on STEP's Latin-American Council and Global Board. He has been part of FERC Academic Board 2018–21. He has published and edited books and book chapters on Colombian family businesses.

Nupur Pavan Bang is Associate Director at the Thomas Schmidheiny Centre for Family Enterprise, Indian School of Business (ISB), India. She specializes in family business and finance and has 19 years' experience as an academic. Nupur is an astute observer of "families" in family businesses and has interacted with several of them to understand their challenges and issues. She is a frequent speaker at several industry forums on issues related to family govern-ance, role of a family office, and the role of women in family businesses. Her current areas of interest and research are performance of family businesses and roles of and challenges faced by women in family firms. She is a Postdoctoral Fellow from ISB, holds a PhD in Finance and is a Fellow of the Association of Certified Chartered Accountants (ACCA) of the UK.

Rodrigo Basco, as part of a fourth-generation family-owned Argentinian firm, has always been interested in the nuances of family businesses. He is currently a Professor at American University of Sharjah (AUS)–United Arab Emirates and holds the Sheikh Saoud bin Khalid bin Khalid Al-Qassimi Chair in Family Business. He is the Board Chairman of the STEP (Successful Transgenerational Entrepreneurship Practices) Project Global Consortium and Associate Editor of *Journal of Family Business Strategy*. He is also Visiting Professor at IMT School for Advanced Studies Lucca (Italy). His research focuses on entrepreneurship, management, and regional development with special interest in family firms, and he has taught economics, management, and family business courses at universities in Spain, Chile, and Germany. His research has been published in international academic journals and he edited several special issues on the topics of "Family Business and Regional Development",

"Entrepreneurial Families in Business Across Generations, Contexts, and Cultures", "Family Business and local development in Ibeoramerica", and "Family Business in the Arab World".

Andrea Calabrò is Director of the IPAG Entrepreneurship and Family Business Center and Professor of Family Business and Entrepreneurship at IPAG Business School, France. He is Global Academic Director of the STEP (Successful Transgenerational Entrepreneurship Practices) Project Global Consortium. He has published journal articles on family firms, internationalization, and corporate governance in leading international journals such as: *Strategic Management Journal, Entrepreneurship Theory & Practice, Family Business Review, Harvard Business Review, Journal of Business Ethics*, and *Journal of Small Business Management*. His latest book, *A Research Agenda for Family Business: A Way Ahead for the Field*, has been published with Edward Elgar Publishing and sets the stage for a shift in the family business debate.

Albert E. James is Associate Professor in the Rowe School of Business at Dalhousie University, Canada. A late bloomer, after 25 years working for family businesses he became an academic in his 50th year. Research and teaching interests are focused on family business topics, entrepreneurship, indigenous entrepreneurship, decolonization in our curriculum, and stewardship theory.

Georges Samara is the winner of the Extraordinary Doctorate Award (2018), the Academy of Management best family business paper award (2019), and the best published paper award by the International Association of Business and Society (2020), in addition to more than ten international best research paper nominations and awards. Georges is currently an Assistant Professor at the University of Sharjah, UAE. He also acts as a family business consultant and has participated in setting up programmes and delivering many executive education courses for family businesses. His research has been published in top-ranked journals such as *Entrepreneurship Theory & Practice, Journal of World Business, Business & Society, Human Resource Management Review, Journal of Family Business Strategy*, among others. He serves as Editor in Chief for *Business Ethics, the Environment and Responsibility* and member of the editorial board of the *Journal of Family Business Strategy*.

FOREWORD

Pramodita Sharma

The case study method of teaching and learning is a frequently used pedagogical tool not only in business education, but also in history, law, medicine, and family studies, among other disciplines. The dilemmas faced in the hybrid organizational form of family enterprises inevitably deal with multidisciplinary issues. Thus, case studies are particularly suitable for family business education at all levels as they can bring the contextual idiosyncrasies as they challenge students to place themselves in the position of a case protagonist.

Typically, there are no right answers as the students challenge each other to view the issue from multiple perspectives of family and non-family members of different generations, genders, and level of engagement with their family enterprise. By applying their critical thinking, and often relying on their experiences and training, they debate the pros and cons of different courses of actions as they work through complex problems faced by leaders of family enterprises. Students learn the important skills of mindful listening and asking important questions. The intellectual energy in a typical case classroom can be infectious drawing out the most reserved or introverted into the discussion. Emotions may run high as some topics discussed cut too close to a student's lived experiences or anxieties.

The power of case method in family business education is evident from the remarkable success of the Global Family Enterprise Case Competition held annually by the Grossman School of Business at the University of Vermont. Student teams and judges descend from around the world to test their prowess at finding solutions to tenacious problems faced by family enterprises today.

As a former Global Academic Director and part of the Successful Transgenerational Entrepreneurship Practices (STEP) Project Global Consortium, I am aware of the contribution of the STEP research community in developing case studies to capture the journeys of family businesses from different parts of the world. This book presents an important collection of 19 cases from 18 countries spanning four continents.

Topics addressed range from strategies family firms have used to persist amidst global lockdowns during a pandemic, as they find ways to keep themselves, their families, and employees safe from the disease, unemployment, and safety. Some draw insights from the behaviours that enabled their legacy businesses to survive historical external shocks like wars, revolutions, financial crisis, and internal turbulence of losing family members to health issues or death.

Each case in the book follows a storytelling narrative and sheds light on a different region and aspect of work–family life. The authors have done a remarkable job of keeping the narrative focused to guide students to explore different pathways and possibilities, before suggesting a course of action. Family business educators and advisors will enjoy the breadth of topical and geographical coverage in this book, and business leaders will be able to learn how other families in similar situations to them have attempted to overcome adversities and create value across generations.

As the editors highlight *this Casebook nurtures the contextual empathy of learners, which is important in educating family business owners, rising-generation members, advisors, and students in general. It also challenges learners to critically evaluate why practices work in some families but not the others.*

–Pramodita Sharma
Professor and the Schlesinger-Grossman Chair of Family Business,
Grossman School of Business, University of Vermont

FOREWORD

Daniel Trimarchi

A common question from business families that I often hear is "What are other families doing? How are they dealing with these issues we are facing?" This carefully curated list of case studies from across the globe helps to answer these questions in a very practical and insightful way, acknowledging also the heterogeneous nature of family firms and avoiding the often-misguided pursuit of "best practice" in the development of potential solutions or frameworks.

Research in the field of family business has continued to flourish in recent times and groups such as the Successful Transgenerational Entrepreneurship Practices (STEP) Project Global Consortium have led the way. As a global community of distinguished researchers and scholars the group continuously combines the rigour of academia with the practical realities of operating a sustainable and successful family business. This Casebook is one more example of these high-quality insights, applying concepts and theories to these practical realities in an informative and educational way.

As Director of the Family Business Global Network at KPMG Private Enterprise, I have had the pleasure of working with the STEP Project Global Consortium in a variety of co-produced pieces of thought leadership and I am privileged to be able to introduce this extensive collection of *Family Business Case Studies Across the World*.

The collection provides an exclusive inside view of the decisions, strategies, and actions that business families across four continents have taken in response to COVID-19. Perhaps more importantly, it is designed to provide practical examples of how different family businesses are preparing for future disruptions that may have a meaningful impact on their succession plans and governance practices.

With succession and governance topics ranging from diversity, next-generation development, leadership, corporate social responsibilities (CSR), managing family conflicts, to business exits, the Casebook is an excellent reference for educators, family business advisors, and a unique resource for family business owners and leaders.

As an advisor to family businesses, I recognize the uniqueness of every family – and the businesses they lead. There is no "one-size-fits all" solution as to how they deal with challenges and look for new opportunities. Using a case approach allows family stories to be told, providing readers with an appreciation for why certain decisions might work in one family business and not for others. Context is important for any insights to be relevant and practical, and the opportunity to "learn from your peers" has unbeatable power and influence. The authors and editors have been able to overlay this context in a very practical manner, making many of the lessons learnt transferable and adaptable for the reader.

As next-generation family members begin to take leadership and senior managerial roles in many family businesses, issues of leadership, succession, and governance are rising in parallel. *Family Business Case Studies Across the World: Succession and Governance in a Disruptive Era* will be a key resource for many family businesses and their advisors in navigating these changes.

–Daniel Trimarchi
Director – Family Business Global Network, KPMG Private Enterprise

ABOUT THE STEP PROJECT GLOBAL CONSORTIUM

The Successful Transgenerational Entrepreneurship Practices (STEP) Project Global Consortium is an independent not-for-profit global research initiative launched in 2005 to explore entrepreneurship practices within family businesses across generations with over 50 academic affiliates and collaborators. The STEP Project is committed to collaboratively research transgenerational entrepreneurship to produce highly relevant, applied research which makes a tangible difference to the business families and their stakeholders around the world. The focus is on promoting *rigorous and relevant research*, *teaching excellence*, and *industry engagement* offering knowledge and practical insights to sustain entrepreneurial families across generations. Over the years the STEP Project community has designed and executed several Global Family Business Surveys collecting responses from over 5,000 family business leaders from around the world. Scholars belonging to the STEP Project disseminate their research outputs, based on the jointly collected qualitative and quantitative data, in leading international peer-reviewed journals. The STEP Project Global Summits with their unique structure offer the ideal context for family business owners and managers, academics, and practitioners around the world to meet in an ideal setting promoting open exchange, learning, and networking. Being multidisciplinary, multicultural, and inclusive are only a few of the qualifying attributes of the STEP Project Global Consortium network. Learn more at: http://thestepproject.org

The STEP Project affiliates (2021) are as follows:

- American University of Sharjah
- Audencia
- Cátedra de Empresa Familiar de la Universitat de València
- Chinese University of Hong Kong
- Dalhousie University
- Dublin City University
- ESPAE Graduate School of Management at ESPOL
- ESSCA School of Management
- Grand Valley State University
- Indian School of Business
- Instituto de Estudios Superiores de Administración
- IPAG Entrepreneurship & Family Business Center
- Saginaw Valley State University
- Siegen University
- Universidad de Jaén
- Universidad de los Andes
- Universidad de Piura

- Universidad Francisco Marroquín
- Universidad ICESI
- University of Extremadura
- University of Salerno
- University of Vermont
- Windesheim University of Applied Sciences
- Witten/Herdecke University
- Zhejiang University

ACKNOWLEDGEMENTS

We would like to express our heartfelt gratitude to all family business leaders and their families who participated in this Casebook of the STEP Project Global Consortium. Their generosity and their wisdom in managing all the ups and downs in their own settings make this Casebook truly unique. We are also grateful for all reviewers who dedicated their time to make suggestions that improved the quality of the narratives in the cases, making sure that the issues and dilemmas raised in the cases are relevant to learners. Our appreciation also goes to the continued support of all STEP Project affiliates and collaborators and our sponsor KPMG Private Enterprise. Finally, this Casebook would not have been possible without the commitment, dedication, and support of Arpita Vyas, Project Manager of the STEP Project Global Consortium.

1

Family firms across the world: succession and governance in a disruptive era

Nupur Pavan Bang, Georges Samara, Rodrigo Basco, Andrea Calabrò, Jeremy Cheng, Luis Díaz-Matajira and Albert E. James

As one of the most enduring forms of organizations, family firms are not new to facing challenges due to external disruptions. The most recent external disruptions, such as Industry 4.0, (de)globalization, the US–China Trade War, and the COVID-19 pandemic, have, however, exposed family firms across the world to new scenarios they need to experience, understand, and adapt to. In addition, family firms are continuously exposed to internal disruptions due to the continuous search for balance between economic and non-economic goals, the entrance of next-generation members within the firm, and perhaps unexpected departures of family members. As disruptions become the "new normal", the key question is: how do family firms across the world respond to these disruptions?

To answer this question, it is important to focus on strategic decision-making and the processes that family leaders formally or informally follow to take certain types of decisions in such challenging times. In a family firm, strategic decision-making is even more complex because of the intermingling of emotions, family relationships, and an ultimate desire to preserve legacy. Many family leaders face dilemmas while deciding upon succession, professionalization, governance, ownership transition, preserving control, and nurturing legacy. Sometimes, family leaders may find themselves overloaded, overwhelmed, and on a lonely journey while tackling all these issues. Learning from the experiences of other family leaders who have already faced similar challenges or who currently are in the same situation offers a unique opportunity to reflect, learn, and react.

Further, we, at the Successful Transgenerational Entrepreneurship Practices (STEP) Project Global Consortium, want to better understand family firm behaviour under disruptions and across different contexts. Therefore, the STEP Project facilitates learning experiences through the continuous and collaborative effort of our affiliates and collaborators, who help families understand the internal and external disruptions, benchmark with families-in-business globally facing similar challenges by sharing common and successful practices. Through this learning journey, those families-in-business prepare for successful generational transition by understanding different generational outlooks on succession and governance while considering the role of cultural and institutional differences.

CASE STUDIES AS A LEARNING TOOL

Learning from our own mistakes is considered as a continuous path for personal and professional growth. However, we learn from our mistakes after having made them. Sometimes, the mistakes can get very costly, especially in a family firm context. In a family firm, it can cost wealth, family and business relationships, livelihoods, reputation, and much more. Therefore, if family firms can learn from the mistakes and good practices adopted by other family firms, they can avoid making some of these mistakes or at least be aware of the existence of potential problems that accumulate as more generations become involved in the business and demographic changes occur.

To facilitate this learning, being committed to knowledge transfer among family firms, the STEP Project has focused, in the last 16 years, on developing case studies as a tool to capture the journeys of family firms across the world. With the intention to bring a few of the dilemmas, challenges, and strategic decisions that were faced by family firms while considering the perspectives of different demographic groups, the STEP Project, in this latest initiative, has put together a collection of case studies compiled into a comprehensive book. This Global Casebook is a unique collection of cases covering family firms in 18 countries spanning four continents, from founder-led small and medium enterprises, to multi-generational family conglomerates and business groups, from agriculture to tourism businesses, and from families in the owner-manager stage to the cousin consortium stage. This Casebook facilitates comparisons of family firm practices around the world. Learners do not need to "shop around" different case publishers for a dedicated collection on succession and governance issues.

Through these case studies, we want to convey that these challenges are not specific to any one firm. They are common. Founders and current family firm leaders are not alone, and while every family firm is different and every problem or dilemma occurs under various circumstances, investigating what others have faced and what they have done may result in critical and strategic thinking about issues that controlling families might encounter in their own firms.

THE RESEARCH PROCESS

By using an applied research approach, we convert the tacit knowledge that family firms have gained into explicit knowledge that can be transmitted across generations and family firms. In this sense, enduring and resilient family firms are those which can learn and assimilate knowledge from their own previous generations and from their external context. Family firm leaders, managers, and advisors can highly benefit from these novel insights.

As the first part of this initiative, the STEP Project launched a survey to understand the impacts of changing demographics on succession, governance, and firm performance in

2018/19. To get deeper insights about the results of the STEP Project 2019 Global Family Business Survey,[1] STEP Project affiliates and collaborators were asked to conduct a case study in their own country in 2019/20.

The cases were based on semi-structured interviews, examining specific sets of phenomena in family firms worldwide. The interview questions were reviewed by leading family firm academics who thought that such questions have not yet been studied, and there needs to be more knowledge and discussion about them. Hence, while our approach to present and analyse the cases was practice-oriented, our methodology, in other words, our quest for knowledge, followed a common protocol, guidelines and a scientific way of processing and codifying what we present and conclude from those cases. The qualitative approach adopted allowed us to get an in-depth context-specific understanding of the businesses and their owning families.

The interview broadly comprised the following questions:

1. *Differences in generational outlook*: How do generational differences affect succession and in turn performance of family firms?
2. *Retirement planning*: How do the age of the current leader and/or age of the successor affect succession and in turn performance of family firms? How does personal retirement planning affect succession and performance?
3. *Gender and societal change*: What is the role of gender, family configuration, and societal changes in influencing succession and in turn performance of family firms?
4. *Unexpected succession:* How does the family firm prepare itself for unexpected illnesses, severe accidents, or sudden death of the family firm leader? How does the preparedness or planning for all these contingencies affect firm performance?

In early 2020, witnessing how the COVID-19 pandemic affected the world, our STEP Project affiliates and collaborators were interested to know how families responded to this crisis. The members approached families-in-business they interviewed in 2019 and asked them an additional set of questions about their management and learnings from the pandemic and how they were preparing for the future. The discussions were around how the pandemic affected their succession planning, governance, and relationship with their employees as well as with the environment in which they operate. This resulted in collecting a unique set of cases showing the pros and cons of their succession plans and governance systems. The collected case studies are also highly diverse in terms of generational involvement, cultural aspects, institutional settings, and industries.

STEP PROJECT CASE STUDIES

To maximize the learning process among our readers, in this Casebook, learners will find business family and family firm stories, unique thoughts and reflections from family firm members, and additional materials to stimulate discussions among students, family firm

---

[1] Retrieved 29 September 2021 from http://thestepproject.org/wp-content/uploads/2020/09/STEP2019GlobalFa mBizSurvey-Report1.pdf

owners, rising-generation members, and advisors. Beyond exploring generational shifts and institutional crises, some of the main features of the case studies in this Casebook are:

- *Heterogeneity and diversity*: Family firms are heterogeneous. Every family firm presents a unique set of features stemming from the family structure and culture to the business structure, industry, and culture combined with the institutional environment in which the family firm is embedded. These cases show the difficulty of decision-making processes across generations and that some succession and governance dilemmas of family firms are similar across cultures, although the solutions to these dilemmas may differ depending on the institutional setting and geographical context. In addition, the Casebook also showcases some unconventional wisdom – such as Jewish wisdom in succession and rising-generation development, and Islamic tradition and Sharia Law on succession.

- *Stories of success and failure*: This Casebook brings together stories of success that took the family firm to greater heights and stories of failure and broken families that fought until the end for a piece of wealth that finally led to the destruction of the entire family firm. Families learn from success and good practices, but we know they benefit more from others' failure experiences – which are rarely disclosed to the public. A few families featured experienced feuds. A few cases also show complex family dynamics because of divorce and multiple marriages. In a way, this pushes families to redefine what they mean by "family" in leadership and wealth succession. We have cases where the family shared how they lived through the bankruptcy order, and where heirs faced unexpected succession given the sudden death or critical illness of the incumbent (which were much more common than expected). How these experiences reshaped the development of the respective successors, families, and businesses are highly interesting. In cultures where talking about death could be a taboo, learning from these unexpected succession cases can advance open dialogue in the family, preventing the odds of deep conflicts.

- *External adversity*: Families are facing an unparalleled rate of change in the internal and external environment. The cases focus on unexpected crises, such as the recent and unexpected emergence of the COVID-19 pandemic, and how they changed and transformed the family firm. The cases address traditional family firm questions such as "how do families own, govern, and manage their firms to succeed, yet some, if not most, fail across generations?" We hope to show how families have adapted their succession and governance practices to manage risks and to respond to adverse external events.

- *Differing perspectives*: Many cases in this Casebook are written from the protagonist's perspective, coupled with potentially different angles of the business or the family. This allows the learners to gradually identify positional differences, viewing the same issue from different positions. It also allows for debate and differing viewpoints to emerge in a discussion. Thus, the cases can be controversial at times, perhaps intentionally so. There may not be a single right answer. Different solutions can be justified through arguments from personal experience, theories, observations, and abstract reasoning.

- *Nurturing contextual empathy*: A typical case provides a bit of the history, background of the dilemma or decision point, trigger point for the issue, and the urgency to solve the dilemma or make a decision. The cases enable the learners to put themselves in the role of the protagonist in the case. The cases attempt to recreate the emotional part of the protagonist that allows the learners to bring contextual empathy and their own experience to decode the emotional complexities of different stakeholders in the case.

- *Written by research-based case writers*: The case studies result from the collective efforts of 45 scholars who are experts in family firms research and practice in their countries and globally. As the case writers are also steeped in research, they can blend the conceptual knowledge gained through an extensive amount of published scholarship with the practical experience.

- *Cross validation of potential learnings*: The cases followed a rigorous peer-review process. We required that the protagonist families were duly informed of the case development and in cases with identifying information a sign-off from the protagonist's family, often represented by the protagonist himself/herself. This ensures that the cases present real learnings as assessed by both scholars and families.

- *Power reading*: For pedagogical reasons, the cases are deliberately kept short. We acknowledge the reduced attention span and the need for compact cases. Hence, we keep the length of the case such that it is short but manages to represent a selected part of the story and truth, focusing on the protagonist's angle of the story.

- *Compelling stories*: The cases cover a real situation or dilemma faced by an individual family member, the family, or the family firm. The compelling storytelling narrative is primarily designed as learning materials to nurture contextual empathy and decision-making capabilities of families facing internal and external disruptions. To retain the discussion of sensitive issues, the identity of the business and the family are masked in a few cases to honour the request for confidentiality by the protagonists.

- *Keeping it real*: Representing the reality may often mean that the cases contain facts and inevitable exogenous circumstances that families-in-business may encounter. Responses to these circumstances are neither standardized nor straightforward; rather, the decisions are sometimes made with irrelevant, random, and unsorted information or missing details to cope with the uncertain environment.

LEARNING NOTES

These cases are accompanied by learning notes that serve different users. They can guide instructors to teach the cases, and they can help practitioners think carefully and strategically about issues that they may encounter in the family firm. The cases are meant to stimulate discussion in a classroom if used to teach a group of graduate or undergraduate students who are directly or indirectly associated with family firms. The cases may also resonate with family firm leaders and managers who face similar circumstances but may manage the situation differently or those who are set to face similar situations. The cases may serve family firm advisors to get different perspectives on challenges faced by the family firms they advise and the potential solutions that might come out. Hence, while learning from our own mistakes can be a great route for growth, learning from the mistakes and the successes of others may be an alternative rewarding strategy that alleviates the negative ramifications of learning from our own mistakes.

HOW IS THIS CASEBOOK ORGANIZED?

This Casebook provides a compelling narrative on how families have navigated the roadblocks of succession and governance in the context of continuous disruptions and across cultures. Chapter 2, "Family Business Case Learning: How to Maximize Learnings from this STEP Project Global Casebook", shares what the case learning approach is about, how to read and analyse a family business case, and encourages the learners to create the best learning journey for themselves. Chapters 3 to 21 are each a different case study. We organize the 19 cases in this Casebook by four key themes described below, to help learners quickly orient themselves to their desired learning goals. Chapter 22 draws lessons learnt and conclusions from all the cases in this Casebook.

Part I, "Conflicts, Sudden Death, and Succession" exposes learners to tensions in the family enterprise system and family feuds which happen for different reasons. The cases examine how succession and potential heirs' expectations can trigger anxiety in the system and how the issues can be escalated by the sudden death of the incumbent or an important family member.

- Chapter 3, "Aborted Succession: We Need Both Succession and Retirement Plans" (France) by Miruna Radu-Lefebvre and Ameline Bordas discusses the importance of initiating appropriate succession and retirement plans and shows how the absence of these measures can inhibit the succession process.
- Chapter 4, "Mending the Fence Before the Family Fell Apart: Succession in the Shampoo Family" (India) by Kavil Ramachandran and Nupur Pavan Bang shows how conflicts and competing points of view in the extended family (between the son and the son-in-law) can cause serious problems at the time of succession.
- Chapter 5, "The Silence Before the Storm: Intragenerational Conflict for Succession" (Turkey) by Özlem Yildirim-Öktem and Irmak Erdogan also emphasizes that family conflicts inside the nuclear family (this time between brothers) can lead to major disputes on who will be the next successor, and this is especially likely in the absence of open communication between the founder and his children.
- Chapter 6, "Lessons Learned from Being NextGen" (Germany) by Peter Klein and Stefan Prigge portrays the problems that may arise at the time of succession when the next generation (third generation in this case) are not interested in joining the business and the alternative routes that the family can take to ensure business continuity.
- Chapter 7, "Florax Group: When Unintended Succession Leads to Unfulfilled Promises" (the Netherlands) by Rosemarie Steenbeek, Judith van Helvert, and Jolanda D.A. Knobel alerts to the problems that may accompany the sudden death of the family firm leader when the next generation is not prepared to collaborate as a team to take on the business reins.
- Chapter 8, "Succession Turnaround at the Avendorp Group: A True Family Tragedy" (the Netherland) by Daniël Agterhuis, Julian van den Akker, and Judith van Helvert

highlights a major turnaround of events, where the sudden death of the wife of one of the owners led the family to deviate from the original succession plan and created an unexpected trauma in the family firm.

Part II, "Governance for Transition Planning" shows how families-in-business can make use of their formal and informal governance systems to manage leadership transition and ongoing internal and external disruptions.

- Chapter 9, "Valuing Our Values: Family Values Driving Business Success" (Ireland) by Eric Clinton and Stephen Browne shows how deeply ingrained family values as informal governance mechanisms can drive the family to continuous success and navigate the uncharted waters, in this case, the COVID-19 pandemic.
- Chapter 10, "Time to Hang up the Boots?" (Spain) by María Jesús Hernández-Ortiz, Francisca Panadés-Zamora, Myriam Cano-Rubio and Manuel Carlos Vallejo-Martos showcases the importance of leadership agility and effective decision-making to navigate through a crisis, COVID-19, but also points at the importance of governance and succession planning for effective leadership transitions.
- Chapter 11, "A Woman at the Helm: Growth and Succession at Inversora Lockey C.A." (Venezuela) by Nunzia Auletta and Patricia Monteferrante discusses the governance and succession challenges when the female CEO was forced to suddenly leave the country to follow her husband's new work endeavour.

Part III, "Unconventional Wisdom in Unusual Times" features cases with idiosyncrasies in family structures (e.g., divorce and multiple marriages), evolutionary patterns such as early succession leading to the quest for early retirements and shifting practices due to disruptions the protagonist family faces.

- Chapter 12, "'Should I Stay or Should I Go?' Filipe de Botton's Dilemma" (Portugal) by Alexandre Dias da Cunha and Remedios Hernández-Linares discusses the dilemmas that Filipe faced at the time of his retirement and what processes he decided to set up to ensure a smooth transition from a family business to an enterprising family, and how he should select the future leader of this enterprising family.
- Chapter 13, "Can I Retire? An Early Successor's Dilemma" (Saudi Arabia) by Dalal Alrubaishi focuses on retirement, with particular consideration to the dilemma that a successor faces when he has dreams and opportunities outside the family firm, but, at the same time, his family firm needs him to stay.
- Chapter 14, "Which Family Prevails During Divorce and Succession? The Wagner Avila Case" (Colombia) by Luis Díaz-Matajira and Stefano Wagner brings together a succession challenge under the circumstances of COVID-19, a divorce, and an unwilling successor.
- Chapter 15, "'Chemical Reaction': Choosing a Successor in a Mosaic Family" (Russia) by Elena Rozhdestvenskaya exhibits the challenges of succession when you have multiple successors from different marriages, leaving the family wondering who they should name as the successor given the complex family dynamics.

- Chapter 16, "Clease Auto: How a Global Pandemic Allowed a Family to Maintain Their Family Business Legacy" (Canada) by Elizabeth Tetzlaff, Britany Kraus, and Albert E. James discusses how the COVID-19 pandemic shapes whether and how the incumbent decides on his succession plans.
- Chapter 17, "The Ricci Durand Family in the COVID-19 Pandemic" (Peru) by Carmen Pachas Orihuela, Antonio Martínez Valdez, and César Cáceres Dagnino exhibits the challenges that COVID-19 brought to the Durand family whose main line of business is in tourism and travel.

Part IV, "Rising-generation Leadership in Ongoing Disruptions" is about future. The cases explore the critical leadership roles of the rising generation in navigating their traditional family firms through crises, transforming the business model, and creating new brands and ventures in the portfolio.

- Chapter 18, "Pineola Nurseries: Family Business Succession under Fire" (United States of America) by Steve Gaklis outlines how COVID-19 and its consequences forced a next-generation member to sacrifice herself, to postpone her entrepreneurial dreams to ensure survival of the family firm amidst its bankruptcy threat.
- Chapter 19, "DC International: Riding out of Disruption as a Third-generation Successor" (Hong Kong, China) by Marshall Jen, Jeremy Cheng, Kevin Au, and Kelly Xing Chen discusses the impact of an ongoing set of disruptions on the third-generation leader's plan for strategic venturing and how the leader can rally the family's support for the new venture.
- Chapter 20, "Am I Ready for This?" (Philippines) by Andrea Santiago exposes the strategic dilemmas that a successor faces when a sudden unexpected succession occurs.
- Chapter 21, "Universal Cement Corporation: Doing 'One Thing at a Time' in the Crisis of Multiple Needs?" (Taiwan) by Yi-Chun Lu, You-Fong Wu, and Hsi-Mei Chung exhibits the difficulties faced by two rising-generation successors when they see the need to transform the business but struggle to balance the resource allocation between the 60-year-old traditional family firm and the ten-year-old rising star, given the complexities with a multi-family firm.

CONCLUSION

This Casebook is the first of its kind to include global family business cases related to the COVID-19 pandemic to our best understanding. The cases examine under-explored yet important questions surrounding governance and succession planning amidst the COVID-19 crisis and amidst unexpected disruptions such as a sudden death of a founder, or a sudden change of plans in controlling owners and their offspring.

From these cases, we see the challenges and opportunities of each family-in-business in various important issues that they encounter. For example, in cases where families faced challenges in their generational transition, because of their failure to grow and identify capable and willing successors or a lack of agreed-upon mechanism in choosing one, they could teach important lessons to other families and prevent them from committing the same mistake. Many cases portray the importance of establishing either formal or informal governance mechanisms to manage the unprecedented and unusual contingencies that family firms may encounter throughout their business lifecycle. The cases also delve into the importance of communication and the dangers associated with the absence of open communication for family firm survival across generations and for family relationships amidst demographic changes. Similarly, learners can learn how experience managing prior crises such as the Asian Financial Crisis or the Global Credit Crunch could enhance resilience and agility in these families, especially if the families could institutionalize the experience in their governance system.

With the rich context provided in each case, learners can appreciate why an individual or a family makes a particular decision and why some decisions might work for some family firms and not for others. Instead of prescribing "best practices" which do not warrant universal applicability given the heterogeneous nature of family firms, a well-crafted case can afford learning of real family firm situations, matching concepts and theories to succession and governance problems, and testing learners' own reaction to the decision dilemma. In other words, this Casebook nurtures the contextual empathy of learners, which is important in educating family firm owners, rising-generation members, advisors, and students in general. It also challenges learners to critically evaluate why practices work in some families but not in others. We encourage you to embark on the learning journey with us using this Casebook.

2
Family business case learning: how to maximize learnings from this STEP Project global casebook

Jeremy Cheng, Andrea Calabrò, Luis Díaz-Matajira, Nupur Pavan Bang, Rodrigo Basco, Albert E. James and Georges Samara

How can we learn from family business cases? Every day we come across stories about very successful family businesses in our community and stories about feuding families that fight until the end for a piece of wealth that destroys the family fold. Business families like to learn from their peers by extracting good practices and avoiding fatal mistakes that others incur. Advisors are often asked to share real cases on how to build a future-proof succession plan or a family governance structure that can secure a harmonious and prosperous future for their client families. Family business scholars want to share intriguing stories in their class, while taking the opportunities to identify "unexplained" phenomena and build better theories to explore them.

At the Successful Transgenerational Entrepreneurship Practices (STEP) Project Global Consortium, we are cognizant of the need for quality stories to serve all these purposes. This STEP Project Global Casebook brings together carefully crafted cases from family businesses of different sizes and generations, and from different countries and industries. What differentiates these cases from other cases is the focus our STEP scholars place on crafting them and the academic rigour to examine the underlying phenomenon in each case. We offer a holistic understanding of what happens in the family and the business, calling into the history and developmental trajectory of the family enterprise system. We stay neutral in the issues identified but give stakeholders their own voice to let readers grow their contextual empathy and multi-perspective view of the issues. The ultimate objective is to inspire critical reflections of one's own position and actions necessary to drive the common good – for the individual, the family, the business, and the community. To achieve all these, each case follows a specific paradigm of development and ways to "code" the underlying messages.

In this chapter, we propose a way of analysing and learning from family business cases, from the perspectives of families, advisors, and scholars. We share how to "fish" knowledge that will maximize learnings from well-crafted cases, what the case learning approach is about and how to read a case in general. Moreover, we discuss how to analyse a family business case, paying specific attention to factors unique to family firms. Finally, we explain how families, advisors, and scholars can best utilize the materials in this Casebook.

THE STEP PROJECT CASE STUDY METHOD

This STEP Project Global Casebook collection covers *real* cases of families-in-business. While fictitious cases may simulate complex situations families may face, these may reduce learners' contextual empathy of the unique background of each family enterprise system. Our contributors carefully crafted challenges and/or dilemmas an individual or a family faced and provided necessary background using a storytelling narrative. All issues described are real: the case families went through relevant decision points, and they struggled. We broadly categorize the decisions into two types. The first type of decisions is encountered by families as they are planning for or undergoing their own generational transition. These decisions are more structured in nature, and stakeholders are oftentimes expected to make such decisions in a specific timeframe. Many families will reach relevant decision points as they set their path for leadership and ownership succession. The second type of decisions is more situation-driven, often less structured in nature, and quick decisions are usually required in a disruptive time: high-stake family conflicts, sudden death of family leaders, or disruptions in the COVID-19 pandemic. Not all families will experience all these decisions in their trajectory, but they train learners to think about the what-if scenarios.

Unlike typical family business cases which are quite lengthy at times, the cases in this collection are much condensed. They provide a succinct history of the family and the business, background of the decision due at hand, trigger of the issue, and the decision needed or issues to be resolved. This tailoring implies that the cases focus more on the perspective of main characters (also known as protagonists or decision-makers) and necessarily represent only part of the complete story. Learners are put in the shoes of the protagonists through the curated reality. Given this, learners are required to make *informed* assumptions based on the limited information they have from the case when they recommend actions or interventions. This mimics the real-life situation where information asymmetry is present amongst different stakeholders in the family enterprise system. Through discussions in the class or amongst the family, learners gradually identify positional differences from different stakeholders, even if they are discussing the same issue. It is important to be aware of multiple meanings, from the protagonist's viewpoint and from others' perspectives. Ultimately, learners explore what to do for the best for the family enterprise system by taking all different perspectives into account.

ACTIVE READING FROM THE PROTAGONIST'S PERSPECTIVE

After understanding the nature of the cases in this collection, it is important to know how to decode the messages embedded in the cases. Active reading is the first step to do so. It is about reading with purposes in mind. Learners should ask what the case is about after all. The questions below are fundamental in all cases:

- Who is the protagonist?
- Who are other major characters?
- Who may be the hidden figures?
- How are all these characters related?
- What are the main issues?
- How does each character perceive the issues?
- Why do these issues exist?
- What are the alternatives to face the issues?

These questions help learners understand and relate information in the case. Very often, learners find themselves reading back and forth to confirm or refuse some of their thoughts. To facilitate this process, a good practice is to skim through the case first, and then go deeper in the subsequent readings. Knowing when to read fast or slowly can help learners grasp the gist of the cases in a shorter period. All cases are structured so that the opening paragraphs often highlight the major dilemma or issue the protagonist must handle in the case. Similarly, the closing paragraphs sharpen all these and usually specify in greater details the issues in place. So, it may be worthwhile spending a bit more time to understand the opening and the closing paragraphs. It is also useful to read slowly when a new character comes into play. Learners often find it useful to draw a genogram if not provided in the case and/or relate each character using the three-circle model (Tagiuri and Davis, 1996).

After reading the opening and closing paragraphs, learners may offer an educated guess on what may cause the issues at hand. This process reinforces active reading and opens learners' assumptions, usually originated from their own experience. Another thinking process learners may apply is to reflect on whether the same or a similar issue had been encountered by themselves, their own families, or their clients' families before. Again, this can help raise the contextual empathy as learners go through the case. Yet, learners should be mindful that they may selectively attend to certain information in the case to reconfirm their own beliefs and biases. A good way to break the assumptions is to challenge oneself with questions: Is this the only way to explain the phenomenon? Will there be other perspectives from different stakeholders? What could the protagonist have done differently?

As learners start reading in greater detail, they seek to build a more holistic view of the issues surrounding the protagonist and the family enterprise system in focus. It is a good practice to start organizing information using basic visual tools such as a genogram (with age, roles, relationships, work, ownership shares, etc.), organizational chart, and timeline with key events in each of the systems. In the reading process, it is useful for learners to put themselves in the role of the protagonist and ask questions such as: Why is this person in this dilemma? What would I do if I were the protagonist? Learners should keep in mind that the protagonist is immersed in the overlapping family, business, and ownership systems, and that the interlocking systems may change as time passes or when some critical events happen.

TRANSFERRING ACTION-DRIVEN LEARNINGS TO LEARNER'S SETTING

The ultimate goal of reading and analysing a case is not only to solve the problems of the case protagonist, but also to transfer such learnings to the learner's own setting. As learners may appreciate, this involves a two-stage process described below.

Stage 1: Solving the dilemma or issues of the protagonist

Identify the problem and analyse the family enterprise system. At this stage, the first task is to identify the family, business, and ownership problems which the protagonist must resolve. A good number of tools are available to help explore and analyse issues and paradoxes in each of these systems, and we highly recommend the article "Analyzing family business cases: Tools and techniques" (Sharma, Blunden, Labaki, Michael-Tsabari, and Algarin, 2013) which covers a solid list of these analytical tools. Next is to evaluate the health of the family enterprise system. Learners should list the strengths, weaknesses, opportunities, and threats (SWOT) of the system while keeping its goals in mind. Learners should remember that there is no single answer in the analysis. It is about educated guess, where arguments are based on evidence from the case, and alternative explanations can be reasonably ruled out. A suitable theory can help frame the analysis. At times, learners may need to combine a few theories to get a better understanding of the issues at hand. Cases in this Casebook are tailored so that learners can bring in different theoretical lenses to understand and perhaps solve the issues. It is key to understand that there is no perfect theory as well. What learners need to do is to train themselves to be a critical user of theories.

Plan and execute a course of action with necessary preparation. Producing a concise and precise analysis of the situation should not be seen as the end of case learning. Learners should be able to come up with a clear course of action that the protagonists and their families can take to navigate through the challenges, given the conditions and restrictions mentioned in the case. In the planning process, learners should ask a few fundamental questions:

- What actions or strategic choices are available to the protagonist?
- Are there any hidden options which may be "unlocked" with external help?
- What will be the result of each action or choice?
- What are the risks behind?

Laying down answers to these questions can generate a plan balancing pros and cons of different actions and choices. But the power of this kind of planning is often discounted when execution is not thoroughly thought through. Learners should devise an execution plan with due consideration of the following questions:

- What power or authority do the protagonists have in their family enterprise system? Can the power or authority be legitimately used to achieve their goals?
- Who should be involved? How can the protagonists get the buy-in from these stakeholders?

- What resources are needed to execute the plan?
- How much time is required to realize the immediate, medium-term, and long-term goals?
- What if the intended outcome does not show up?

Planning is about identifying a new course of action to achieve the intended goals of the protagonists while execution is how the protagonists resource their plan and get people to work. Two elements are important here: (i) control/monitoring, and (ii) trust. Oftentimes, however, families forget an important dimension – preparation – which bridges between planning and execution. No single person – even seasoned professionals – can automatically know all loopholes in the system to be perfect on the control and monitoring role. Similarly, no one will automatically trust people in the team so that decisions can be made in the most effective manner. Preparation is the process for stakeholders to socialize with the goals and learn their way to execute. Learning – in its broad sense – is important here to achieve this planning–preparation–execution linkage.

Check what happens in the Learning Notes. At the end of each case, learners can find *Learning Notes.* These are directed to (i) scholars who plan to adopt the cases in the class, (ii) families who may use the cases to initiate family learning, and (iii) family advisors who may want to share successful or failure stories with their client families. The *Epilogue* in the *Learning Notes* usually describes what happened to the family or family business after the case ended. This provides unique insights into the actual choice of the protagonists and/or the real course of action that the protagonists embarked on, sometimes with brief explanations to why such an option or action was chosen. After reviewing the *Epilogue,* learners should compare their own position with what the protagonists had picked. This is, however, not to locate the "right" solution – which does not exist universally – but to explore what contingencies or factors may drive a different choice or action.

Stage 2: Transferring learnings to the learner's context

This stage builds a solid understanding of issues families-in-business may face. This may grow the intellectual capital in the learner but may have little take-home value if not applied in the learner's context. We recommend that learners assimilate what they learn to their own settings and initiate actions in their own families while recognizing the heterogeneous nature of family businesses.

Assimilate the learning back to the learner's real-life role/position. Every individual, every family, and every family business are different, even though research tends to find generalizable patterns in families or businesses falling under a particular set of criteria. Learners should not aim to transplant all learnings from a case to their own setting. Instead, they should critically reflect on their own situation, and recognize unique factors that may shape different choices and actions. Below are several sources of heterogeneity of family firms.

- Individual differences such as gender, lifecycle, and personality; the positional difference in the family enterprise system can influence the perspective one may take; in addition, being an incumbent and a rising-generation member can depict a very different set of preferences and expectations.

- Family differences such as family structure, relational closeness, temporal orientation, historical impasses, family involvement in the business, and governance mechanisms.
- Business differences such as industry structure, governance mechanisms, group and/or portfolio nature, and experience navigating through prior disruptions.
- Ownership differences such as owners' involvement in the business, ownership concentration, ownership structure (e.g., using a holding company, trust and/or foundation, and family office) and types of non-family owners (dispersed non-family ownership, institutional investors, or government).
- Generational differences such as being in the owner-manager stage, sibling partnership, or cousin consortium.
- Cultural differences such as being placed in a collective or individualistic culture.

Initiate family conversations. Case learning offers a unique opportunity for families to engage in directed conversations, build shared language and cognition, and ultimately enhance family cohesion. A shared conversation planned around a case allows the learner's family to enjoy a meeting around an inspiring story. It also presents a relatively neutral starting point to engage the family in a difficult conversation by sharing what happens in other families, thereby helping members ask more sensitive questions about the situations they are facing.

ADVANCING FAMILY EDUCATION USING THIS CASEBOOK

To maximize the outcomes, learners are encouraged to turn ad hoc family conversations into a series of structured learning opportunities. This is what we call "family education", usually serving the following goals:

- Develop a community of practice embracing the ethos of learning together as a family, which sustains the family's power to adapt to the highly disruptive environment.
- Grow the rising generation as assets, not liabilities.
- Function as a call for serving the family to the rising generation; signal that the family welcomes them and invites them to take leadership roles.
- Nurture the rising generation as responsible shareholders and stewards of the family wealth if they do not want to be directly involved in the daily operations of the family business.
- Psychologically prepare the incumbent generation for "letting go" by showing them that the rising generation speaks their "language" and they can manage potential issues in the business when they occur.
- Prepare for the transition from family business to entrepreneurial family. Unity of a family comes with alignment of vision, missions, and values, and it takes time and effort to educate and socialize family members.

Family education can be institutionalized by building a family learning curriculum. Such a curriculum should be built based on the family's assessment on their current and future talent needs. In some families, a chief learning officer (who can be a family or non-family member) is engaged to conduct the assessment, and plan and execute relevant work. The assessment requires a critical and genuine reflection of the following questions:

- Where is the family now? Can the family agree on where they want to go in the future?
- What are the major talent gaps to build the shared future for the family?
- What are the short-term, medium-term, and long-term learning needs?
- How should the family acquire the necessary knowledge and skills?
- Who will be the learners? Who will teach? Who will be the "dean"?
- When should the learning opportunities be offered in-house? When should the learners go outside of the family to acquire the necessary knowledge and skills?
- How should the family assess whether the learning objectives are achieved?

A few remarks deserve attention here. First, as the learners may appreciate, the curriculum for each family can vary substantially. Interested learners should visit the work of Schuman and Ward (2011) and Peppet (n.d.). In this Casebook, our contribution is to convert the tacit knowledge of families-in-business into explicit knowledge that can be transmitted across families and learners. Table 2.1 maps the education topics suggested by Schuman and Ward (2011) with the cases in this Casebook. It should be noted that even though we map a particular topic to each case, this does not mean that the case only serves one single education topic. Rather, "curriculum designers" or chief learning officers should review the *Learning Notes* to better comprehend how each case can contribute to the desired learning goals. Second, case learning contributes to part of the learning curriculum, and this should be used in conjunction with other valuable learning methods, such as experiential learning. Third, learning is rarely a linear process. From awareness to mastery of a particular practice, families may have to apply the knowledge and skills learnt in structured and unstructured scenarios. Our cases provide such scenarios in the planning–preparation–execution process.

Table 2.1   Family education topics and suggested cases in this Casebook

Education Topic	Case
Development Area 1: Family Skills and Understanding	
Family values and family history	• Chapter 9. Valuing Our Values: Family Values Driving Business Success
Family dynamics and interpersonal skills	• Chapter 3. Aborted Succession: We Need Both Succession and Retirement Plans • Chapter 4. Mending the Fence Before the Family Fell Apart: Succession in the Shampoo Family • Chapter 5. The Silence Before the Storm: Intragenerational Conflict for Succession • Chapter 14. Which Family Prevails During Divorce and Succession? The Wagner Avila Case

Education Topic	Case
Impacts of personal health (sudden death)	• Chapter 7. Florax Group: When Unintended Succession Leads to Unfulfilled Promises • Chapter 8. Succession Turnaround at the Avendorp Group: A True Family Tragedy
Development Area 2: Career Development	
Career planning and coaching	• Chapter 15. "Chemical Reaction": Choosing a Successor in a Mosaic Family
Vocational preferences	• Chapter 18. Pineola Nurseries: Family Business Succession Under Fire
Management development	• Chapter 20. Am I Ready for This?
Development Area 3: Ownership Knowledge	
Business history	• Chapter 17. The Ricci Durand Family in the COVID-19 Pandemic
Financial literacy (financing new ventures)	• Chapter 19. DC International: Riding out of Disruption as a Third-generation Successor
Estate planning	• Chapter 16. Clease Auto: How a Global Pandemic Allowed a Family to Maintain Their Family Business Legacy
Living with wealth	• Chapter 6. Lessons Learned from Being NextGen
Understanding family offices	• Chapter 12. "Should I Stay or Should I Go?": Filipe de Botton's Dilemma
Development Area 4: Preparation for Governance	
Understanding boards and business governance; preparation for board service	• Chapter 13. Can I Retire? An Early Successor's Dilemma
Understanding business strategy and culture	• Chapter 21. Universal Cement Corporation: Doing "One Thing at a Time" in the Crisis of Multiple Needs?
Understanding family constitution, family council, and family governance	• Chapter 10. Time to Hang up the Boots?
Family leadership and facilitation skills	• Chapter 11. A Woman at the Helm: Growth and Succession at Inversora Lockey C.A.

A SPECIAL FOCUS ON ENTREPRENEURIAL LEARNING

Transgenerational value creation is what we focus on when crafting this Casebook. We are cognizant of the challenges families-in-business face in this disruptive era, characterized by ongoing internal and external disruptions. To survive and thrive, families must know how they can create new values by better deploying their resources to explore and exploit opportunities around them. Oftentimes this involves new venture creation by the rising generation while respecting the family tradition. Entrepreneurial learning is the process of acquiring skills and knowledge necessary to initiate, manage, and develop a venture (Cheng, Ho, and Au, 2014). We believe that learners can grow their entrepreneurial learning repertoire by analysing family business cases in this Casebook. Immersing themselves in the "overlapping communities of practice" of the case protagonist, learners can identify the key type of knowledge behind the entrepreneurial legacy in each case and how the overlapping family, business, and ownership systems may create an influence, positive or negative, on the sustainability of this legacy (Hamilton, 2013). While all cases discuss the issues of the rising generation, we highlight the following cases in Part IV of this Casebook, which features rising generation venturing and leadership in the ongoing waves of disruptions.

- Chapter 18. Pineola Nurseries: Family Business Succession under Fire
- Chapter 19. DC International: Riding out of Disruption as a Third-generation Successor
- Chapter 20. Am I Ready for This?
- Chapter 21. Universal Cement Corporation: Doing "One Thing at a Time" in the Crisis of Multiple Needs?

CONCLUDING REFLECTIONS

Active reading of family business cases from the protagonist's perspective creates unique learning opportunities for family business members, advisors, academics, and students. Solving the dilemma or issues of the protagonist is, however, not the only goal of analysing a family business case. Instead, learners should proactively generate and transfer practical insights from the cases to their own settings. Yet, as mentioned, every family is unique in their own way. Learners must keep in mind the different sources of heterogeneity in the protagonist's family enterprise system when they attempt to transfer the learnings to their own families.

To maximize the benefits of this Casebook, we advance the concept of family education, and we encourage the learner's family to adopt some of the cases in constructing their family learning curriculum. The selection of the cases begs the question of what purposes, goals, values, and challenges of the learner's family are, and how the family seeks to prepare the current and rising generations as responsible shareholders and stewards of the family legacy while creating value through transgenerational entrepreneurship. Entrepreneurial learning, we propound, is of particular importance in the disruptive era. To learn or not to learn, this is the question!

We tailor this Casebook not only for families-in-business. Family advisors can follow similar steps to grow their clients as learning families. The Casebook is also a tool to train advisors' critical awareness of the issue of family firm heterogeneity. Advisors are responsible for customizing plans and interventions that fit the idiosyncrasies of their client families. By exposing themselves to different cases, advisors should be in a better position to appreciate that the cookie-cutter approach or the "one-size-fit-all" mentality cannot be a sustainable practice. Advisors should learn to be a critical user of research, including case studies. This Casebook also provides academics with a dedicated collection to bring high-quality discussion in the class. More importantly, it serves Miller and Le Breton-Miller's (2021) call for family business researchers: "Look closely at the subjects first, theorize later" (p. 2); "To garner inspiration, read stories as much as studies" (p. 2); and "Study change, evolution, history" (p. 3). We strongly believe that cases in this collection can inspire our colleagues in our fast-growing field.

We invite all stakeholders in the family business field to read this Casebook as you think you will take the most from it, but more importantly by creating learning opportunities that best fit your role.

REFERENCES

Cheng, C.Y.J., Ho, H.C.F., and Au, K. (2014). Transgenerational entrepreneurship and entrepreneurial learning: A case study of the Associated Engineers, Ltd. in Hong Kong. In P. Sharma and P. Sieger (eds), *Exploring transgenerational entrepreneurship: The role of resources and capabilities* (pp. 62–87). Cheltenham, UK and Northampton, MA, USA: Edward Elgar.

Hamilton, E. (2013). *Entrepreneurship across generations*. Cheltenham, UK and Northampton, MA, USA: Edward Elgar.

Miller, D., and Le Breton-Miller, I. (2021). Brief reflections on family firm research and some suggested paths forward. *Journal of Family Business Strategy, 12*(1), 100410. doi: https://doi.org/10.1016/j.jfbs. 2020.100410

Peppet, S. (n.d.). *Creating a 5- to 10-year, five capitals family learning curriculum*. Retrieved 29 September 2021 from https://scottpeppet.com/articles/for-family-members/creating-a-5-to-10-year-five-capitals -family-learning-curriculum/

Schuman, A.M., and Ward, J.L. (2011). *Family education for business-owning families: Strengthening bonds by learning together*. New York: Palgrave Macmillan.

Sharma, P., Blunden, R., Labaki, R., Michael-Tsabari, N., and Algarin, J.O.R. (2013). Analyzing family business cases: Tools and techniques. *Case Research Journal, 33*(2), 1–20.

Tagiuri, R., and Davis, J. (1996). Bivalent attributes of the family firm. *Family Business Review, 9*(2), 199–208. doi:10.1111/j.1741–6248.1996.00199.x

PART I
CONFLICTS, SUDDEN DEATH AND SUCCESSION

3
Aborted succession: we need both succession and retirement plans

Miruna Radu-Lefebvre[1] and Ameline Bordas

Gustave Etoffe – the founder, CEO, and President of Etoffe Group, a €100 million euro manufacturing company located in Vendée, France – was getting old. At 67, Gustave felt quite clearly that his wife, Andrée Etoffe, together with their two sons, Steven Etoffe, 33, and Stanley Etoffe, 39, were increasingly concerned about when he would decide to pass the baton to his sons. Notably, in France, the usual retirement age was 62. Gustave was in relatively good health but was less likely to work for long hours and over the weekend as he did over the last decades. His company had experienced rapid growth and needed an agile pilot to be able to make quick decisions and exploit the opportunities offered by the market for verandas, swimming pool shelters, terrace shelters, pergolas, mobile homes, and outdoor hotels. However, as Andrée and Gustave's sons confessed, the CEO had neither prepared a formal succession plan nor discussed his retirement projects. His family and employees expressed increasing anxiety about the future of the company and its leadership position in the region. The family dilemma was that *something* had to be done to make Gustave aware that he needed to address these concerns to secure the company's future development, but without giving him the feeling that he had become useless and must be replaced as the head of the company. The question was how to raise discussions and persuade Gustave to set up an effective succession plan without making him feel that retirement was the end of the road or a symbolic death.

THE FAMILY BUSINESS HISTORY

In 1975, Gustave Etoffe and his brother, John Etoffe, joined forces to create a family business. They launched a company named Etoffe Frères in the region of Vendée in the west of France. The company specialized in the manufacture, installation, and marketing of wooden frames, garden shelters, and joinery. They ran the company together from 1975 to 1994. John had an

[1]   Corresponding author.

Certain details in the case have been disguised. The case is developed solely as the basis for class discussion. Cases are not intended to serve as endorsements, sources of primary data, or illustrations of effective or ineffective management.

operational role in the company, whereas Gustave oversaw the company's strategy, marketing, and management. John decided to leave the family business in 1994 because their relationship had deteriorated. "After my brother left, we did not get along any more ... It's like in a marriage, there are divorces sometimes. It was a divorce that went very well," said Gustave.

At the same time, Gustave's spouse, Andrée, had also been involved in the company since 1975, but had no specific functions assigned. She played essential roles in the company's communication and marketing, and she was highly involved in the activity of leisure habitat, an alternative to tents and mobile home. Gustave called her his business "partner", in that she played an informal but important role in the company's strategy and governance over several decades.

After a humble start in 1975, Etoffe Group significantly diversified its activities over the ensuing years, investing in manufactured verandas, swimming pool shelters, terrace shelters, pergolas, mobile homes, and outdoor hotels, and became the French leader in aluminium verandas, while maintaining 100 per cent family ownership. Consequently, the company had experienced significant growth, now employing 688 people with an annual turnover of €100 million.

FAMILY HISTORY AND DYNAMICS

Gustave's father was also an entrepreneur. He owned a house construction company where he worked alone as a carpentry-frame artisan. In 1965, at the age of 13, Gustave joined his father's company as an apprentice in carpentry; this arrangement lasted for more than three years. In 1971, his father asked Gustave to take over the family business, but Gustave refused. He described this decision as follows: "So he wanted me to go back to his business. But I never wanted to go back there ... I wanted to live my life, and I was too young at the time! I was 18 years old." Gustave worked in other companies while studying for his building technician certification before starting up his own company with his brother, John.

Almost two decades after John's departure from the company, Gustave's two sons, Stanley and Steven, also became involved in the family business. Stanley and Steven started working in the company in 2012 and 2015, respectively. Stanley, the older son, was 39, and worked as a Regional Director of the Île-de-France and Northern France area, whereas Steven, the younger son, was 33 and worked as a Director of the Lyon Agency.

The family dynamic was characterized by strong family bonds and love but also by a lack of open communication on succession and retirement issues. Andrée and her sons, as well as internal stakeholders (employees, Director of Human Resources) and external stakeholders (clients, suppliers, financial partners), were anxious due to of the risk of unplanned succession. Family and others estimated the risk of illness or death as significant, given Gustave's advanced age. These worries were enhanced by the shared family awareness that Gustave still played a major role within the company regarding not only strategic aspects, but also his daily involvement with management, innovation projects, customer relations, and external communication. Indeed, Gustave had difficulties positioning himself solely on strategic issues. He continued organizing daily meetings with the company's three main directors: "when you are attached to your job, you continue to develop things. We have ideas, we share them."

However, despite the fear of unexpected succession, neither the parents nor the children have initiated discussions aimed at elaborating succession and retirement plans. In addition, nothing has been done to change the governance mechanisms to enable the two sons to take control of the company (including management and ownership transfer), while still allowing Gustave to "keep an eye" on the strategy. Gustave saw family succession as something "natural" and "normal" and explained that he thought he did not need to explicitly discuss it with other family members. His desire was that his sons felt they should take over the company but without their father explicitly asking them to do so. This was because Gustave felt constrained in the past by his own mother, a woman he described as "authoritarian" and "directive": "We went three years without talking to each other. It still marks the life of a man, even when your mom is not there anymore; it keeps coming up in my memory. I think that strong people should not try to impose themselves on others' decisions. We must leave room for everyone to express their intentions."

Secretly, however, Gustave confessed that he perceived the family life of his two sons as a barrier to succession: "My two sons will come, but this will depend on their wives and their children." His two daughters-in-law had professional careers in sectors of activities far outside the Group's scope (they worked for health and tourism companies). Consequently, his daughters-in-law, whom he called "the outsiders", had difficulties in finding their place in the family. In addition to mentioning that his daughters-in-law had prioritized their professional careers over the family business, Gustave also expressed his irritation regarding their influence over his two sons' succession intentions.

The Communications Director had therefore described succession planning as "a taboo subject" for both the family and employees. Indeed, Gustave said that he wanted "to transmit [to his sons] an entrepreneurial spirit and a certain lifestyle" (freedom, creativity, good living standards). However, his act of avoidance regarding open communication on succession and retirement signalled his fear of giving up his CEO life and his unspoken refusal to lose the power he had over his company.

GUSTAVE'S AMBIVALENCE ABOUT SUCCESSION AND RETIREMENT

Gustave's position was highly ambivalent, which explained the inconsistency between what he said and what he appeared to be doing in relation to succession and retirement. On the one hand, he had confessed his desire to pass on the business to his sons during informal discussions with his employees, HR Director and Communications Director. On the other hand, although he said he had "begged" his sons to join the family business, he had not openly discussed succession and retirement with them. "The family business must stay in the family," asserted Gustave in discussion with his directors. That was why he had invited his sons to join the company: "because it's a family business and it's my will. They joined the company." According to Gustave's estimates, his sons had eight years to show their desire to run the business: "We must let people take their place. It is important. Given the age of the company's directors, we have about eight years in front of us." Interestingly, this period of eight years did not correspond to the age at which Gustave planned to retire, but instead, to the age at which his directors would retire from the company. Indeed, since 1998, several external directors have been hired to head the Group's strategic entities. However, Gustave refused to share ownership with them because he wanted to "preserve the family business' independence and autonomy".

To elicit his sons' interest in taking on an entrepreneurial role in the company, Gustave included them in the launching and development of new projects, although these were "marginal" to the company's activities. He explained this as follows: "It's through small victories that they will be inspired to act as entrepreneurs!" However, Gustave did not want to give them the feeling of being obliged to take over the family business: "We cannot impose this. Many business leaders do this. We impose our decisions, and we are not aware of the damage we do all around." Aware of the freedom and joy of being an entrepreneur, Gustave estimated that anything was possible if his sons wanted to launch new entrepreneurial projects in line with their aspirations: "And if my sons really want to run a business, we can buy other companies. We can have fun. But there has to be a match between a person and a project. My two sons may come to do this, but it will also depend on their wives and children." However, his inability or unwillingness to speak openly about succession and retirement left his sons in doubt regarding their father's real intention to pass the business on to them one day. This state of uncertainty became increasingly tense over the years because of the lack of open communication. Gustave maintained that he was "hurt" by the lack of commitment and involvement of his sons regarding succession, while his sons confessed that they did not know if succession would ever happen.

STANLEY AND STEVEN'S HESITATION

Stanley and Steven were motivated to take over the family business, but they did not want to open a discussion about succession and retirement with their father. From their point of view, their perceived lack of commitment was related to their father's lack of communication regarding the agenda of his future retirement. The feeling of not being on track for succession was also reinforced by the presence of external directors at the head of the Group's strategic entities. Stanley and Steven both expressed the desire to emancipate themselves from their father's power at the head of the company. Before joining Etoffe Group, they both had successful professional careers outside the company, "where they were both very good". They were committed to their independence and wanted to be recognized and accepted by the company's stakeholders as capable of running the company legitimately. This probably explained why they worked in family business centres located far from Vendée. They lived in Paris and Lyon, respectively, and it seemed unlikely that they would settle in Vendée, where the company's headquarters and production sites were located. They wanted to prove themselves and show their father what excellent managers they were.

The lack of open communication and succession planning seemed to undermine the entrepreneurial spirit of Gustave's two sons. Even if Gustave trusted them to launch and manage various development projects for the company, these were "marginal" projects in relation to the Group's main activities. The father's omnipresence in the company was detrimental to his sons' ability to find their place in it. Indeed, having little or no autonomy in making strategic decisions for the company, they may have doubted their ability to step out of their father's shadow.

ANDRÉE AS THE MEDIATOR

Andrée wanted her sons to take over the reins of the family business, but she was also concerned about how this might affect their personal lives and the overall family dynamics. She feared family conflicts; she explained that this was why she and her husband had avoided "the discussion about how succession should take place in the near future". She did not want her sons to take over the business "at any cost", and she prioritized their "well-being". However, in the tense family atmosphere, Andrée decided to play a mediating role in addressing succession planning with both father and sons. She facilitated the exchange of information and preventing the emergence of a family crisis.

Thanks to Andrée's efforts, the succession process was formally initiated. The succession plan was finally announced to the staff by Gustave during the General Assembly of March 2020. However, by the end of 2020, the two sons had not changed their positions within the company, and management succession had not yet been scheduled. Ownership transfer was planned to begin in 2021, but Gustave still had to decide how management and ownership transfer would be distributed between his two sons. Gustave was uncertain about who would lead the company and how to divide the shares between his sons. Despite Gustave's public announcement, uncertainty continued to reign in the company. The risk of aborted succession always seemed high to the two sons, who feared that without a proper retirement plan, their father would never effectively implement succession.

LEARNING NOTES

Case synopsis

Gustave Etoffe – the founder, CEO, and President of Etoffe Group, a €100 million manufacturing company located in Vendée, France – was getting old. At 67, Gustave felt quite clearly that his wife, Andrée, together with their two sons, Steven, 33, and Stanley, 39, were increasingly concerned about when he would decide to pass the baton to his sons. Notably, in France, the usual retirement age was 62. Gustave was in relatively good health but was less likely to work for long hours and over the weekend as he had over the last decades. His company had experienced rapid growth and needed an agile pilot to be able to make quick decisions and exploit the opportunities offered by the market for verandas, swimming pool shelters, terrace shelters, pergolas, mobile homes, and outdoor hotels. However, as Andrée and Gustave's sons confessed, the CEO had neither prepared a formal succession plan nor discussed his retirement projects. His family and employees expressed increasing anxiety about the future of the company and its leadership position in the region. The family dilemma was that *something* had to be done to make Gustave aware that he needed to address these concerns to secure the company's future development, but without giving him the feeling that he had become useless and must be replaced as the head of the company. The question was how to initiate discussions to persuade Gustave to set up an effective succession plan without making him feel that retirement was the end of the road or a symbolic death.

Learning objectives

The case exposes the challenges of intra-family succession in a context marked by a genuine lack of intergenerational communication. We take the founder's perspective to highlight his perception to explore why succession had not yet happened, even though the incumbent generation and the two heirs were expecting it.

The case discussants should be able to establish the following:

- The need for transparent intergenerational communication.
- The need for succession planning.
- The need for a retirement plan.
- The role of family members and employees in pushing for succession planning and decision making.

Discussion questions

1. What are the challenges faced by the Etoffe Group in the context of an ageing incumbent (67 years old)? How does the family business currently address these challenges?
2. What is your assessment of the family dynamics in the Etoffe family?
3. How do family dynamics affect how the management and leadership transition are managed?
4. What should the incumbent and the two potential successors do to better address the challenges of succession?

Epilogue

Gustave publicly announced his willingness to transfer his company to his two sons during a General Assembly with the firm's employees. The two sons' positions within the company have not changed, and leadership succession has not yet been scheduled. As for the transmission of capital, Gustave said it "is planned to start during the next months". Uncertainty still reigned in the company, despite the public announcement of Gustave's intention.

Suggested readings

Aronoff, C., McClure, S., and Ward, J. (2011). *Family business succession: The final test of greatness.* New York: Palgrave Macmillan.

Brun de Pontet, S. (2018). *Transitioning from the top: Personal continuity planning for the retiring family business leader.* New York: Springer.

De Massis, A., Chua, J.H., and Chrisman, J.J. (2008). Factors preventing intra-family succession. *Family Business Review, 21*(2), 183–99. https://doi.org/10.1111/j.1741–6248.2008.00118.x

4

Mending the fence before the family fell apart: succession in the Shampoo family

Kavil Ramachandran and Nupur Pavan Bang[1]

Dr Raveendra Sheth, popularly known just as Doctor, and his son-in-law Vipul Shah, continued talking about the latest movies and music, as Doctor's son Rajesh Sheth, Managing Director (MD) of Herbal Hair (P) Ltd, talked about his plans for the company to the family members gathered around the table. Doctor found these monthly family meetings a waste of time. However, Rajesh had been taking the initiative to organize these meetings for the past five months. Doctor went with the flow but was neither convinced about the need for these meetings nor his son's ability to make any positive changes. Doctor was more aligned to the working style of Vipul. However, Vipul and Rajesh were not aligned, and this was a cause of worry for Doctor.

Doctor understood that growing differences between Vipul and Rajesh in the conduct of the business were taking tolls on family harmony and the smooth functioning of the business. In 2018, Rajesh brought in Nirmal Pandey, a family business consultant, to iron out the differences between Vipul and Rajesh and perpetuate their family and business. However, he did not help matters by trying to professionalize the board of Herbal Hair without consulting with Vipul and Doctor. Doctor wondered if his decisions – or lack of them – brought them to this point. What was it that he could do to ensure that Vipul and Rajesh took the family and the business forward together rather than being at opposite spectrums? Was splitting the business an option?

FROM A HUMBLE START TO THE UNPLANNED IN-LAW ENGAGEMENT

Doctor (70) had two sons, Rajesh (45) and Tejas (35) and a daughter, Sumitra Sheth (39), who married Vipul (45), the son of a close friend (see Figure 4.1 for the genogram). Herbal Hair was set up by Doctor in 1978 to manufacture herbal shampoo. He developed a shampoo based on his father's knowledge of traditional Indian medicine. They experimented with several herbs available in Gujarat, India, and finally came up with a product that later came to be known as "Jeeva", meaning "life". They found it effective not only for washing hair but also for controlling loss of hair, controlling dandruff, and controlling the temperature of the scalp. Doctor built the business up steadily with the help of a few trusted employees. Within a few years, it became a well-known brand in Gujarat and neighbouring areas. Since Doctor and his wife, Anuradha Sheth (65), were busy building the business, they could not devote much time to their children.

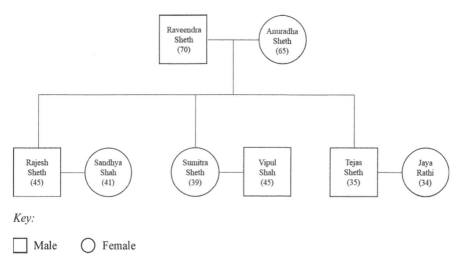

Key:

☐ Male   ○ Female

Note: The number in parentheses indicates the age of the family member.

Figure 4.1   The Sheth family genogram

In 1998, when Rajesh was in the final year of his engineering degree, his father had a mild stroke and was forced to be out of action for nearly a year. Tejas had just joined a junior college in Singapore when this happened. At that time Doctor wanted some reliable help, and his son-in-law, Vipul, was the first name that came to mind. Vipul had completed his Bachelor of Arts and was not sure what to do when Doctor contacted him. There was no plan then for Doctor to make him a partner in the business. But as Doctor reduced his involvement in day-to-day operations and started depending more and more on Vipul, Vipul became an integral part of the business. Rajesh too joined the business after finishing his studies in 2000 and started looking after the marketing and finance functions, while Vipul took care of operations, general administration, and Research and Development (R&D).

Doctor realized that Rajesh resented the fact that he had asked Vipul to join the business. Rajesh felt sidelined. As Vipul often said, "If I had not come running when Doctor needed someone to help him, this company and wealth wouldn't have been created." Rajesh never liked these words. "But what option did I have then?" thought Doctor. "Rajesh was still studying, and Vipul was available, capable and willing to help, when I had a stroke in 1998."

WIDENING FAMILY INVOLVEMENT FROM THE SECOND GENERATION

Rajesh got married to Sandhya Shah after he formally joined the business in 2000. Sandhya was the daughter of a well-known surgeon in the city. She earned a Bachelor of Science in Home Science from a local women's college and was very independent in her views. She resented the fact that Rajesh and she lived with his parents even after marriage. She wanted him to build an independent bungalow like Vipul, who lived in the neighbourhood with Sumitra. Sandhya often told Rajesh, "As the future MD of the group, you also need a bungalow of your own."

Sandhya had found a formal position in the company in 2011 when their existing R&D manager resigned. Rajesh then suggested to his father that Sandhya would fit in that role as she was getting bored at home and had the necessary qualifications. Doctor also thought it was a good idea. She reported to Vipul, who took care of R&D.

After completing an engineering degree in Singapore, Tejas did an MBA in the United Kingdom (UK) and worked in London in the finance department of a fast-moving consumer goods (FMCG) company. In 2012, he returned to India to join the family business since Herbal Hair badly needed someone to take care of human resources (HR). Tejas did not have much of a choice, but to accept what the elders instructed. His wife joined him after winding up her legal practice in London. She was not interested in the business activities of the family.

Despite not being very enthusiastic to take charge of HR, within a short period of time, Tejas streamlined the HR processes such as performance appraisal, recruitment and reward, and competency development. A senior manager mentioned, "Tejas has the best attributes of Rajesh and Vipul. Hope he will build this place." However, Tejas was not too happy with the fact that his talents were not fully utilized. Once he told his father that he contemplated going back to the UK. On a few other occasions, he said that he would start something of his own. However, his father wanted him to continue in Herbal Hair, taking greater interest in the business.

AN UNUSUAL TRIANGLE

Despite sharing the same blood, Doctor often saw less commonalities with his son, Rajesh, especially when compared with Vipul. Vipul and he bonded over their mutual love for music. They enjoyed going together to programmes such as the "garba" (a traditional Gujarati dance form) festival spread over ten days every year. On the contrary, Rajesh was an introvert and disliked noisy festivals. He liked Hindustani classical music and read serious fiction and books on philosophy when time permitted. He did not have many friends.

Doctor often suggested to Rajesh to learn from Vipul. Vipul was an extrovert, made friends easily, networked effortlessly, and sold the brand Jeeva wherever he went. Rajesh and Vipul had very different styles of working. Vipul used to shout at even senior managers, which Doctor believed helped him extract work from the employees. Doctor told Rajesh many times to be very firm with his staff howsoever qualified they were. "Never fully trust anyone. They will come and go, but we are here to stay" was his philosophy.

The entire family met from time to time, particularly on birthdays and festivals. These were occasions for Doctor to catch up with Vipul on gossips on musicians and artists. Rajesh used to spend more time with the children on such days. Once he told Sandhya, "My father never had any time for me when I wanted; in any case, if we start talking about this, the lunch will be spoiled. Why create a scene? Better avoid talking about it!"

INCREASING DISTANCES

In 2012, the company had a turnover of Rs. 900 million (US$12.3 million) and about 500 employees. Doctor, Rajesh, Vipul, and Tejas each had 25 per cent shareholding in the company. Doctor remained the Chairman and MD with his wife, children, and all children-in-law as board members. The board met once a quarter as per statutory requirement. Over the years, these board meetings became somewhat tense and often acrimonious, with Doctor and Rajesh shouting at each other. Vipul never intervened in such situations and once told Sumitra that he was, after all, an outsider, an argument she found difficult to accept. Tejas was present on two such occasions and intervened to calm down the situation. He used to say, "this is a board meeting, and we should behave like professionals here". They had discontinued board meetings since October 2013, when during a board meeting Doctor shouted at Rajesh and challenged him to prove his worth. Rajesh walked out of the meeting room.

In November 2014, Rajesh suggested that they form a separate company called Herbal Marketing Ltd with all eight members of the family as the owners and directors and Doctor as the Chairman. The company was formed, and Rajesh became its MD. Herbal Marketing marketed all Herbal Hair products but had a separate office in the posh Navrangpura area, 3 km away from the Herbal Hair head office, which was in the lesser known Osmanpura area. Sandhya also decided to operate from the new Navrangpura office, although her small team of R&D had their laboratory in Osmanpura. She took special interest in choosing the interiors of the new office. Doctor and Vipul were sceptical of the whole idea of having a separate company and made indirect comments on the new-look approach of Rajesh.

At Herbal Marketing, Rajesh recruited a young HR head from a garment manufacturing and marketing company who took advice from Tejas but reported directly to Rajesh. He also had a senior accountant who looked after the finance function under the General Manager (Finance) of Herbal Hair. During the process of setting the salaries for employees, Rajesh ensured that the Herbal Marketing team did not have much to complain about. There was, however, no simultaneous change in the salary of Herbal Hair staff members, who often mockingly described Herbal Marketing Limited as the "Heavy Money Liability" pocket of Rajesh.

Rajesh had hardly any time to visit the Herbal Hair office after opening Herbal Marketing. Doctor continued to visit his Herbal Hair office at least three times a week. He always had a cup of tea with Vipul if he was around. They had their offices adjacent to each other. Tejas occupied the office vacated by Rajesh. Doctor did not have an office in the Herbal Marketing premises since Rajesh thought that it would be unnecessarily duplicating an office that Doctor would not be using anyway. Several new executives of Herbal Marketing hardly recognized Doctor.

OUTSIDE ADVICE AND CORPORATE RESTRUCTURING

In 2018, owing to the growing differences between Vipul and himself, Rajesh approached a family business consultant, Pandey, and sought his advice on perpetuating the Sheth family and business. Rajesh was very optimistic about Pandey's recommendations while the rest of the family was, in general, ambivalent about the idea. In fact, Doctor said, "We have no problem now; why waste money on a consultant?"

Pandey's recommendations covered several areas. First, based on the "vision exercise" that he conducted, the family identified shared vision and values for themselves. They envisioned to have a unified happy family that practised values such as full transparency, caring, and honesty among themselves. Second, he recommended the merger of Herbal Hair and Herbal Marketing into an integrated unit with Rajesh as the MD and Vipul and Tejas as directors. He had multiple rounds of discussion with all the directors on this matter who all thought that Rajesh, being the eldest son of the Doctor, was the right person to be the next MD of the merged entity. Third, a core committee consisting of all heads of operations from Herbal Hair and Herbal Marketing was formed. The committee met once a week to review and coordinate different activities. Reports of this committee were sent to Rajesh, Vipul, and Tejas regularly. Fourth, Pandey wanted the Herbal Hair board to be revamped with the induction of independent directors.

Rajesh, on redesignating himself as the MD of Herbal Hair, appointed two well-accomplished professionals, with whom he shared a warm relationship, as independent directors at Herbal Hair, although it was a private limited company and was not mandated by law to have independent directors. All female family members from both generations were withdrawn from the board since the focus had shifted to value-added discussion. The board resumed regular meetings.

Doctor and Vipul often came to the board meetings together. Since the meetings were held in the small but posh boardroom of Herbal Marketing, Rajesh used to walk in from his cabin along with the independent directors once he was informed that Doctor and Vipul had reached the boardroom. Doctor continued to be the Chairman but preferred to keep quiet during most parts of the meetings or attended to the phone calls he received. They regularly had detailed presentations by marketing, HR, and finance heads.

INCREASING GAPS IN COMMUNICATION

As part of the restructuring suggested by Pandey, a new marketing head was appointed by Rajesh. The marketing head recommended that there was a need to integrate R&D with marketing and thus the R&D head should report to Rajesh. He also recommended the candidate for the R&D head, who was appointed by Rajesh. Vipul attended the recruitment meeting for the R&D head but did not ask many questions. He told Rajesh that he got information about the interview only the previous afternoon and did not have time to review the CV in detail. Rajesh apologized for the oversight. Doctor did not get involved in the recruitment as he was travelling.

In another incident, Varsha Jain, Chief Purchase Officer (CPO) at Herbal Hair, who reported to Vipul, received a mail from a senior manager in marketing that one lot of the shampoo container caps had a slightly different colour from what was approved as per branding norms. Jain was responsible for sending to the marketing department a sample of each consignment approved by her for purchase. Responsibility to ensure quality of materials remained with the CPO. Jain shot back with a strong message challenging the judgement of the marketing department. She copied the marketing head in the mail. He immediately replied, threatening Jain for using strong words and for questioning the commitment of his team. Jain copied Vipul and Doctor in her strongly worded reply, seeking an apology from him and his team. During lunch, Doctor told Tejas about the email chain and wondered as to what kind of professionals Rajesh had recruited at Herbal Marketing. He added that Vipul was also unhappy with the high-handed approach of the marketing team. Tejas promised Doctor that he would take care of it after verifying the facts.

Tejas sent a crisp but polite note to Jain and the marketing head with copies to Rajesh, Vipul, and Doctor asking them not to have any more emails on that issue. He decided to have a meeting with Jain and her counterpart in marketing to streamline the process involved and prevent recurrence of such instances.

While Tejas was walking into his cabin the next morning, he thought he heard Vipul shouting at someone on the phone. Later that day, he walked into Vipul's cabin and asked him about it. Vipul was upset with the R&D head for not having consulted him while testing some new herbs and perfumes. He was all the more annoyed that he no longer knew what was happening in R&D. Incidentally, he checked with Tejas whether Rajesh was planning to recruit a new General Manager for coordinating all factory operations. He warned Tejas against any such moves. He added that Herbal Hair and Herbal Marketing were still two companies.

While the Doctor remained the Chairman of Herbal Hair and Herbal Marketing, sometimes he learned about the functioning of Herbal Marketing from existing and old employees visiting him and his wife. Doctor told Pandey, the family business consultant, that he came to know about a major change in the packaging of the shampoo from his old secretary who had retired from the company.

THE DILEMMAS IN PERPETUATING THE FAMILY AND THE BUSINESS

Both Rajesh and Vipul worked very hard to make Herbal Hair a Rs. 1.25 billion (about US$17 million) company over the years, but the foundation of success seemed to be shaken. Despite the efforts to mend the fence with the new governance mechanisms and practices, Doctor saw that the growing difference between Vipul and Rajesh was taking tolls on family harmony and the smooth functioning of the business. In one of his reports, Pandey underlined the need for both Rajesh and Vipul to rebuild trust and communication. He noted, "they both should constantly remind themselves that the business is one entity with multiple arms whose synergistic performance is essential for business success."

During one of the interactions, Doctor told Pandey that he was facing a dilemma. Although he had allowed Rajesh and Vipul to take care of the management, he had not decided about the future ownership of the company after him. He was increasingly uncertain about what to do, especially after Tejas joined the company and proved his potential. Also, he did not want to take a decision that would hurt his daughter. Should the siblings (and Vipul) continue the collaboration and divide the shares amongst themselves? Or should they divide the company and be in charge of their own one? Doctor was simply not sure.

LEARNING NOTES

Case synopsis

Herbal Hair (P) Ltd was founded by Dr Raveendra Sheth (Doctor) in 1978 to manufacture herbal shampoo in Gujarat, India. By 2020, his two sons, Rajesh Sheth and Tejas Sheth, and his son-in-law, Vipul Shah, were actively involved in the running of the business. Rajesh and Vipul had very different personalities and leadership styles. Differences between Rajesh and Vipul were growing and threatened the smooth running of the business as well as family harmony. Rajesh brought in a family business consultant, Nirmal Pandey, to help them perpetuate the family and the business but it did not seem to work very well. Doctor also faced challenges of succession going forward. What was it that he could do to ensure that Vipul and Rajesh took the family and the business forward together rather than being at opposite spectrums? Was splitting the business an option?

Learning objectives

The case traces the challenges of succession in a typical small and medium-sized family business. The family brings a rich resource basket in terms of family members readily available to step in when needed. But when there is a lack of understanding, profession-alism, and governance amongst family members, it becomes challenging to take decisions in the best interest of the firm. Added to the challenge in this case was the non-assertive behaviour of the family business leader (Doctor).

The case discussants should be able to establish:

- The need for clear roles and responsibilities.
- The need for a decision-making framework and clear communication between family members.
- Discussions about differences in leadership style of each family member to arrive at possible solutions to the succession challenge at hand.
- The role of the external advisors and independent directors in pushing for governance.

Discussion questions

1. What are the challenges faced by the Shampoo family and how are they being addressed?
2. What is your assessment of the leadership styles of Doctor, Rajesh, Vipul, and Tejas?
3. How is the family managing leadership succession?
4. What should Doctor, Rajesh, Vipul, and Tejas do? Why?

Epilogue

During the middle of 2020, Doctor was forced to split the company into three. The divide was geographical: Rajesh got the market for Northern and Eastern India; Tejas was given Western

India; and Vipul Southern India. The assets and market sizes were approximately equal at the time of division, although Vipul was able to influence his father-in-law to get the prime market of the South.

There had been harmony at home since the division. The entire family met for festivals and special occasions such as birthdays and wedding anniversaries. Vipul had aggressive plans to expand with other products. Rajesh and Tejas had built more steady growth plans. However, in this setting, they would be less able to leverage their complementary strengths and resources in the bigger family.

Suggested reading

Carlock, R.S., and Ward, J.L. (2010). *When family businesses are best: The parallel planning process for family harmony and business success*. Basingstoke: Palgrave Macmillan.

5
The silence before the storm: intragenerational conflict for succession

Özlem Yildirim-Öktem[1] and Irmak Erdogan

After a long discussion with his brother for a new supplier contract, Sinan Sayla was alone in the meeting room, staring out at the view of one of Istanbul's chaotic business centres. He was tired of his brother's insistence on taking part in each decision, regardless of his area of expertise. It had been only a few weeks since the first board meeting of 2019, and Sinan was about to sign a contract with a new supplier for one of their business lines. Purchasing and sales were Sinan's responsibility, and he believed the new contract would not only reduce the company's dependence on a few suppliers but also boost the revenue. His brother Hakan Sayla was not convinced, however.

Sinan was sure that the board would abide by his opinion as usual, but conflicts with Hakan about every single managerial decision often left him frustrated. Although their responsibilities did not overlap, consensus was sometimes needed to proceed in the business, but it always ended up with tension and stress. Sinan recalled a conversation with his mother the other day: "We can't get along, mom. We are fighting all the time," he complained. "But Hakan believes you can work together, like a team," his mother replied. Sinan said, "No mom, that doesn't work. Besides, the company needs a leader. My father thinks so, too. You know it was me whom he prepared for this role."

Sinan reached for his phone to call Ali Karaman, the company's general manager, to ask for intermediation, as always. Staring out the window, he felt miserable, thinking that a major family crisis was inevitable, and it did not seem so far away anymore. Sinan wondered how he could solve this problem. Something had to change in the company.

---

[1]   Corresponding author.

Certain details in the case have been disguised. The case is developed solely as the basis for class discussion. Cases are not intended to serve as endorsements, sources of primary data, or illustrations of effective or ineffective management.

THE SAYLA COMPANY

The Turkish business environment was dominated by small and medium-sized enterprises (SMEs) that were typically owned and managed by families. As Turkey was a late-industrializing economy, most of these family businesses were run by first- or second-generation family members. The top management team generally overlapped with the board of directors, which was dominated by family members. Given Turkey's patrimonial culture, male family members held executive positions, and the eldest normally assumed a paternalistic leadership role. Business relations were trust-based, and social capital was a critical asset in the business environment, which was characterized by considerable political and economic uncertainty. Both the external and internal social capital resided in family members.

The Sayla Company was founded in 1979 by Kemal Sayla to sell automotive spare parts in Istanbul. It started as a small shop with only one full-time employee. The company acquired a building from an American firm where Kemal had previously been employed, and as the company expanded its operations, new warehouses were acquired in Istanbul and other cities in Turkey. As of 2019, the company had 57 employees: 22 warehouse workers, 23 salespeople, and 12 administrative staff. The main office was located in an area that was once considered the outskirts of Istanbul, but in the last decade, it had become one of the city's bustling business centres. The business had grown four times since the involvement of the second generation and had an annual sales revenue of $14 million. The company had three product lines: heavy-duty vehicles, German passenger cars, and Asian passenger cars. The product range had also been expanded with the second generation; the number of brands the company offered had increased from four to 72, and the number of dealerships had increased from two to 40. Relationships with stakeholders had also changed. They had evolved from a trust-based relationship with very few customers to contractual commitments in a wide range of customers, and from an efficiency-based concern with personnel management to a resource perspective that invested in human growth. The company was no longer dependent on a sole supplier; the original sole supplier now provided only 40 per cent of the company's needs, and the remaining 60 per cent was sourced from a number of other companies.

The automotive spare parts market in Turkey was a dynamic and continuously growing market. New product lines were introduced as the range of vehicles expanded in the industry. There were three large companies in the sector, each with revenues over $100 million. The Sayla Company was a medium-sized company in its sector with respect to its revenue, but it had a very high growth rate. Operating with a small number of employees, the company was quite profitable compared to its competitors, most of whom were more revenue focused. Automotive spare parts were a reliable sector, even in times of crisis. Regardless of the macroeconomic environment, the industry maintained its growth pace; in favourable economic conditions, the demand for new cars increased, whereas during periods of economic turbulence, when people could not afford to buy new cars, they repaired their cars, which in turn increased demand. In the Turkish market, overall spending for automobiles was much higher than the European average. The industry was still in its growing phase; the company needed fast decision-making and could not afford weak leadership. The only threat to the future of the business was electric cars, but the Sayla family did not expect that to come for another 20 years.

They perceived hybrid cars as a bigger threat, so over the past five years, they had enlarged their product portfolio accordingly.

The Sayla family owned 100 per cent of the shares of the business – 80 per cent belonged to the founder, Kemal, and the remainder was shared equally by his two sons, Hakan and Sinan. The organizational structure was divisionalized according to business functions: logistics, information technology, finance, sales, purchasing, and human resources. The company's rapid growth had required the establishment of managerial levels. The top management team consisted of two family members and two non-family members, all males. The two sons were managing the logistics, IT, sales, and purchasing departments. The finance manager and the general manager, on the other hand, were not family members. Each had a very high tenure of above 30 years in the company, which was almost a precondition for holding an executive position in a business context that was characterized by trust-based relationships. An "outsider" manager was tried once, but he did not work out. However, he later worked as a consultant for the Sayla Company.

Like other SMEs in Turkey, the board of directors was composed almost exclusively of members of the top management team. There were five board members, including the founder. The board was diverse in terms of age, experience, and skills. The general manager, Ali Karaman, acted as a balancing point: he was a referee when tension between the brothers prevented a decision. He too was actively engaged in the decision-making process, but he would leave the final decision to the family. "In the end, this company is yours, you decide," Karaman usually said to the brothers. Kemal was president of the board, and his only job was to approve decisions. He was actively involved in another family firm he had established abroad, so he did not interfere with even the most strategic decisions of the Sayla Company. Board meetings, held monthly, provided a platform where disagreements emerged and different ideas were discussed.

Contrary to common practice in other SMEs in the same industry, no member of the extended family worked in the Sayla Company. In the early days of the company, a few relatives had worked in various divisions, but this practice was stopped after a short time because there were so many disagreements. No external mechanisms (such as management consultants or a family constitution) were in place for the governance of the company.

The family members of the Sayla Company owned no property; everything belonged to the company, including all its buildings and cars; the residences where the two sons lived and their personal cars were also company owned.

THE SAYLA FAMILY

Kemal Sayla was born in 1952 in the Black Sea Region in Turkey. In 1971, he moved to Istanbul to study business at university and then started working in an American firm after graduation. In terms of formal education and work experience, he had an above-average profile for his generation in the local business context. He eventually left the American firm to establish his own business in the same industry. At the beginning, he sustained his business thanks to good ties with his previous employer. He did not like risk and therefore preferred to operate in business lines where there was almost no competition. He was so involved with his work that his children complained he did not spend enough time with them. "I have three children," he often said, referring to the family business as another child.

Kemal's two sons were both born in Istanbul. Hakan was born in 1979, one year before his younger brother, Sinan. After high school, Hakan did not go to college and instead started working in the family business. He had two children and, like his father, had a desire to pass the family business down to his children. Sinan, on the other hand, went to college and studied economics at one of the prestigious universities in Istanbul. He was married but had no children. Unlike his father, Sinan loved risk and competition.

Mine Sayla, Kemal's wife and the mother of Sinan and Hakan, did not own any shares in the company, nor did she have an official role in business. However, she still played an important role in that both Sinan and Hakan turned to her when they had a conflict. Often she served as an intermediary when the two brothers did not communicate with each other directly.

INVOLVEMENT OF THE SECOND GENERATION

The involvement of second-generation family members was not a surprise, as both brothers had been groomed to take part in the family business. Sinan had wanted to become an architect, but his father manipulated the family's friendship circle to convince him not to work in "somebody else's" firm. After obtaining a bachelor's degree in economics, he had wanted to go abroad to pursue an MBA, but this was impossible because he had to take over the family business. Hakan, on the other hand, was very interested in music and would like to have done something related to music if he had had a chance to pursue his own way. Neither of them was able to avoid the social pressure and soon found themselves competing for leadership in the family business. "The winner is Kemal Sayla," the brothers would joke among themselves.

Neither brother was an extrovert, but Sinan was the one who established relationships with new suppliers and customers and developed better ties with the company employees. He later became responsible for the sales and purchasing departments. IT, on the other hand, was Hakan's domain, an area that seemed to become more important in the long run because the nature of industry was evolving, but it was an office job that required little face-to-face interaction. This functional division of responsibilities between the brothers was their own choice. Differences in their experience, character, and educational backgrounds seemed to account for this choice. Despite their differences, the two brothers trusted each other completely. Once Sinan had to give power of attorney to Hakan for a business matter. This legal document would allow Hakan to make decisions on behalf of Sinan. As they read the document to be signed, Sinan said, "Hakan, I don't think you should sign this. You are granting me all the authorization with this document," to which Hakan replied, "No problem," and then signed without hesitation.

SUCCESSION AND THE POWER STRUGGLE

In 2015, Kemal handed over control of the business to his children. He no longer had an executive role in the company, and he went to the office only a few days a week. Unless key performance indicators signalled a problem, he did not interfere much, even with big investment decisions. When he was asked for his opinion on an investment, he often responded, "If you believe it's a good investment, then do it." This was quite an extraordinary attitude compared to that of the founders of competitor firms. Kemal had the final say on family matters, but not on the business, which had reached an incomparable size during his time in terms of annual revenue, customer range, and product lines. "Thanks to me, the company has grown four times. That wouldn't have happened if I hadn't left," Kemal often said.

The power struggle between the two brothers became more evident after their father handed over the reins and became more involved in their business abroad. Although they were trying hard not to interfere with each other's part in order to avoid conflict, their areas of responsibility were interrelated, so interaction between the brothers was inevitable when a final decision had to be made. This created tension between the brothers, both of whom were quick-tempered, a characteristic often attributed to people originating from the Black Sea Region.

The two brothers had different opinions about their father's continued role in the business. Sinan thought their father's experience, intuition, and judgement helped them a lot. Hakan, on the other hand, believed he and Sinan should lead the company together as a team. "We can move so much faster without our father," he said.

The two brothers also had different visions for the future of the business. Sinan aspired to grow the business and sell it at the right time. Neither his father nor Hakan knew about this idea, however. "This is not only a business, it's also something I can pass on to my children," Hakan once said to Sinan. Their father, on the other hand, was strongly against the idea of selling the business: "I would rather go bankrupt than sell the company," he often said.

Within the company, there was a general acceptance that power would be transferred to the second generation, but there was not yet any consensus within the family about who would be the future leader of the family business. Like the majority of medium-sized family businesses in Turkey, the Sayla Company had no formal mechanism for succession – no family constitution, no written succession plan, no external advisors. Kemal knew that once he retired completely, one of his sons should take the lead, but this topic was never discussed openly within the family. "I have full confidence that Sinan will take care of the business very well," he once said to his wife. But he also wished to include Hakan in the business. For him, it was important to continue the business to the third generation, and Hakan was the one with children. "How I wish to see the day when my grandchildren are running the business," Kemal often said at family gatherings.

The leadership role was informally assigned to Sinan from the beginning, despite the common practice of the older brother taking the lead. In a typical family business in the industry, the founder was president of the board of directors, and the eldest son was CEO. In the Sayla Company, however, Sinan had been prepared for the leadership role. When he was 18 years old, for example, he started travelling extensively throughout Turkey to visit their corporate customers and learn about the products. Hakan, on the other hand, spent most of his time in the office. As a result, it was Sinan who acquired knowledge and experience in the business. Sinan was consulted on final business decisions because the core functional departments (sales and purchasing) were under his responsibility. This was a problem since primogeniture, as a social norm, was in the background. Despite his limited knowledge about the business, Hakan always wanted be part of the managerial decision-making process, which often left Sinan stressed and frustrated.

A SHORT BREAK-UP

Due to internal conflicts and stress, Sinan once left the company for seven months. "Forgive me, but I cannot continue," Sinan said to his father.

In such hard times, the family consulted a member of the extended family, a retired high-ranking army officer whose administrative experience and skills were admired by the family. A gathering of the nuclear family and this elderly relative functioned as an informal family council. After Sinan announced he wanted to leave, the family council convened. "Hakan doesn't meet with customers, he doesn't know the products, he doesn't know the market. He never leaves the office; he is not prepared for this role. But he is in the middle of every single decision. Either he goes, or I will leave," Sinan explained to the family council. His mother was worried: "But what can your brother do if he leaves the company?" she asked. Sinan replied, "Mom, you are too emotional when it comes to Hakan. He can keep his shares or sell them to us, I don't mind." In the end, the family council decided it was best for Sinan to leave because he was under a lot of stress, and his health was more important.

During Sinan's absence, the revenues of the Sayla Company dropped by 30 per cent and the company's debt increased significantly, so they had to call him back. Kemal had to ask him several times. Hakan sent an indirect message to his brother via his mother: "OK", he told her, "I won't interfere anymore." Sinan returned, and as soon as he returned, the company got back on track.

SINAN'S DILEMMA

After yet another heated argument with Hakan, Sinan was waiting for the board members to arrive for the board meeting. He was questioning his own motivation for working in the family business. He would not even have started working in the family business if it had not been for his father's pressure. When he was younger, his father used to say he was working for his children. Now, Sinan would tell his father, "You used to work for us, and now I am working for you." It seemed like a vicious cycle. Sometimes he could not stop thinking that he was facing all this stress because of a major shareholder who did not even come to work anymore. Unlike his older brother, he had no children to whom he could pass on the business. At times he was so frustrated with his brother that he considered leaving the company again. But he had done that once, and the company had not been able to function without him. He owned a stake in the company which he did not want to put at risk. However, it was clear to him that he could no longer tolerate working with his brother in this way. He had a feeling that there was an unspoken consensus about his future leadership in the company and that his father was always on his side. But what if something happened to his father? His brother and mother would hold the majority of the shares, which might imply the continuation of this dual leadership.

Sinan wondered if he should just keep the things as they were and avoid confrontation so as not to provoke a big family crisis. Should he avoid confrontation and continue to manage conflicts with the help of intermediators? Or should he take a step towards making changes? If so, what kind of change should he suggest to the board of directors? Sinan was not sure which decision would be the best for the interests of both the business and the family.

LEARNING NOTES

Case synopsis

The Sayla Company was founded by Kemal Sayla to sell automotive spare parts in Istanbul, Turkey, in 1979. The family owned 100 per cent of the shares of the business, 80 per cent of which belonged to the founder. The remaining 20 per cent was shared equally by his two sons, Hakan and Sinan. Kemal did not interfere much with the business anymore, and his two sons had a clear division of responsibilities: The elder brother, Hakan, managed logistics and IT, whereas the younger brother, Sinan, was responsible for sales and purchasing. Although Sinan was managing the core areas of the business and had more knowledge about the various product lines, Hakan wanted to be part of the decision-making process, and there was always a tension between the two brothers. Despite the traditional norms of primogeniture, Sinan was perceived by various stakeholders as the potential leader of the Sayla Company. However, the family had not reached any consensus on who the future business leader would be. The family members had avoided open communication about the succession issue for a long time. A sudden dispute among the family members was very likely. Sinan wondered what he could do to prevent a family feud.

Learning objectives

The case provides an example of family conflict in the second generation where two brothers each expect to assume leadership in the family business. The conflict becomes more challenging when one of the potential successors intends to break the primogeniture tradition. The case shows how intragenerational conflict between two successors can have a significant impact on the functioning of the business, especially when open communication among the family members is lacking.

The case also highlights the buffering role of non-family managers in managing conflict within the family. Without open and timely communication between family members or a succession plan, resentment and separation within the family are inevitable.

The case discussants should be able to establish:

- A need for timely and open communication within the family to resolve conflicts.
- The necessity of formal mechanisms for succession such as a succession plan and external advisors.
- The role of the first-generation family members and non-family executives in managing the succession conflict.
- The consequences of putting pressure on disinterested members of the next generation to join the family business.

Discussion questions
1. What are the main challenges faced by the Sayla family? 2. What are the main reasons for conflict between the two brothers? 3. How would you describe the communication process among the main actors? 4. Would you consider appointing a non-family executive as an immediate solution to an enduring problem? Or would it be better to seek a long-term solution in the absence of a succession plan and the confusion that results from it? 5. On which criteria would you base your choice for the successor to Kemal Sayla as the company's leader? Why? 6. What should Sinan do? Why?

Epilogue

As the tension between the brothers increased, Sinan complained about this during a board meeting at the beginning of 2020 and suggested dividing the company into two. At that point, the father had to intervene (in favour of Sinan), and the board of directors decided that Hakan would no longer be a board member. Hakan got very upset and resigned from all his executive positions (in the IT and logistics departments), without any concern about leaving his duties to a successor. The company decided to outsource the IT department and collaborate with an external consultant for the logistics division.

Hakan still owned 10 per cent of the company and his income had not changed. He had not started a new business and for now, he was spending time with his family. Sinan still had concerns what would happen when their father passed away; Hakan might return to the family business with their mother's support. Kemal continued not to interfere with the business, leaving the decision-making to the remaining three members of the board, which was now able to proceed quickly. The company grew by almost 100 per cent in 2020.

At the beginning of the pandemic period, the Sayla family lost many of its relatives, including the elderly member in the family council and later Kemal's brother. During the pandemic period, Sinan displayed a paternalistic leadership style, giving priority to the health and safety of the employees. He managed to convince the board to shut down for a period, to provide private health insurance for all employees, and to make incentive payments for motivation. Competitors in the industry, on the other hand, were very greedy during the pandemic period; just to meet the rising demand, they continued to operate as if nothing had changed and failed to take adequate precautions. As a result, numerous owners and sales personnel in the industry passed away. The Sayla Company managed to sustain its workforce as well as the top management team, and it has responded better to the increasing demand that shifted from competitor firms. This was attributable to the human resource perspective of Sinan and to the experience of Kemal, who predicted a rise in demand at the very beginning of the pandemic and suggested increasing inventory, as he had always done in times of crisis.

The company almost tripled its revenues during the pandemic. With demand increasing at an unprecedented pace, Sinan increased his focus on the business. He postponed his plans for early retirement and for the establishment of a new business in organic agriculture. However, he still planned to sell the family business if he found a good opportunity. This might be the right time, given the industry's growth during the period and the fact that foreign companies planned to enter the market through acquisition. The Sayla Company was still not big enough to face competition with big foreign firms.

Suggested readings

Calabro, A., Minichilli, A., Amore, M.D., and Brogi, M. (2018). The courage to choose! Primogeniture and leadership succession in family firms. *Strategic Management Journal, 39*(7), 2014–35. https://doi.org/10.1002/smj.2760

Caputo, A., Marzi, G., Pellegrini, M.M., and Rialti, R. (2018). Conflict management in family businesses. *International Journal of Conflict Management, 29*(4), 519–42. https://dx.doi.org/10.1108/IJCMA-02–2018–0027

Cosier, R.A., and Harvey, M. (1998). The hidden strengths in family business: Functional conflict. *Family Business Review, 11*(1), 75–9. doi:10.1111/j.1741–6248.1998.00075.x

6
Lessons learned from being NextGen

Peter Klein[1] and Stefan Prigge

On a warm summer evening in 1990, Marianne Graf and Johannes Stein, both members of the third generation of the Schmidt family, withdrew with their tall glasses of red wine to a quiet secluded corner in the garden of a restaurant where they were celebrating the baptism of Julia Graf, Marianne's first child. The happy occasion was attended by many guests, including stakeholders of MaxTec AG, their family business. It was a nice reunion, but they missed their eldest brother, Paul Stein, Jr, who did not come. As the two siblings sat down after the long, exhausting day, the absence of Paul, Jr and their father, who had passed away five years back, made them melancholic.

Paul, Jr, the most eligible to run the business, had disassociated himself completely from the business and the family following an incident that did not go down well with him and he felt hurt. Marianne was held back due to the patriarchal traditions and her own lack of conviction about her leadership skills. Johannes was pursuing other interests. The siblings reflected upon what the future held for the family and the business.

The christening of the first child in the fourth generation forced Marianne and Johannes to think of ways in which they could provide a better environment for their children to grow up in. They did not want their children to inherit the burdens and chaos of the family business that they felt. They also contemplated the implications of getting a non-family CEO to run the company. Would that be the most optimal solution?

---

[1]   Corresponding author.

Certain details in the case have been disguised. The case is developed solely as the basis for class discussion. Cases are not intended to serve as endorsements, sources of primary data, or illustrations of effective or ineffective management.

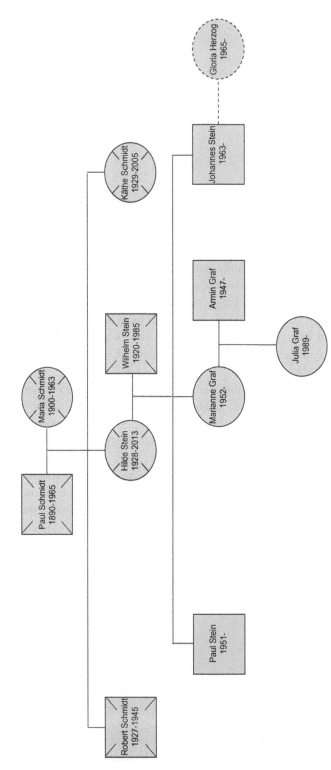

Key: A rectangle represents a male and a circle a female. The lines indicate relations, that is, spouses and children. The dashed line represents an engagement.

Figure 6.1 Genogram of the Schmidt family

MAXTEC'S JOURNEY

MaxTec was founded in 1950 in Wittenburg, North Rhine-Westphalia, Germany, by Paul Schmidt. Paul put the mechanical engineering company on a well-defined growth path. He had three children. His son, Robert Schmidt, was killed in World War II. One of his daughters was not interested in the company and had been paid off early. Hilde Stein, his other daughter, was the only one interested in the family business. Hilde's husband, Wilhelm Stein, soon joined Paul in the running of MaxTec and became the CEO after Paul's death in 1965 (see Figure 6.1 for the genogram). Hilde grew into the role of the matriarch and was closely involved in the management of the company during Wilhelm's lifetime as a majority shareholder.

Wilhelm passed away unexpectedly in 1985. After being at the helm of MaxTec AG for more than 25 years, during which time, together with his wife Hilde, he determined the fate of the company, his death left a deep void. Upholding the tradition that her father Paul had established, namely that MaxTec AG was always managed by a family member, Hilde stepped in as the CEO. Hilde was also the majority shareholder of the company with almost 100 per cent shares. Marianne and Johannes held a small number of shares. There were no non-family shareholders.

By 1990, MaxTec's annual sales amounted to about €200 million. It employed close to 2,000 people, mainly in facilities located close to Wittenburg. It was also strongly integrated into the local networks in the state of North Rhine-Westphalia, the industrial heart of Germany. From its beginning, the company had specialized in mechanical technology, developing engines for all kinds of machines. Always an innovative leader in its niche, MaxTec felt the pressure to remain innovative to maintain its market share, particularly as the cards were reshuffled in the global economy after the fall of the Iron Curtain. It had begun to take energetic steps towards foreign markets.

PAUL, JR WALKING OUT

Paul, Jr, the first child and eldest son of Hilde and Wilhelm, bore the name of the founding father. Marianne was born relatively soon after Paul, Jr, and Johannes was the latecomer by a margin of more than ten years. MaxTec was an integral part of the growing up years of all children. Business was often discussed at the dining table. Paul, Jr grew up with the impression that he was the natural successor to his father. He was even sent to Italy in a fairly responsible position at a very young age to build up a new branch there. The Italian branch turned out to be a success story. Hilde and Wilhelm, however, came to the conclusion that their Italian success materialized not because of Paul, Jr but in spite of him, and that he didn't have what it took to be a CEO. So, they did not want to entrust him with the company.

Marianne recalled, "I remember how proud he [Paul, Jr] was when he returned from Italy to the headquarters. It saddened and enraged him when our parents did not install him as crown prince in the company. Instead, they gave him a position as head of department, which many people would have been happy about. But for Paul, Jr, it was like a resounding slap on the face, especially since he was clear that everyone else would easily recognize the vote of no confidence that this new position came with."

That incident changed everything for the family. Paul, Jr was quick to react. He turned away completely from everything; from the family with whom he had had no contact since then, and from the family firm, where he received a prepayment for the inheritance. The separation was complete.

"It's really too bad Paul, Jr completely withdrew and didn't even come to the baptism of the first child in the next generation. I really didn't expect that. We were always so close," Marianne said sadly.

"I think we all underestimated how much the whole thing really hurt him. Father, mother, all of us, certainly didn't see it coming," said Johannes.

JOHANNES, THE YOUNGEST BROTHER, RELEASED FROM FAMILY BUSINESS DUTIES

One year after Paul, Jr's departure, their father Wilhelm died rather suddenly. While Hilde stepped in as the CEO, she never wanted that position. She wanted to keep the family and the business together, but not as CEO. "As Paul, Jr was no longer available, spotlight was on you, Johannes. Mother hoped that you would follow in her footsteps one day. She told me several times about how happy she was that you were interested in finance. She must have had it crystal-clear that the leadership of MaxTec was assured," recalled Marianne.

However, that was not in line with Johannes's plans for his future. Indeed, he had developed a strong interest in finance and considered it to be the preferred area of his professional life. However, Johannes did not see his future in managing the family firm's finances and being its CEO. In addition to his interest in finance, a strong desire had emerged in him to get something of his own off the ground. Enjoying individual freedom was central to his vision for his own future. As Johannes explained in his own words to his sister: "The three of us, Paul, Jr, you and I had been trained from an early age to work for the company. When I started at our company, I quickly realized that this wasn't what I really wanted to do. Sure, I'm incredibly attached to our company. But I also wanted to do my own thing."

Hilde, the matriarch, underestimated this strong urge in Johannes in the beginning. Fortunately, as latecomer, being 12 years younger than Paul, Jr, Johannes always had more leeway than Paul, Jr and Marianne. It took some time, but ultimately Hilde was very understanding. She realized that Johannes would be unhappy in the company and, therefore, she "released" him. Johannes had his own little investment company that was doing well, which had not gone unnoticed by his mother.

For Marianne and Johannes, it was surprising that their mother had let Johannes pursue his own passion even though she needed him at the family firm. However, they felt that the incident with Paul, Jr might have demonstrated to her that pushing and predetermining things can backfire. And she might have wanted to avoid conflicts with Johannes at all costs.

MARIANNE: NOT IN THE CEO'S RACE

Marianne was only one year younger than Paul, Jr. She had been working for many years in a very responsible position in the marketing department of MaxTec. She should have been a natural replacement for Paul, Jr following his breaking completely with the family. However, she had never been considered as a potential CEO; neither in her childhood when Paul, Jr thought he would be the natural successor, nor in the emergency situation when her father died and her mother stepped in, and not now. In the end, MaxTec was simply a reflection of the long-standing tradition in Germany and many other countries of having only male family members in leading management positions. The fact that their mother Hilde had to take the helm as the first female in the company's history was the outcome of the emergency situation that arose due to Wilhelm's sudden death.

Hilde always considered herself as an interim CEO. She was willing to remain the main shareholder and the matriarch; however, she wanted to hand over the CEO position to someone else, preferably to a family member. But the outlook on keeping managerial leadership in family hands was bleak. Marianne said: "Even though mother demonstrated how a woman could assert herself in a male-dominated world, I have always lacked the motivation to do the same at some point."

The future leadership of MaxTec now stood at crossroads.

FUTURE CHALLENGES

Marianne and Johannes contemplated the future of the company and the family. The absence of Paul, Jr at the christening of the first child of the fourth generation made them think about the family environment in which the next generation would grow up. They felt that, in retrospect, their own growing up had not been optimal and that they would like to improve the environment for their children.

They also realized that the only option for the company was to move away from management by family members to outside management. For that to happen, the role of the family in the family business would have to be redefined. While they identified with the company, felt committed to their traditions, and realized that the company had kept them together as a family, for the future of the company they would have to look at a professional CEO to take the company forward.

Marianne and Johannes spent another quarter of an hour discussing initial ideas about how they could help their children grow up better. At the same time, they were moved by the question of what the transition to outside management would mean for the company and the family. More freedom for the family? But they were both very attached to the family business and would like to pass their dedication on to their children. How was that supposed to work if the company no longer sat at the dinner table, especially since Marianne and Johannes and their respective children would not be sitting at the same dinner table, as had been the case with the previous generation?

LEARNING NOTES

Case synopsis

Founded in 1950 by Paul Schmidt in Wittenburg, Germany, mechanical engineering firm MaxTec AG had grown to be a global company in 1990 and was 100 per cent family owned. After Paul's death, Wilhelm, married to Paul's daughter Hilde, became CEO. Hilde, owning almost 100 per cent of the shares, played the role of matriarch and remained behind the scenes. However, after Wilhelm's unexpected death, she became the CEO. The outlook for her successor from the third generation, her children, appeared gloomy. Paul, Jr, her eldest son, who was the natural successor, turned his back on the company and the family after a major row. Her daughter, Marianne, had no ambition to succeed as top manager and she was also not considered by her parents as a candidate for the post. The third child, Johannes, chose to set up his own business in the financial sector. On the christening of Marianne's first child, Marianne and Johannes looked back on their time as NextGen and discussed what went wrong. They were concerned about how to do better as parents so that their children, the next NextGen, grow up happier while developing a strong bond with the family business. Moreover, as there was no family member at hand for managerial succession, they contemplated opting for a non-family management and its implications for the business and family.

Learning objectives

The case of MaxTec provides an opportunity to discuss a wide range of topics such as succession, impact of non-family CEO, and the environment in which the NextGen grows up in a family business. As the problems for the current generation go far back to how they were raised as children and how they were introduced to the family business, the case deals with childhood and early adulthood of the next generation in a business family in a long-term preparation for succession. Moreover, as the experience of the current generation, particularly with the two brothers, Paul, Jr and Johannes, provides strong arguments for shifting from management by owners to that by professionals from outside the family, the case also offers an opportunity to discuss topics such as how to keep the family's identification with the family business intact when its management is handed over to non-family managers. In addition, the potential benefits from family governance tools to support the development of both the family and its business in this direction can be discussed on this occasion.

The case discussants should be able to:

- Understand the need for clearer and more open communication between parents and children about the future roles, responsibilities, and opportunities for the NextGen in the family business.
- Reflect on traditional succession procedures (primogeniture; to force, or at least have strong expectation, that children will work in the family business; preference for male children) and their impact on the family and the family business.
- Develop a contemporary view on succession and the future role of NextGen in the family business.

- Understand the effects it has on the family business and the business family when the family business shifts from owner management to that by professionals from outside the family.
- Explore and evaluate potential benefits family governance tools might have for the growing up of the NextGen and for the company as it moves from being an owner-managed entity to a non-family managed company.

Discussion questions

Looking back:

1. What are the reasons for Paul, Jr to leave the business family and the family business?
2. To what extent can the events surrounding Paul, Jr have influenced how things develop with Johannes?

Looking ahead:

1. What challenges will the family and the family business face in the coming years? What can be done to keep identification with the family business strong, even when the company is no longer family-managed?
2. What can Marianne and Johannes do differently for their children, so that the problems of their generation are avoided and their children still develop an identification with the family business?
3. How can instruments of family governance contribute to the development of the business family and the family business on their path?

Epilogue

Johannes ultimately returned to the family business as a member of the supervisory board after many years of self-employment in the financial sector. Marianne and Johannes each introduced their two children to the family business but did not create any pressure on them of great expectations. Family governance has been strengthened by a family constitution, which, among other things, stipulates that, apart from the supervisory board, family members may only work in the family business either as interns or as CEO. Family members are free to develop their professional careers in any field they prefer, but they must be qualified, for example, by taking business management courses to act as able owners in the family business upon acquiring shares. Although they were kept away from the family business during their childhood, the four children of Marianne and Johannes are very interested in it and participate as qualified shareholders. One child is the second family member on the supervisory board along with Johannes, where he brings to the table his extensive experience with start-ups. This in turn shows that entrepreneurial orientation has also developed in the next generation but, as with Johannes, it is outside the family business. Another child has taken on the family governance of the family business and yet another is doing a doctorate on family businesses. Marianne and Johannes are very pleased that their children were able to grow up without pressure and yet (or therefore) have developed into committed and qualified shareholders of the family business.

Suggested readings

Botero, I.C., Gomez Betancourt, G., Betancourt Ramirez, J.B., and Lopez Vergara, M.P. (2015). Family protocols as governance tools: Understanding why and how family protocols are important in family firms. *Journal of Family Business Management*, 5(2), 218–37. https://doi.org/10.1108/JFBM-01-2015-0001

Prigge, S., and Klein, P. (2021). Tilling the soil – and wait and see how the next generation develops. In M.R. Allen and W.B. Gartner (eds), *Family entrepreneurship* (pp. 85–95). Cham, Switzerland: Palgrave Macmillan.

Zellweger, T.M., Nason, R.S., and Nordqvist, M. (2012). From longevity of firms to transgenerational entrepreneurship of families: Introducing family entrepreneurial orientation. *Family Business Review*, 25(2), 136–55. https://doi.org/10.1177/0894486511423531

7

Florax Group: when unintended succession leads to unfulfilled promises

Rosemarie Steenbeek,[1] Judith van Helvert and Jolanda D.A. Knobel

December 2018 – Ulrich van Noorden, founder of the Florax Group, lay on his deathbed surrounded by his wife and two sons. He was worried and wanted a private talk with his eldest son, Sjak van Noorden. Ulrich said: "You and your brother Paul are both well educated. Please sell the business, the way I intended to, and find a job. The partnership between you and your brother has always been difficult. You do not want to jeopardize your relationship with your brother over a company, the firm is not worth it." Sjak was shocked. This company meant everything to his father, it was his life. He had always assumed that his father wanted him to take over the business.

Ulrich had never considered the possibility of an early death and the potential consequences for the firm. His plan was to sell the firm upon retirement because his sons were too different to succeed the family firm together, and he did not want to favour one son over the other. But Sjak refused to go along with the plan of selling the firm. He wanted his father to know that he would do everything to make sure that the company and the family would be taken good care of. So, he said: "Don't worry dad. I promise that I will take care of mom and Paul financially. I believe that the best way to do so is to continue the family firm together." Whilst making this promise to his father, Sjak knew it was a hard one to live up to. He and his younger brother Paul van Noorden never agreed on anything, they were just too different. Ulrich's death left his wife, Mieke van Noorden-Demandt, with 50 per cent of the shares, and the other 50 per cent was divided equally between their sons, Sjak and Paul.

Now, two years later, Sjak felt that he was failing on his promise. Although the business was continuing satisfactorily the family harmony was far from perfect. Sjak felt the urgency of acting and further developing and structuring the firm. However, he did not know how to do

[1]   Corresponding author.

Certain details in the case have been disguised. The case is developed solely as the basis for class discussion. Cases are not intended to serve as endorsements, sources of primary data, or illustrations of effective or ineffective management.

this. Even though Paul and his mother were owners and Paul was a member of the management team, Sjak felt that the firm's operations depended entirely on him. As the family faced one crisis after another, they could never take the time to consider their roles in the firm, nor the way that the leadership and ownership was currently arranged.

THE ORIGINS OF THE FLORAX GROUP

Florax Group was an entrepreneurial, medium-sized pharmaceutical firm. In accordance with the guidelines of Good Manufacturing Practices (GMP), Florax Group manufactured, developed, and distributed Active Pharmaceutical Ingredients (APIs) for both the veterinary and human markets. These active compounds were distributed worldwide. Florax Group also had its own laboratory, which analysed not only APIs produced by Florax Group, but also APIs for external clients. Florax Group consisted of two independent firm units: Florax Lab and Florax Trade. Florax Lab was the oldest firm unit and the core of the firm. At Florax Lab, approximately 50 products (APIs) were produced and distributed worldwide. Florax Trade dealt in APIs, which were mainly imported from India and China and then exported to the rest of the world, with a focus on the European market. The combination of these firm units enabled Florax Group to offer a complete solution to its customers.

Florax Lab was founded as a chemical firm by Ulrich and Mieke in 1982. Ulrich was a scientist with a PhD in organic chemistry. He started his first business activities in the garage of his home. Together with his wife, Ulrich worked hard for years to build the family firm into a functioning firm, performing chemical syntheses on an assignment basis. After a few years, the firm moved to an old milk factory in the couple's village. There, the firm started to operate well. After ten years, the firm moved to Winschoten because the village community refused to have a chemical factory in their village centre. Moreover, Ulrich received a subsidy to move to Winschoten to stimulate employment there; the community provided him with a laboratory that was only two years old. Ulrich added a small factory and started operations here.

From the moment that the pharmaceutical sector showed interest, Florax Lab increasingly concentrated on the production of APIs, which were the active ingredients of both human and veterinary medicines. With approximately 15 persons employed, Florax Lab was a financially healthy firm. In the late 2000s, the firm experienced a big setback when new quality standards were introduced for the production of APIs in Europe and America, which required a substantial investment. From 2013 onwards, firms had to define how and under what conditions a product was manufactured. To follow those guidelines, Florax Lab had to make a substantial investment. Simultaneously, European firms had to compete with Chinese and Indian producers that did not follow these quality standards and offered their products at much lower prices.

Florax Lab's future was uncertain because of these developments. In 2015, Ulrich decided to expand his firm. That year, the trading firm Florax Trade was bought as an extra firm unit. Together with Florax Lab, the new firm unit made up the Florax Group.

DISCORD IN THE FAMILY

Ulrich and Mieke had two sons: Sjak (born in 1986) and Paul (born in 1990). Sjak was a hard worker, eager to achieve the best possible results, but always humble. He finished his PhD in neurochemistry in 2018. Paul, on the other hand, did not care much about work. He sought status in driving nice cars and wearing expensive watches. Because Paul never held a job before he started working at Florax, he lived off his parents' money. He was still, and had been for a couple of years, in his last year of his Marketing Management study and the family seriously doubted whether he would ever graduate. These differences in character between the brothers were obvious but never discussed.

Even though their sons were still studying in 2013 and not involved in the business, Ulrich and Mieke wanted to engage them in important, strategic firm decisions. They reasoned that it was important to involve their sons at an early stage, to figure out whether they would be willing and competent to have a role in the family firm in the future. The implementation of the new quality standards, as well as the substantial investment required for this implementation, was the first issue that caused a serious disagreement between the family members. Ulrich was convinced that when Florax adhered to the new standards, they would become players in the top league and provide high quality products, and consequently, they would be able to set higher prices. Sjak agreed with his father; he was convinced of the future potential of this approach. However, his brother Paul saw things differently: "I did not see a reason why my father would even try to implement those guidelines. It was clear how much money was needed to be invested. And those Chinese and Indian producers would outcompete us anyway with their low prices. Frankly, I did not consider it as a serious option. The costs were huge; it would inevitably result in low profits."

Several meetings were held in which the family members talked about this strategic decision and its implications for the future. However, they were not able to reach consensus. Mieke tried to stay as neutral as possible in this decision. She agreed with her husband and eldest son but made sure of backing-up Paul in the discussions.

Due to the different opinions of the family members, no decision could be made, and slowly, the firm started to deteriorate. There were many problems: the loss of clients because Florax did not adhere to the new standards, the physical condition of the buildings, and the machinery. Also, Ulrich started having doubts about the possibility of his sons taking over the firm together. The family harmony, although it seemed fragile at times, was most important for Ulrich. He feared that choosing one of his sons as his successor would only make matters worse, and their opposite characters would possibly prevent them from working together successfully. As such, without informing his family members, Ulrich planned to prepare the firm for sale. He figured that this would prevent him from having to choose between either Sjak or Paul as possible successors. He had not updated the buildings and machinery, but one fortunate coincidence was that the trading firm bought in 2015 became profitable within only two years. This development freed up some money. In January 2018, five years after the discussion within the family, Ulrich decided to introduce the GMP standards in his firm after all, to be able to sell his firm at a better price. Paul was not sure why this should happen: "I could not believe that my father chose to implement the GMP standards. What is the point of involving me in the decision-making when nobody ever listens to me? I just do not get it. Why would we invest so much money in the firm, what about the dividends for this year?" However, Sjak fully agreed with the decision made by his father: "It is absurd how my brother reacted to the decision to implement the new quality standards. Doesn't he realize that we need to invest to guarantee the continuity of the firm? All he speaks about is dividends. I wish my mother would stop defending him all the time, Paul can handle this just fine for himself."

Ulrich tried to listen to both his sons' wishes by implementing the GMP standards using the additional profits generated by Florax Trade. However, he learned that his decision was too late because in September 2018, a few months before his death, the Food and Consumer Product Safety Authority (NVWA) visited them, and they received terrible news. Florax had three weeks to comply with the standards, otherwise the firm would be closed. Ulrich moved mountains and met the demands of the NVWA.

FAMILY DYNAMICS IN THE FIRM

Meanwhile in February 2018, Sjak finished his PhD in neurochemistry and pharmacy education, and was working part time as a pharmacist. He was thinking about what to do when Ulrich asked him to help with implementing the new quality standards in the firm. Implementing these guidelines was a process that could take years to fulfil and because of the bad condition of the machinery, Ulrich did not know where to start. Sjak decided to help his father: "My father wanted to achieve the implementation of the GMP standards in any way he could. So, I decided to work four days a week at Florax Group and one day per week as a post-doctoral fellow at the university."

Even though Paul was still studying Marketing Management with no clear prospect of graduating soon, Ulrich reached out to him as well and asked for a marketing plan to convey the new focus on quality to the firm's main stakeholders. This was the first time that Sjak and Paul worked together in the family firm where the irritations between them piled up.

And then, unexpectedly, in December 2018 Ulrich died at the age of 59. Sjak felt responsible for continuing his legacy:

> So, I took his place as CEO in the firm. I had just turned 30 and had only worked at the firm for a few months. There was little time to think about a plan and consider what I really wanted. But I was curious, and I liked having the challenge of running a family firm with one main objective: to continue the firm. But I worried whether this was going to work. Paul never finished anything and was mostly busy with his social life. The week after my father died, the bank came by and asked about our plans concerning the firm's strategy. In a very short period, I had to learn a lot about how to lead a firm. I knew that I must be willing to work hard, I would be an entrepreneur 24 hours a day. For that reason, I thought it was best that I run this firm on my own because I was concerned that Paul was not as committed to this challenge as he needed to be. I could always consult my brother and my mother when needed. After all, they do own 75% of the shares together.

Mieke was devastated by the sudden death of her husband. She took time to grieve and distanced herself from the daily business activities. Paul's view on the situation was different from Sjak's ideas. A few weeks after the funeral he asked Sjak to meet him and told him: "Since I am now one of the owners of Florax Group, I believe that I deserve a nice job in the firm. You said that you wanted to continue as successor to the firm, but I will not let you do so without me. I have talked to our mother about it, and she agrees that I should quit my studies and become the Manager of the Florax Trade Business unit. That sounds like a job for me."

Although Sjak never saw his younger brother as a responsible person, he felt that he had to give him a chance in the family firm. He was a co-owner after all, and his mother had agreed to it. For continued operation of the family firm, quick decisions needed to be made. Since Paul had now become the manager of the trading unit, Sjak intended to involve his brother in important decisions. But already after a few weeks, the brothers' different visions and ways of working became clearer than ever, and Sjak stopped trying to get Paul involved. Despite the ongoing tensions between the brothers, Sjak did his best to lead the Florax Group to the best of his ability.

YET ANOTHER CRISIS

In the early months of 2020, the brothers had to deal with another crisis. When the pandemic struck, Sjak needed to take action. Protocols had to be drawn up to ensure that the general rules about social distancing and hygiene were obeyed. When possible, the employees were asked to work from home. However, due to the nature of the job, few people were able to comply with this guideline. The Netherlands never went into a full lockdown, so it was still possible to continue working in the lab. However, the employees started to work in shifts to limit the amount of personal contact in the lab. Sjak explained: "It was a strange time. Employees were scared of the virus and of getting sick. It was hard to shift to a new way of working. We were lucky that the pharmacies needed our medication more than ever."

Despite the pandemic causing many difficulties, it also hindered trade with China, where all Florax's competitors were located. The pharmaceutical industry realized how dependent they were on other countries and wanted to change that. Sjak realized that he faced a huge opportunity and soon decided to scale up the production of high-quality APIs. This strategy turned out to be successful. Pharmacies all over Europe started to order an increasing number of products from the Florax Group.

Sjak never consulted with Paul on this decision. He figured that Paul was not knowledgeable about the developments taking place in the market and he needed to act as fast as possible. Paul was annoyed that he was not informed about this major decision, but he was pleased with the additional profits made. Without informing Sjak, Paul prepared a plan with his mother to pay out higher dividends instead of reinvesting the profit made by the firm. Together, Paul and Mieke had a majority of the shares, so Sjak had no choice but to listen to them. This development made it harder for Sjak to continue with the firm's new strategy and the current crisis and the family troubles made Sjak think about his own life: "My concern for the firm is constant. Seven days a week, I am here, if only to confirm that there are no issues. If I could share these concerns with someone, I think that would make a difference … I do not talk about these things any longer with my brother and mother. It always ends in an argument which makes things even worse."

This crisis made clear that things needed to change for Sjak. He admitted that it had been difficult and challenging to succeed his father, especially since he did not feel that he could rely on Paul. Sjak only had a background in pharmacy, lacking any education or training in business administration. So, besides the troubles in relation to his brother, he was not sure about his own role either. Sjak had three goals for the near future: (1) he wanted to educate himself in business administration matters, (2) he wanted to manage his work–private life balance, and (3) he needed to determine his future role in the firm and where he wanted to take the firm. Sjak explained: "I am looking for support on various firm matters, for example, how to structure this organization. In addition, I need to know what kind of a person I am. Over the last few years, I have had very little time to think … I have been extremely busy, primarily with operational tasks. The firm was a mess when my father died. All I did was make sure that the firm could continue."

All Sjak wanted was to have a healthy family firm and a healthy family. Where was he supposed to start?

LEARNING NOTES

Case synopsis

Florax was founded as a pharmaceutical firm by Ulrich and Mieke van Noorden in 1982. Ulrich and Mieke worked hard for years to grow the family firm but over the years the intention to sell the firm upon retirement grew. Their sons, Sjak and Paul, were too different to succeed the family firm together and Ulrich did not want to favour one son over the other. For that reason, Ulrich neither discussed succession with them, nor took effort in keeping the buildings and machinery up to date. Then, Ulrich suddenly passed away. On his deathbed, he told Sjak to take care of his mother and brother and to sell the company like he had planned. Sjak did not know about his father's plans for the future, and he promised him to take care of his mother and little brother, Paul. He believed the best way to do so was to continue the family firm. Sjak was aware of the differences between him and his brother and he would soon learn about the big problems within the company, but he was eager to make the family firm successful, together with Paul. The years passed, problems in the company piled up and the fights in the family grew worse. It became harder and harder for Sjak to keep his promise. What should he do?

Learning objectives

This case discusses multiple implications of transitions from the first generation to the second generation after the unexpected death of the founder. A sudden death can lead to tremendous changes in both the family and the business system which can potentially harm the continuity of the business and the family harmony. The next generation is forced to make important decisions about the family firm during an emotional period. When the succeeding generation is in charge of the firm without succession planning, and the firm does not have proper governance instruments in place and lacks professionalism, a crisis like this might be the end of the family firm and the family harmony.

The case discussants should be able to discuss:

- The importance of communication.
- The importance of succession planning.
- The role of ownership in decision making.

Discussion questions

1. What are the challenges faced by Sjak and how are they being addressed?
2. What does a successful succession mean to the van Noorden family? Take at least the perspectives of the family, successor, management, and the incumbent into consideration.
3. What are the options for the family for the succession in ownership and leadership? Which option would you recommend to the family? Why?
4. What are the options for family and business governance to help Sjak and the Florax Group. Which governance mechanism would you recommend to the family? Why?

Epilogue

The pandemic turned out to be good for business. Since it was next to impossible to trade with China for a long period of time, pharmacies all over Europe started to order more and more products from the Florax Group. This business success, although Sjak never forgot the dark side of it, forced him to think about the future: his own future, that of the family, and the family firm. During the summer months of 2020, Sjak decided he wanted to continue with the family firm, but only when some changes were made regarding the family and business governance. With the support of a family business advisor, he decided to start an advisory board. This advisory board would help him in structuring and professionalizing the family firm. Simultaneously, Sjak started to work on the family harmony. Sjak hired a mediator specialized in family business to talk to each of the three family members individually and together. These conversations helped them communicate and see the situation from each others' perspectives. Together they decided that it was best if Sjak would continue with the firm alone, since he embodied the soul of the firm. Sjak bought out his mother and brother, but promised to keep them engaged through an annual family council.

Suggested reading

Bloemen-Bekx, M., Van Gils, A., Lambrechts, F., and Sharma, P. (2021). Nurturing offspring's affective commitment through informal family governance mechanisms. *Journal of Family Business Strategy*, *12*(2), 100309. doi: https://doi.org/10.1016/j.jfbs.2019.100309

8
Succession turnaround at the Avendorp Group: a true family tragedy

Daniël Agterhuis, Julian van den Akker and Judith van Helvert[1]

May 2021 – Klaas Avendorp celebrated his 70th birthday with friends and family. However, his brother Erik, with whom Klaas had led the Avendorp Group for more than 25 years, as well as his nephews and nieces, Erik's children, were not present at his birthday party. Five years after Klaas's decision to transfer the family business to his son Steven Avendorp, the brothers were able to resolve their disagreement, but the relationships with his nephews and nieces were still severely damaged and they refused any type of contact. Klaas wondered whether he had made the right decision at the time and how the family relationships could be restored.

In 1985, Erik and Klaas succeeded their father in the Avendorp Road Construction Group. They had worked in the business since they were kids, and they were enthusiastic to develop the family business further. The firm grew tremendously under their dual leadership, although the brothers did not always see eye-to-eye. Both Erik and Klaas were short-tempered and regularly disagreed over important decisions that needed to be made. They noticed that their children had an even harder time tolerating one another, and their personalities regularly collided. Erik and Klaas worried that their children would potentially have a harder time working together than they had themselves. They deemed it impossible for both third-generation branches of the family to lead the firm together. They faced a dilemma, because they had to decide which branch of the family would get the opportunity to succeed the family business. They eventually decided that Erik's children were going to be raised with the idea to take over the leadership and ownership of the firm one day, while Klaas's son was raised to pursue a career outside of the family business. Klaas recalled, "My brother and I believed in this decision and thought it was the best for the continuity of the family firm. When reaching my retirement age, I would sell my shares to Erik, and he would pass them on to his children."

---

[1] Corresponding author.

Certain details in the case have been disguised. The case is developed solely as the basis for class discussion. Cases are not intended to serve as endorsements, sources of primary data, or illustrations of effective or ineffective management.

Their plans for the future of the family business tragically changed in 2012 when Erik's wife suddenly passed away. The stress and grief became too much, and Erik decided to stop working in the business. As a consequence, he had to sell his shares to his brother Klaas. In the past, Erik and Klaas established some ground rules for their positions as family business owners, and one of those was that one can only be an owner when one works in the family business, preferably in a management position. Unexpectedly, at the age of 61, Klaas became the sole owner of Avendorp Group. He carried on leading the business, and he actually enjoyed being the sole decision-maker. He started reminiscing about the good times he had with his father in the business and wondered whether it would still be possible to transfer the business to his son, Steven. Steven had a master's degree in psychology, but was still not sure about his plans for the future. After his studies, Steven had been engaged in multiple jobs. However, he had always shown interest in the family business multiple times, and he seemed concerned about the long-term continuity of the firm. Although Steven was not raised with the intention to succeed the firm, Klaas believed that his son was qualified enough to lead the group. The idea of his son representing the next generation in the firm made him proud, but it would mean that he had to disappoint his brother and his brother's children. Erik's children were already preparing for their future in the family business and Klaas knew that Erik, as well as his nephews and nieces, would be furious if he suggested a change of plans.

SHORT HISTORY OF THE FAMILY FIRM

The history of the Avendorp Group dated back to 1951, when Piet Avendorp established the Road Construction Company, P. Avendorp. The company was founded in Zwolle, the Netherlands, but soon moved to Hattem due to the availability of 24.7 acres of land and the strategic location of being closer to the IJssel River. In its first years the company carried out some regional projects, but the firm quickly became known nationally for their high-quality services.

1985–88: The early years

After 34 years at the head of the family business, Piet transferred the firm to his two sons, Erik and Klaas. The brothers had big plans for the future of the company. The first thing that they decided to do was to acquire another firm that focused on private building activities because they felt that solely focusing on road construction made them too vulnerable. The expansion of activities enabled the Avendorp Group to diversify its portfolio and to be less sensitive to the economic cycle. Under the dual leadership of Erik and Klaas, the Avendorp Group grew tremendously – both in terms of employees and revenue.

The early years, however, were not solely characterized by success. The brothers often disagreed about financial policies and the strategic direction of the family firm. Erik was always busy expanding their current reach and making a name for the company on a national level, investing heavily in it. Klaas on the other hand was more committed to strengthening bonds with current clients and aimed to retain a solid liquidity position. They realized that if their different views on the future were not quickly resolved, it would disrupt the relationship between them and threaten the smooth running of the firm. They decided that they needed a mediator to facilitate a constructive discussion.

The brothers were adviced to take a moment every week to work on their communication. They made a tradition to meet every Sunday afternoon. They would discuss the upcoming week, but it was also a time to catch up with each other personally.

The brothers both had children who always came along to play with their cousin(s), while Erik and Klaas talked business. In the beginning, both families enjoyed the tradition, but as the children grew older, they started fighting more and more. It became clear that they, just like their fathers, had very different personalities. Their attitudes towards each other collided regularly until the point that they did not want to play together anymore. It sometimes worried the brothers that the cousins did not really get along well, but Erik and Klaas hoped that it was just a phase that would resolve itself as the children got older.

The relationship between the cousins stayed the same for a long time. This, however, changed when Steven (Klaas's son) and Martine Avendorp (Erik's oldest daughter) were asked to help sort out some items in the warehouse one day. They accidentally bumped into each other, which led to a fight. Two employees had to split them apart. It was a breaking point and a wake-up call that the cousins might never be able to cooperate.

Erik was out of the office that day to meet some customers on the other side of the country, so he did not know about the incident that had occurred between the two cousins. Klaas called his brother later that evening with the following idea:

> I know we envisioned that our children would continue the business together, but the situation does not seem tenable any longer after this clash. I think that we have to make a new decision about the future of the company. As far as I am concerned, there are four feasible options to choose from: (1) All of the children that show interest will have the opportunity to succeed the business and we will wait and see how their collaboration unfolds; (2) we will divide the business into branches between all of the children that show interest (e.g., one branch will lead the road construction, and another branch will lead the private building for instance); (3) only one branch of the Avendorp family will have the opportunity to succeed the business; and (4) when we both reach our retirement age, the business will be sold to an external party.

Erik agreed with his brother. The situation was getting worse, and they had to find a solution quickly.

1989-2012: Raised with roots or wings

Since the brothers wanted to safeguard the continuity of the firm and prevent conflict among its future leaders, the first option was soon excluded. Option two was also not considered possible. The family business was large enough to be divided into two or even four branches, but this option would still require some form of collaboration among the cousins occasionally. Selling the company to a third party was also out of the question, because the brothers had a strong desire to continue the business within the Avendorp family. In the end they decided that the third option would be the most preferred situation as it would safeguard the continuity of the business.

Yet, this created a new problem. The brothers had to decide which of their children would be considered as potential successors, and who would be encouraged to pursue a career outside of the business. Weeks passed by until the decision was eventually made. Even though Klaas was concerned that conflicts between the siblings could still create problems in the future, the brothers decided to give Erik's children the opportunity to succeed their father, while Klaas's son, Steven, would be encouraged to seek employment elsewhere. The brothers based their choice on a couple of reasons. First, as the family business had grown significantly over the last decades, there was now room (or even a need) for more than one business leader. Since Steven was an only child and Erik had three children, Erik's side of the family was a more logical choice. Tasks and responsibilities could potentially be divided between a general director, a sales director, and an operational director. Second, Erik's children had spent much more time in the business in their youth. They completed many school projects and internships at either the Avendorp Group or at their mother's place of work. Erik's wife was financial director at a large industrial firm. Steven did not seem to feel an affiliation to the family firm at all. He showed much interest in music and creative activities. He was inspired by his mother, who was a concert pianist. As such, Steven was not troubled by the decision that his cousins would take over the firm at all. Lastly, there was a higher chance that the business would stay within the family if three children succeeded the business, instead of one. It would be more likely to find a suitable fourth-generational leader, and it also prevented the business being sold to a third party if a successor potentially lost interest in the business.

Agreements were made ensuring that Klaas would sell all of his shares to his younger brother when he reached his retirement age, which Erik would then pass on to his children. After Erik's retirement, Erik's children would be the sole owners of the Avendorp Group, obstructing Steven from having a chance to succeed. Erik's children supported their father's and uncle's decision, and Steven also agreed on the outcome. He was proud of the family business, but he had also already considered following in his mother's footsteps.

Now that there was more clarity about the future of the children, more "targeted parenting" was possible. When working in the business during holidays, Erik's children, Martine, Sjoerd, and Rachel Avendorp, had a chance to observe their father and uncle performing their career tasks and roles. As a result, the business became a frequent subject of conversation at the kitchen table. Later, all three siblings successfully finished their relevant study programmes and received their degrees. They had ensured that they were well prepared for their future roles in the family business.

The Avendorp Group continued to blossom under the leadership of Erik and Klaas. By August 2000, the brothers had been leading the business for 15 years. To celebrate this anniversary, family members, staff, and friends gathered at the headquarters in Hattem. Erik remembered,

My father Piet was a great father and husband, in particular, he was a clever businessman. He was deeply faithful to his core values, especially trust, integrity, and teamwork. After my brother and I succeeded the family firm fifteen years ago, we tried our best to incorporate these values and continue his legacy. I definitely think we were on the right track, and I was very excited about the next fifteen years.

2012: A change of minds

The brothers' entrepreneurial enthusiasm continued in the following years but came to an abrupt stop in 2012. Erik's wife suddenly passed away and he lost the joy of working in the family business. He became burnt out and decided to stop working in the family business as a result of the stress and grief from living in a house with so many memories of his late wife. Erik needed a new start and he wanted to move. However, because Erik and Klaas had decided in the past that family members could only hold shares when they had a management position, Erik had to sell his shares in the family business to Klaas, who then became the sole owner of the Avendorp Group. Looking back on the sale of his shares Erik said, "I never imagined that by selling my shares to Klaas, I would risk the future career of my children. It never crossed my mind that Klaas would be able to change his mind and exclude my children from a succession in the family business."

Klaas had the full intention of proceeding all of the shares to Erik's three children when he took over Erik's share of ownership. However, the joy of working in the family business and the successes of his last projects made him remember the good times that his father had enjoyed in the business. He also remembered the succession process that he and his father had enjoyed. So, Klaas started to wonder about the idea of proceeding the family business to his son, Steven, and having a successful collaboration just like Klaas had experienced with his father. Klaas was also not fully confident that the continuity of the family business would be safeguarded by the sibling partnership. Klaas mentioned:

> I knew that my brother's children were 'rooted' into the business and had suitable educa-
> tion and experience to succeed the family business, whilst Steven did not. Passing on the
> shares to my brother's children would be the obvious decision to safeguard the continuity
> of the family business. However, I was not fully confident that the siblings would get along
> and have a successful collaboration. I was much more optimistic that Steven would be
> able to develop himself to become the next CEO. He was successful as treasurer of a study
> association and showed entrepreneurial qualities by organizing events and connecting with
> people in his field of psychology.

The Avendorp Group, but mostly Klaas, was now facing a difficult decision. Should he choose successors who were intensively prepared to take over the family business, but did not always see eye-to-eye? Or should he go for a successor without any relevant experience, but who showed great learning ability? What would the rational decision be, and when should an entrepreneur trust his gut feeling?

PRESENT DAY

Having come to this realization and knowing that his son did not want to fully commit himself to working as a psychologist, Klaas decided to call Steven one evening. Klaas wanted to share his thoughts on the situation and on the future of the family business. At the end of the call, he asked his son to consider succeeding him in the business. Steven recalled:

> It was a lot for me to consider at the time. I was not raised with the knowledge, education, and experience that is needed to lead a business. The firm had evolved to become a large company, so there was a lot of responsibility on the shoulders of the management team; the business leader was responsible for 343 employees in 2012. My father, uncle, and cousins all worked regularly within the business from an early age, but I did not.

Steven thought long and hard about the decision at hand. He was still unsure about his plans for the future, but:

> I eventually decided to succeed my father in the business. My father and I knew that there were just a few years left to transfer the family business. We had to start making a succession plan, in which we defined the skills and knowledge required to become CEO and lead a management team. I started with a one-year internship abroad, as I had no experience with entrepreneurship whatsoever, nor did I know what the construction industry looked like. We owned an operational firm in Montevideo, the capital of Uruguay – where I could gain this experience. After that, my father and I worked closely together for four years from 2012 until 2016. During this time, implicit knowledge was transferred, and we could discuss our visions of the future.

Avendorp remained financially robust and witnessed an appreciable growth in revenue in the past two years (see Table 8.1). Over these seven years Steven acquired all the shares and became the CEO of the Avendorp Group (see Table 8.2). Steven had many plans for the future of the family business but lacked the experience of working in the firm. Klaas reflected:

> When I look back, I have mixed feelings about my decision to succeed the business to Steven instead of Erik's children. I am satisfied about how well Steven was able to lead the business and I am happy with the progress that the family business has made over the last years. On the other hand, the relationship with our family members, my brother and nephews, has been severely disrupted. It has become quite a family tragedy. Our intention has always been to maintain family control over the firm and to avoid family conflicts. I have been able to realize the first but at the cost of a huge family feud. Will I ever be able to solve our family problems?

During his 70th birthday celebration, Klaas pondered what he could do to mend the fence and restore the harmony in the two branches. Was it truly possible to resolve the deep issues and prevent this unintended family tragedy going beyond the third generation?

Table 8.1 Financial information of the Avendorp Group

Figures	2018	2017
Revenue	€199.02 million	€138.76 million
EBITDA-margin	3.92%	5.42%
Net profit-margin	2.34%	3.17%
Total assets	€87.91 million	€86.03 million
Fixed assets	€32.11 million	€30.60 million
Current assets	€55.80 million	€55.43 million
Equity	€45.46 million	€42.28 million
Long-term liabilities	€8.95 million	€9.15 million
Short-term liabilities	€33.50 million	€34.60 million
Employees	380	356

Table 8.2 Ownership information of the Avendorp Group

1951–85	1988–2012	2012–14	2014–present
Piet Avendorp (100%)	Erik Avendorp (50%) Klaas Avendorp (50%)	Klaas Avendorp (100%)	Steven Avendorp (100%)

LEARNING NOTES

Case synopsis

The Avendorp Group was founded by Piet Avendorp in 1951 and started as a small road construction company in the Netherlands. After 34 years at the head of the business, Piet passed the baton to his two sons, Erik and Klaas Avendorp, who diversified the business activities. The firm grew tremendously under their dual leadership. The brothers, however, did not always see eye-to-eye, but were able to work out their differences and hoped to pass on their success to the next generation. Their children, on the other hand, had very different personalities which regularly collided and led to (small) fights. It worried the brothers that a situation where the cousins had to work together might endanger the continuity of the family business, and they decided that only one branch of the family could succeed. Erik's children were designated as potential successor(s) and raised with the idea of taking over the firm, while Klaas's son, Steven Avendorp, would be encouraged to seek employment outside of the family business. Both Erik and Klaas believed in this idea and that it was the best option for the family business.

Their vision of the future, however, changed in 2012 when Erik's wife suddenly passed away. The stress and grief became too much, and Erik became burnt out working in the business. Klaas, who still enjoyed his time as entrepreneur, took over the shares of his brother and became the sole owner of the Avendorp Group. The plan was still for Klaas to pass on all the shares to Erik's children when he would reach his retirement age. In the following years, the joy of working in the family business made Klaas question their decision of who the successor(s) should be. Without consulting his brother about the change in the succession plans, Klaas asked Steven to succeed him in the family firm. Erik and his children were devastated by Klaas's decision to ask Steven instead of Erik's children, as they had planned for. Klaas struggled to see how he could rebuild the relationship with Erik's branch of the family.

Learning objectives

The case discusses the implications of a family firm that evolved from the work of a simple first-generation entrepreneur towards an increasingly complex sibling partnership and cousin consortium. The case highlights the complications that may occur when key players in a business succession process make sudden, yet impactful changes to succession planning. To avoid the situation where appointed successors can be excluded from business succession, families must consider the importance of family governance, business governance, and communication.

The case discussants should be able to determine:

- The valid reasons to prune the family tree and if/how next generation(s) should be raised to succeed in the family business, or pursue a career outside of the family business.
- The impact that sudden changes in one's personal life bring, as well as changes in the vision of the family firm might have on the business succession.
- The implications that these unexpected events have on succession planning and governance.

1. What are some reasons for pruning the family tree – both in terms of ownership and leadership – for the Avendorp Group?
2. If Klaas would have involved you as an advisor during the succession process, what kind of advice would you have given? Could the huge family conflict that occurred in the end be prevented?
3. What possible scenarios for the future could the Avendorp Group consider? How can these scenarios be developed and improved?

Epilogue

The unexpected change in succession severely disrupted the relations between Erik and his brother Klaas, but also between Erik and his children. Erik's children blamed their father for not taking care of their interests in the family business. They not only lost their mother, but also their future at the Avendorp Group. Erik and Klaas were eventually able to resolve their disagreement and leave the past behind them. They regularly visit each other or search through the archives and photo albums of the family business. The relationship between Erik and his children, however, has barely changed. They are still not on speaking terms. Steven is still the visionary CEO of the Avendorp Group and continues to build on the strong foundation that his grandfather, father, and uncle succeeded to him. Under his leadership, the firm has gained a prominent national role as a reliable (road) construction company, as well as recent awards for sustainability acts that Steven initiated.

Suggested readings

Bloemen-Bekx, M., Voordeckers, W., Remery, C., and Schippers, J. (2019). Following in parental footsteps? The influence of gender and learning experience on entrepreneurial intentions. *International Small Business Journal: Researching Entrepreneurship, 37*(6), 642–63. doi: https://doi.org/10.1177/0266242619838936

De Massis, A., Chua, J.H., and Chrisman, J.J. (2008). Factors preventing intra-family succession. *Family Business Review, 21*, 183–99. doi: https://doi.org/10.1111/j.1741–6248.2008.00118.x

Lambrecht, J., and Lievens, J. (2008). Pruning the family tree: An unexplored path of the family business continuity and family harmony. *Family Business Review, 21*(4), 295–313. doi: https://doi.org/10.1177/08944865080210040103

PART II
GOVERNANCE FOR TRANSITION PLANNING

9
Valuing our values: family values driving business success

Eric Clinton[1] and Stephen Browne

In March 2020, Michael Hoey, Managing Director of Country Crest, was in the middle of his weekly accounts review when he heard the news reporter on the radio confirming that all non-essential businesses were to close in Ireland. These measures were in response to the spiralling COVID-19 case numbers across the region. Restaurants, cafés, and all retail stores were to cease trading indefinitely, while difficulties with sourcing supplies and logistics were about to be confounded for the brothers. Consumers began panic buying, supermarket giant Tesco's orders were increasing rapidly, while on-site health and safety protocols had to be adjusted once again due to the pandemic. Michael immediately considered the far-reaching impact this could have on his family-owned firm and the 350 employees who depend upon the business in the local community. He did not know whether to take inspiration or discard the values which had carried them to this point.

Note: Michael (left) and Gabriel (right) Hoey.

Figure 9.1   Michael and Gabriel Hoey

COUNTRY CREST IN THE COVID-19 PANDEMIC

The Hoey family's roots could be traced back to 1910, where the family farmed on their 3,000-acre site in North County Dublin and continued doing so until 1993 (see Table 9.1). It was at this time when brothers Michael and Gabriel Hoey (see Figure 9.1)

---

[1]   Corresponding author.

Certain details in the case may have been disguised. The case is developed solely as the basis for class discussion. Cases are not intended to serve as endorsements, sources of primary data, or illustrations of effective or ineffective management.

established Country Crest to diversify their business offering. Country Crest, a multi-division company, provided potato and vegetable supplies to retailers across Ireland and the United Kingdom. The brothers continued to innovate, when in 2008 they established Ballymaguire Foods, an agri-food business that prepared fresh and healthy chilled meals using sustainable and traceable farm produce. The creation of Ballymaguire Foods enabled the brothers to move toward a farm-to-fork business model, a model which promoted sustainable food practices, while reducing the number of steps between the land and the consumer's plate.

Table 9.1   Country Crest: a timeline

1910	The Hoey family purchase a farm in North County Dublin, Ireland.
1910–1993	Three generations of the Hoey family farm the 3,000-acre site.
1993	Fourth-generation sibling partnership, Michael and Gabriel Hoey, establish Country Crest. The company is set up to grow and pre-pack fresh potatoes for retail customers.
1999	Country Crest opens a new washing, grading, and packing facility for potatoes.
2001	Ireland experiences an outbreak of foot and mouth disease (FMD), affecting supply chains and the national economy.
2005	Country Crest invests €4 million in a state-of-the-art onion washing, grading, and packing facility.
2007	Michael Hoey is nominated as a finalist in the Ernst & Young "Entrepreneur of the Year" competition. Country Crest is involved with a charity promoting educational projects in Haiti, "Soul of Haiti Foundation".
2008	The Hoey brothers expand the family business by establishing a prepared foods division, Ballymaguire Foods.
2009	An 80-metre on-site wind turbine is introduced, supplying over 60 per cent of the company's energy needs.
2011	Country Crest wins the Bord Bia Food & Drink Sustainability Award for their commitment to sustainable business practice.
2013	The horse meat scandal results in a significant decline in sales of beef and beef-related products across Ireland.
2014	Country Crest invests in an on-site cattle-feeding unit to ensure full traceability of beef.
2015	Country Crest's farm shop opens on their Dublin site, specializing in fully traceable beef, craft meats, locally grown vegetables, prepared meals, and artisan foods.
2016	Sweet potatoes are added to the Country Crest catalogue of products.
2017	Country Crest completes its five-year sustainability development project with Origin Green (with the Irish Food Board) and is the first business in Ireland to sign up for a second five-year plan.
2018	Country Crest celebrates 25 years of business with over 350 employees working across all divisions.
2019	Farmers protest and strike against current policies in the beef sector, citing new trade agreements with South America.
2020	First case of COVID-19 is confirmed in Ireland, sparking a nationwide standstill.

Source: Michael Hoey.

Investment in their businesses continued annually, developing industry-leading sustainable farming methods and earning accolades in the process. Their innovative nature was rewarded in 2019 when sales were at a record high with a turnover of €62 million, a 10 per cent increase from the previous year. However, with the recent news of government-mandated business closures, and with restrictions becoming increasingly prevalent across Europe, Michael Hoey was worried about the future.

After hearing the news, Michael took a moment to reflect on their family values on the wall and reached out to phone his lifelong business partner and brother, Gabriel Hoey, to discuss the update. Facing a rising number of internal and external threats, he got the sense that this was incomparable to anything they'd faced in their history. Would their dedication to a values-driven business impede or empower their response to COVID-19?

> Gabriel, have you heard the news? This could ruin everything we've worked for. Can you come in to talk?

GROUNDED IN FAMILY VALUES

The business operations of the Hoey family were underpinned by their family values of respect for the land, environmental reciprocity, sustainable practice, and community embeddedness. The values of Country Crest and Ballymaguire Foods were a manifestation of this, and had been formally identified as:

1. Sustainability
2. Teamwork
3. Integrity & Trust
4. Quality
5. Community
6. Innovation
7. Giving Back

These deeply held values played an integral role in fulfilling their mission of deploying a farm-to-fork business model and were instilled at all levels of the business. A long-standing non-family executive described their demeanour, commenting, "There's always been that ethos [farm-to-fork] promoted by Michael and Gabriel that they are farmers to the core, it's in their blood, it's in their DNA, and they care about the land and they care about the natural resources … and also the 350 people that work here."

These values closely aligned with the company's vision statement of "leading the way in sustainable healthy food innovation". Their commitment to staying "true to nature for the generations to come" also demonstrated their desire to build a sustainable family business built on values. These modi operandi were validated throughout the day-to-day operations of the firm, with another senior member of staff noting, "We don't get everything right but every decision that we make outside the pure financial implications of the decision, we look at the environmental implications of that decision."

VALUING VALUES IN A TIME OF CRISIS

Since the formation of the sibling partnership in 1993, the Hoey brothers enjoyed the highs and at times the lows of family business ownership. Despite facing national and international crises, the brothers consistently showed a devout commitment to their family values which guided their strategic decision making throughout. During periods of great stress and difficulty, Gabriel and Michael Hoey did not stray from these core values.

Global financial crisis – 2007 onwards

At the end of the 2000s, Ireland was facing the repercussions of the global financial crisis. The state of the nation was in ruins, leaving the prosperous times of the Celtic Tiger[2] behind. However, this did not stop the Hoey brothers from investing in their business.

A key development from a commercial perspective followed when they established Ballymaguire Foods in 2008, the same year as the infamous Lehman Brothers collapse. In the midst of this economic uncertainty, they managed to earn a gross profit of over €1.6 million in their first year. Their model of "100% traceable ingredients from their farm and carefully selected suppliers" proved to the Hoey brothers that embedding innovation, alongside a dedication to quality and sustainability, could bring success.

Investing in their own business was not the only priority for the Hoey brothers throughout the global financial crisis. The development of a clear and actionable corporate social responsibility (CSR) strategy, led by co-founder Michael, was a passion for the Dublin natives. This was triggered when in 2007, Michael was nominated for the prestigious "Ernst and Young Entrepreneur of the Year" award. A cornerstone of Country Crest's CSR initiatives was the Christine Valley Model Farm in Haiti as the project was set up by Michael and his fellow nominees of the award.

The project proved to be a resounding success, enabling locals in Haiti to farm sustainably, and providing alternative sources of employment. Commenting on their commitment to CSR, Michael said, "I think we've been fortunate and some days you question that and thank God for what we have. It has to be about giving back."

Throughout the global financial crisis, Gabriel and Michael Hoey not only invested in new business development, but also in sustainable farm infrastructure. This investment included a €1.5 million financing of an 80-metre state-of-the-art wind turbine system.[3] As a result of their efforts and sustainable business model, they accepted an invitation from Ireland's food board on to their industry-leading food and drink sustainability programme. During this period of economic uncertainty, they were rewarded for their commitment to sustainable business

---

[2] Celtic Tiger is a term referring to the economy of the Republic of Ireland from the mid-1990s to the late 2000s, a period of rapid real economic growth fuelled by foreign direct investment. The gross domestic product (GDP) averaged 9.4 per cent annually through 2000 and about 6 per cent a year for the remainder of the period.

[3] "Turbine leading the way in Lusk". Retrieved 29 September 2021 from https://www.independent.ie/regionals/fingalindependent/news/turbine-leading-the-way-in-lusk-27796137.html

practices as they were named as the winner of the "Bord Bia Food & Drink Sustainability Award" in 2011.

Horse meat scandal 2013

As the impact of the global financial crisis was still lingering for many Irish businesses, a crisis of a different kind swept through the nation and neighbouring European countries. Supermarket giants Lidl, Aldi, and Tesco were found to have sold beef products while claiming "full traceability", with horse and pig meat used in parts of their offering.

Although they were not culpable in the use of non-beef products, the Hoeys' portfolio would not escape unscathed. Particularly affected was Ballymaguire Foods as its prepared meals relied on products from external meat suppliers. Sales of their meat-based products dropped by 60 per cent overnight, as consumer confidence plummeted in the industry.

Eager to reassure the Irish consumer of their dedication to sustainable, ethical farming and to reiterate their quality standards, the company undertook a series of self-declared audits, spending large amounts per month on animal DNA testing. Refusing to succumb to the errors of others, the Hoey brothers doubled down on their farm-to-fork model through backward integration. They invested significant capital in an on-site cattle-feeding unit to ensure full traceability of their beef products.[4] Gabriel commented after the project was completed, "Rather than being totally reliant on somebody else's heap of paperwork, we decided to take control of the situation by putting up our own beef unit."

In the wake of the horse meat scandal, albeit after absorbing a significant initial shock, the firm witnessed significant monetary growth as the popularity of their brands soared. Gross profit for Ballymaguire Foods jumped from €0.7 million in 2013 to €1.9 million in 2014, and they added a further 100 employees to their operations in 2015.

Brexit – 2016 onwards

Shortly after the horse meat scandal developments, the country they traded with the most outside of their own, the United Kingdom, voted to leave the European Union (EU) in 2016. This coincided with a significant milestone for the brothers, 25 years since the establishment of Country Crest. Approximately 15 per cent of their business was undertaken with the United Kingdom, along with key supply chains operating through the island. Fears of increased tariffs, duties, and political tensions were understandably high in the agriculture sector. For Gabriel and Michael, reservations over Brexit did not permeate the brothers' psyche; rather, they saw this as an opportunity, with Michael remarking: "We feel more comfortable with it and the feeling is that it may even enhance our business in Ireland …"

Although facing Brexit and further challenges in the form of severe weather conditions, a factor which can make or break an agri-food business, the Hoeys' positive outlook was

---

[4]   "New state-of-the-art beef unit has Country Crest back on track". Retrieved 29 September 2021 from https://www.independent.ie/business/farming/new-state-of-the-art-beef-unit-has-country-crest-back-on-track-30588451.html

rewarded. In a short period in 2017, they were the first company in Ireland permitted to sign up for a second five-year sustainability programme with Ireland's food board. Ballymaguire secured five accolades at the "Great Taste Awards", the leading food and drink awards in the United Kingdom and Ireland. They also secured a multi-million euro contract extension with supermarket giant Tesco, to the value of €60 million.[5] This marked a near 20-year relationship with the retailer. At the time, Sheila Gallagher of Tesco commended the Hoeys on their ability to instil confidence in growers to invest in the future: "We're very proud to continue our relationship with the Hoey family into the future."

Drawing parallels to the global financial crisis, their non-commercial initiatives advanced during Brexit on a local and national level. Locally, they partnered with schools and charities to develop a 10-acre field that was maintained by the school and its pupils to grow potatoes. On an informal basis, the Hoey brothers organized community events for families living near their family farm, further cementing their place in the locality. Nationally, they identified a key role for education in the agri-food industry and forged a strategic partnership with a Dublin university in 2019.[6] The aim of this venture was to foster a culture of culinary innovation for students in the food and drink industry.

ANOTHER HURDLE TO OVERCOME: HOEY BROTHERS LOOK TO THE FUTURE

From its inception in the mid-1990s, the Hoey brothers endured despite a litany of hurdles facing them, from disease to geopolitical tensions and economic crashes. Michael recently remarked on their approach to crisis management: "In business, you will have crises. You must face your crisis. Address it. Then, drive through it to fix it."

Facing a global pandemic provided a new and entirely unique crisis for the Hoey brothers to navigate. By March 2020, many neighbouring countries were already in lockdown, with businesses from various sectors succumbing due to the pressures of COVID-19. Consumer behaviour patterns in Ireland evolved as a result, causing huge shifts in demands in supermarkets, with an extreme effect on the food and beverage industry.

However, the Hoey brothers had a history of intertwining tradition and innovation for over 25 years. In striving to cultivate their agri-food businesses, they embodied their values of staying true to the land, developing environmentally friendly practices, and providing a sustainable business for society to reap the rewards from. The brothers took solace from their past actions and experiences as they prepared to tackle the COVID-19 pandemic.

While uncertainty around COVID-19 remained for the Hoeys, their sense of clarity around the purpose and vision of the family farm was not clouded. Acting as stewards and guardians

---

[5]   "Country Crest extends contract with Tesco Ireland in €60m deal". Retrieved 29 September 2021 from https://www.irishtimes.com/business/agribusiness-and-food/country-crest-extends-contract-with-tesco-ireland-in-60m-deal-1.3371345

[6]   "Country Crest and Ballymaguire Foods driving innovation in TU Dublin". Retrieved 29 September 2021 from https://ballymaguirefoods.ie/country-crest-ballymaguire-foods-driving-innovation-tu-dublin/

of the land was a legacy they hoped to pass on to the next generation and future leaders of Country Crest.

However, worryingly for Gabriel and Michael, the onset of an uncertain, unprecedented, and unpredictable virus provided a sense of jeopardy for their legacy like they had never felt before.

With their on-site turbine providing the soundtrack for their conversation, the Hoey brothers knew that this was a challenge unlike anything seen before, "Okay Michael, you're right. This really is different. Let's get on with it."

LEARNING NOTES

Case synopsis

Agri-food business, Country Crest, was founded by brothers Michael and Gabriel Hoey in 1993. The Hoey business had evolved significantly since its inception, elevating themselves from humble farmers to owners of several multi-million euro agricultural businesses, including Ballymaguire Foods, the largest chilled meals producer in Ireland. With a farm-to-fork model for their businesses, living their core values was a key reason for their overwhelming success. In tandem with their growth was their significant CSR work, led by Michael Hoey. This ranged from initiatives in local Dublin schools to projects spanning several years in Haiti. In Country Crest, their respect for the land and their foresight for the future of agriculture and business distinguished them from many competitors. However, the onset of a global pandemic caused the Hoeys to review their history in light of the numerous business challenges and crises they had faced and to look within to find a way forward.

Learning objectives

This case looks at their history and the role values have played in the success of the Hoey brothers. It provokes learners to consider how the Hoey brothers might face another crisis; a crisis on an entirely different scale, the COVID-19 pandemic.

The case discussants should be able to establish:

- The qualities that may assist a family business during a period of crisis.
- The role values play in an organization and how they can be implemented.
- Understanding of the long-term outlook pursued by a family business.
- The business model of a family business, and the idiosyncratic influence of the family on the model.
- The business case for corporate social responsibility.

Learners can view the following videos about the Hoey family business, which would supplement their understanding:

- Video 1: Entrepreneur of the Year Nominee Video, Michael Hoey (https://www.youtube.com/watch?v=EM0KRKaAcrg) – nominated in the 2007 Ernst and Young "Entrepreneur of the Year" award, this clip profiles Country Crest and how they operate. It gives students a snapshot of the business in the mid-2000s.
- Video 2: Origin Green & Country Crest (https://www.youtube.com/watch?v=-znRp78OlNc) – an initiative with Bord Bia, Ireland's food board, which unites the government, private sector, and full supply chain in order to set and achieve measurable sustainability targets. This clip highlights the company's dedication to sustainability in the mid-2010s.

Discussion questions

1. What role did Michael and Gabriel's family values have on their business?
2. Describe Country Crest's business model of farm-to-fork. How did they implement this?
3. How have the Hoey brothers displayed resilience to this point?
4. In your view, what is their most important metric for success? Consider their decisions through the lens of finance, community, CSR, and the environment.
5. Do you believe their sustainably focused mindset will prove to be a roadblock with COVID-19, and why?
6. How do you think the Hoey Brothers should handle the COVID-19 pandemic? Do they require a change of approach from that taken in previous periods of crisis?

Epilogue

COVID-19 proved to be merely another obstacle for Country Crest to overcome, as they stepped up to fight against it. Keen pragmatists, their consistent communication and adaptability with supermarkets in preparation for Brexit had stood them in good stead for this pandemic. Protocols meant supermarkets were rarely ever out of supply, with Country Crest dealing with an *increase* in demand of up to 30 per cent. Their resilience and dedication to excellence ensured they were rewarded *another* contract extension with Tesco, to the value of €60 million. They continued moving forward with a back-to-basics approach, often amending Ballymaguire food recipes to provide adequate supplies to supermarkets. These were learnings Country Crest would no doubt be thankful for in the future. They continued to employ hundreds of workers, safely and fairly, with Michael remarking: "I was looking at our people coming in to work this morning and I would hate to ever find myself in a position where you are telling them their jobs are gone."

Suggested readings

Aronoff, C.E., and Ward, J.L. (2011). *Family business values: How to assure a legacy of continuity and success*. New York: Palgrave Macmillan.

Chrisman, J.J., Chua, J.H., and Steier, L.P. (2011). Resilience of family firms: An introduction. *Entrepreneurship Theory and Practice*, 35(6), 1107–19. https://doi.org/10.1111/j.1540-6520.2011.00493.x

Sharma, P., and Sharma, S. (2011). Drivers of proactive environmental strategy in family firms. *Business Ethics Quarterly*, 21(2), 309–34. doi:10.5840/beq201121218

10
Time to hang up the boots?

María Jesús Hernández-Ortiz, Francisca Panadés-Zamora,
Myriam Cano-Rubio and Manuel Carlos Vallejo-Martos[1]

Carmen Morillo-Ruiz was in the office of Oleícola Jaén getting the last documents together for the project that would enable their current facilities to be turned into a sustainable oil mill open to tourists. They wanted to launch the project in 2022 and for this to happen it must be passed by the local council. They had been waiting to put this idea into operation for quite a few years. However, it seemed that at last things were coming to a conclusion, as it was very much taken into consideration that they sought to benefit Baeza – the municipality where the business was located in – as much as was possible with their sustainable project.

While Carmen flipped through the project folder, she felt satisfied that she had once again been able to put forward a very rewarding venture for Oleícola Jaén. All the effort and hard work was worth it, as had the change in direction that her life took when she decided to join the family business 15 years ago. Despite this not being the best time because of the circumstances surrounding the COVID-19 pandemic, Carmen and her brothers, Remigio and Joaquín Morillo-Ruiz, continued to put together new initiatives with good results for the company.

This triggered Carmen's thought about her father, Luis Carlos Morillo-Molina. She was very grateful for the values he instilled in her, the experience he passed on, the appetite for innovation, the commitment and passion for the business, as these had enabled her and her brothers to improve and grow the company. As a major shareholder, her father still made decisions, and he intended to go on doing so with his vision for the company "till he dropped", when he would name his successor. A priori, this generational change model envisaged by Luis Carlos did not seem to conform to what his successors, Carmen and her brothers, had in mind.

THE MORILLO FAMILY AND GRUPO OLEÍCOLA

The company was headquartered in the town of Baeza in Spain. Apart from its wealth of historic heritage, the town was based around agriculture; surrounded by a sea of olive trees, the

---
[1]   Corresponding author.

Certain details in the case have been disguised. The case is developed solely as the basis for class discussion. Cases are not intended to serve as endorsements, sources of primary data, or illustrations of effective or ineffective management.

community was largely involved in the olive oil sector. The family, like many others in Baeza, owned multiple olive orchards that had been passed down from one generation to the next, following good practice and expertise in olive cultivation.

Luis Carlos (born in 1949) was the fourth of six siblings and the only one who did not go to college. Luis Carlos's father, Remigio Morillo, suggested that he should help collect tax and manage the family estate. Immersed in the management of the estate, in 1980, Luis Carlos suggested to the family the idea of constructing an olive oil factory to extract oil from olive drupes, a typical business model of the time in the region. He considered that this could be a good business for the family and could add value to their agricultural business. The family conducted a viability study and concluded that it could be profitable. In 1981, Oleícola Jaén S.A. was founded as an olive factory to press the olives from the growers in the region. The factory came into operation during the 1982–83 growing season. Along with his father and siblings, Juan and Felipe Morillo-Molina, Luis Carlos made the required investment, although most of the capital came from Remigio.

The factory set the benchmark in the sector from the very start, thanks to its ability to process large volumes of olive oil and its continuous innovation. Under Luis Carlos's leadership, the factory's oil output grew year on year, and the technology was improved to drive up olive oil production. The company further diversified in 1984 and launched a new activity for the exploitation of olive by-products, such as use of the olive pits for clean energy and pomace oil extraction.

In 1997, Luis Carlos's brothers and father decided to sell their shares to him. As a result, the Morillo Ruiz branch of the family came to own 100 per cent of the shares. This meant a new beginning for the company, with 94 per cent of the shares held by Luis Carlos Morillo and 2 per cent held by each of his children, Carmen, Remigio, and Joaquín Morillo-Ruiz. The ownership structure had not changed since then. Carmen commented, "We do not think it is necessary, as Spanish mercantile and tax law allows us to inherit ownership of the company in equal shares if the business continues as it is."

SUSTAINING THE ENTREPRENEURIAL LEGACY

It was at the beginning of the 21st century that the third-generation members joined the business. Carmen (born in 1978) was the first to join and served as the Chief Financial Officer. Her brothers, Remigio (born in 1976) and Joaquín (born in 1982), followed in her footsteps and worked as Quality and Purchasing Manager and the Head of Production and Marketing, respectively.

After finishing her degree in economics at college in Madrid, Carmen started to make her way in the professional world in the city. Deep in her heart, she wanted to return to her hometown to live and practise her craft there. After two years, she set up a consultancy firm in Baeza with her boyfriend and they ran the business together for some years. Carmen recalled:

> The fact that I had lived in the midst of the family business all my life and heard my father constantly talk about it at home as if it were the family's fourth child led me to the decision

to join the company. Around that time, the business was quite consolidated and profitable in a sector that I knew very well and which would enable me to develop professionally in something I was passionate about. I was convinced that joining the family business was a good move for the company and for me.

Luis Carlos's entrepreneurial spirit was ingrained in the next generation, enabling them to take risks and lead change in the environment. Carmen showed a lot of respect for Luis Carlos:

> My father is a huge visionary; everything we propose, he just says "Do it". It's crystal clear to him and, as he never shows any fear, I would say he is the bravest of us all. He commits to everything we suggest to him. But we four always endeavour to agree.

Joaquín pointed out, "The advice … and above all the security that it can give you when dad is here. He is hugely important. But, you know, we feel we've already got what it takes, we've been here for many years now, over fifteen."

The engagement of the third generation dynamized the company, as they were committed to furthering the company's diversification efforts. They contributed their knowledge of new technologies, marketing, and greater business structuring. They endeavoured to create a working team with all the other employees to secure their greater commitment and a better outcome for the company. They had a permanent labour force that was highly committed to the company. As every year, at the beginning of the harvesting and production season, they hired 70 seasonal employees.

The third generation always wanted to go a step further and innovate. They invested a lot of hope and enthusiasm in their latest business initiative, a subsidiary called AOVELAND. Focused on olive oil tourism, AOVELAND was to launch a theme park based around the world of olives. The park would be built in Baeza, and would introduce visitors and travellers to the family's two great legacies: their olives and their monuments. The family created a foundation that was charged with the commitment to improving society through specific programmes that made people's lives better and increased their involvement in the olive oil sector. One of Baeza's most emblematic buildings, the Aliatares Tower, housed the headquarters of the foundation, with multipurpose rooms for training in a wide range of subjects, olive oil-tasting, holding talks by people in the sector, and spreading the culture of olive oil. Carmen and her brothers were also planning a second project: the conversion of the factory to directly attract international tourists interested in olive oil tourism while simultaneously moving some of the activities that pollute the environment outside Baeza's built area.

MANAGING ONGOING DISRUPTIONS

The company continued to grow, despite the wide spread of COVID-19 in Spain and the world in 2020. The pandemic caused multiple problems for Oleícola Jaén. In March 2020, production operations were closed by governmental order in Spain. But as Oleícola Jaén's activity was regarded as a "basic necessity", it was able to continue with its programmed tasks. At that time, all the harvestings had been completed and it carried on without commercializing the olive oil. There was no slowdown in bulk sales, but the sales of bottled oil fell by 30 per cent as it was mainly intended for hospitality, hotels, and gift items. The new initiatives with AOVELAND and the factory conversion suffered some setbacks in progress as well.

The Board of Directors, made up of Luis Carlos, Carmen, Remigio, and Joaquín, secured actions to contend with the crisis: the administrative and sales teams were reduced; an adjustment plan was put in place and half the staff were temporarily laid off; cleaning personnel were given training to ensure the highest level of hygiene in the facilities; all staff were trained in infection protection; and, lastly, remote working was implemented for those who were able to work from home. The entire staff were reinstated in June and the family began the new seasonal campaign in October 2020 while continuing personnel training to prevent any infections. Not a single employee had been dismissed during the pandemic and they had had no problem at all reaching an agreement with workers on the best possible conditions in challenging times.

On the positive side, sales were boosted by leveraging online sales, which rose by 92 per cent. The business sought to energize the social networks and made investments to attract followers. As it had lost a large part of the market share due to the COVID effect on the reductions of orders in the HORECA (Hotels, Restaurants and Catering) channel, it targeted sales at new sectors such as hospitals and nursing homes, which still required its products for consumption. The new generation of leaders seemed to show great promise in managing the pandemic, which offered Luis lots of confidence in the future sibling team.

TAKING CHARGE AND LETTING GO

The succession process had already been underway. The company reflected Luis Carlos's philosophy and of what he had done throughout his life. Little by little, his children gained experience in all the main functional areas, and "mirrored" what he did:

> We have tried to make the philosophy implemented in the factory and in the company in general a carbon copy. We try to imitate him. We each have our own personality and our own way of doing things but when it comes to the structure and way of working and managing, we look to him and try to mirror him … My father's recognition, his clear delegation of responsibility to us, and his high level of trust have enabled us to become a true part of the company and to become fully involved in its management.

In recent years, all the projects concerning new investments and improvements to the company had come from the third generation. Luis Carlos always supported these new initiatives. Despite his support for the children and his empowerment style, he had no plan as to when he should retire from the company. He felt he could still do the job. He made this very clear to his children when they asked him about his retirement: "Never (laughs). As long as I can still get about with a walking-stick, I'll carry on here." Luis Carlos once said that when it was the right time, he would name one of his children as the visible head (CEO). Carmen showed respect for this choice:

> Personally, I have no problem with this attitude of my father. I consider that my father is determined to choose his successor, possibly because this means that at his 71 years of age, he is still at the helm of the company he created. That's what he wants and we will respect that … There really is no internal struggle going on between us to become the visible head of the company. For us, it is not important for the company to have one particular person who represents us all, but rather that the three of us can continue to exercise the necessary leadership at different times and in different situations.

PREPARING A FAMILY PROTOCOL

The future three-pronged leadership had gradually been shaped by having multiple meetings, working hard on relationships, proposing viable initiatives, and getting results for the company. All this generated Luis Carlos's confidence in his children's abilities and was the key to the business's continuity. The family also wrote a family protocol, which stipulated all the circumstances that the family considered crucial for the business to go forward. It was drafted jointly by Luis Carlos, Carmen, and her brothers, with the consensus and agreement of all the members involved:

> Our aim is to secure the continuity of our work in the company, to avoid any family conflicts, to prevent any cracks splitting the family unit apart caused by the joint ownership of the business, and to clearly set out the way that any future generations might join the company.

The protocol laid down a more elaborate succession plan including how future generations should be included, what the organs of governance and the business management model should be, and how the family should be involved in the business. The family sought advice from an external consultant when drafting the protocol and designing the company and family strategies. They believed that the mediation and vision of people from outside the family could be beneficial. The advisor did not intervene in any decisions but had a voice and put them in their place when feelings and emotions started to come to the surface. As Carmen mentioned, "Someone from outside can see things more objectively without losing sight of what is really important, business continuity."

The protocol envisaged a Family Council and a Family Assembly that would meet once a year. There was an Executive Committee made up of all the family members that work in the company plus a non-voting external consultant. The Committee would meet regularly and every week during harvest time. Main decisions would be set down in the minutes book. Any major issues in any area would be discussed so that they could be endorsed by the other members. A clear strategic plan was also developed. Luis Carlos would deal with fewer and fewer responsibilities but would still be responsible for some things that are very important.

But, little by little, he would begin to delegate them. The family considered that, in the future, the retirement age for all family members working in the business should be 70, and this was written into the protocol.

It had been complicated for the three siblings to reach an agreement, as was the process of Luis Carlos's delegation of the main tasks. When there was any disagreement among the siblings, Luis Carlos did not speak to them as their boss but as a father. Likewise, it was hard to speak to siblings about something that might hurt them. Alignment was reached on all these issues in the written protocol. The question was, though, whether new issues would emerge as the real leadership transition was to unfold and whether the protocol could help manage all these.

THE CHALLENGES AHEAD

The Morillos had a head start in planning for the generational transition. They adhered to professional patterns, with a strong intention to achieve good outcomes. The third generation shared the same vision as their father, and they were committed to the environment, the province, and the olive oil sector. They aspired to build a shared future by learning from the mistakes and successes of the past. The family protocol provided a platform for the entire family to discuss and prepare for potential disruptions.

Challenges unique to the siblings' partnership could emerge, however, and these needed to be addressed in the short and medium terms. In particular, what should the model be for this sibling partnership and who should be the CEO when Luis Carlos stepped down? How would the future CEO be able to secure a seamless transition, where customers would not even notice any change but improvements? This was particularly critical as no one knew who the next CEO would be. Also, what would the ownership structure become? While the siblings had developed a strong sense of collaboration, it was far from certain whether harmony could be preserved after the succession took place.

The third generation, while identifying themselves with the "monarch" father, knew the disadvantages associated with his inability to let go. Succession might be less credible, and authority, power, and legitimacy might not be fully transferred as Luis Carlos might not make way for the succeeding leader. Staff would continue to take Luis Carlos's opinion into account as long as he was part of the business. Carmen was worried that this situation might create a dependency of the staff on their father that might weaken the sibling team's leadership. Also, it would be a reasonable concern that Luis Carlos's ongoing presence could hamstring the sibling team's drive and initiative when they wanted to put new structures, strategies, and projects in place to boost the necessary development. In the future, Carmen and her brothers would continue to behave as they did at present, each in their own small work zone, coming to agreements on decisions when needed. Carmen wondered what the family could do to prepare Luis Carlos for the transition and clear the pathway for the future leader while the family was very harmonious.

LEARNING NOTES

Case synopsis

The Morillo-Ruiz family owned multiple olive grove estates, which had been passed down from generation to generation. In 1982, the family decided to take a step forward and created an agri-food business to sell the final product directly to market. Since then, the business had been successfully restructured several times among the different branches of the family. In 1997, the second-generation leader, Luis Carlos Morillo-Molina, bought out the entire business, and he gradually brought in his children – Carmen, Remigio, and Joaquín Morillo-Ruiz. The third-generation team was well prepared for the leadership role. One of the pillars of the generational change had been the design of a governance system that enabled the effective engagement of the next generation bounded by the shared family values. The father still made decisions and owned the largest share of the firm, and he intended to go on doing so with his vision for the company "till he drops", when he would name his successor. A priori, this generational change model envisaged by Luis Carlos did not seem to conform to what his successors had in mind. The COVID-19 pandemic tested the family's commitment to the company, their employees, and the community. This critical situation led them to take urgent measures to adapt to the new circumstances. The Morillo-Ruiz family's agile decision-making helped to turn around the bad results that the pandemic augured for their company. The question was, however, what the family could do to prepare Luis Carlos for the transition and clear pathway for the future leader.

Learning objectives

This case analyses good practices as well as challenges to succession in an entrepreneurial family owning a medium-sized firm.

Participants in the discussion of the case should be able to:

- Analyse the key aspects of "letting go" and the implications of not doing so.
- Illustrate the importance of shared values in a generative family firm.
- Substantiate the need to understand the facilitators of family harmony.
- Understand the need to establish necessary governance and ownership structures.

Discussion questions

1. What impacts did the founder's leadership style have on the company, now and in the future?
2. What were the key values embraced by the Morillo-Ruiz family? How important were these values in the leadership preparation and transition?
3. What were the challenges faced by the siblings and how could they be addressed?
4. Would the siblings be able to maintain the harmony between them if Luis Carlos left the scene entirely?

Epilogue

The Morillo-Ruiz family took a major step towards generational change from the second to the third generation by signing a family protocol and creating specific governance structures such as the Family Council. The generational leadership transition has already begun given that Luis Carlos's three children occupied management positions that were important for the running of the company with the founder's delegation of responsibility and decision-making power. Therefore, Carmen occupied the position of Chief Financial Officer, Remigio was the Quality and Purchasing Manager, whereas Joaquín worked as the Head of Production and Marketing. However, the equity transfer did not happen, the founder retained the majority of shares (94 per cent). Thus, setting out a process for sharing ownership control among them was one of their challenges. Sharing the same vision as the company's founder (commitment to and concern for the environment, the province, and the olive oil sector) was a key aspect to guarantee the success in the transition. Carmen and her brothers planned to behave as an "all in all owners team", interacting frequently and functioning largely as co-equals. Although they might have different positions, each would have a say in major decisions.

Suggested readings

Aronoff, C.E., Astrachan, J.H., Mendoza, D.S., and Ward, J.L. (2001). *Making sibling teams work: The next generation*. New York: Palgrave Macmillan.
Gersick, K., Davis, J., McCollom, M., and Lansberg, I. (1997). *Generation to generation: Life cycles of the family business*. Boston, MA: Harvard Business School Press.

11

A woman at the helm: growth and succession at Inversora Lockey C.A.

Nunzia Auletta[1] and Patricia Monteferrante

In July 2019, Claudia Visani León, Inversora Lockey's Chief Executive Officer (CEO), was absorbed in her thoughts, watching the evening fall from her terrace in Caracas. Her husband, a senior executive of a multinational company, had just received confirmation of his transfer to Mexico, an excellent opportunity for growth and an expected step in his life as an expatriate.

For more than 15 years, Claudia had dedicated her days to the growth and professionalization of Inversora Lockey, her family's business which employed over 500 people. Inversora Lockey was the leader in the Venezuelan lock and padlock market – through their brands of CISA, Visalock, and Vulkan – exported to other Latin American markets (Colombia, Dominican Republic, Aruba, and Panama), and had two commercial offices in Bogotá (Colombia) and Miami (the United States). Under her leadership, the Visani family had acquired full ownership of the business by buying out the remaining foreign partner, more than willing to avoid the risk of doing business in such a complex environment as Venezuela.

Being a woman leading a metalworking company was not common, but she learned the craft from her father Claudio Visani and shared responsibilities with her siblings. Her brother Andrés Visani had been fundamental in keeping the company operational, and her sisters Marila and Diana Visani had participated in all the crucial decisions. At the same time, she was proud to have gained their trust; when important decisions needed to be made, she felt fully empowered and supported.

Thinking of moving abroad posed a huge challenge for her, in terms of keeping the day-to-day engagement with the operations in Venezuela. As the CEO, she had to manage many unforeseen events, foster relationships with the public sector, maintain a close collaboration with suppliers and customers, and always keep an eye out for the countless threats derived from the economic and social instability in the country.

---

[1]   Corresponding author.

Certain details in the case have been disguised. The case is developed solely as the basis for class discussion. Cases are not intended to serve as endorsements, sources of primary data, or illustrations of effective or ineffective management.

While separating from Lockey was not an option for her, she had to think about the best for the business and the family and propose acceptable alternatives to the board of directors that could contribute to the stability of the company. Entering a new succession process was also a possibility, but even if any of her siblings could make a good CEO, they did not have a formal succession plan.

While separating from Lockey was unthinkable for her, she needed to balance her commitment to the business and the family with the future of her marriage and her personal plans.

FROM A FRIEND'S VENTURE TO A FAMILY BUSINESS

In 1967, CISA SpA, an Italian company among the most important manufacturers of locks and access control systems in the world, decided to establish an assembly plant in Venezuela, back then their main market in South America. CISA's owners, Roberto Bucci and Deo Errani, asked Claudio Visani, a childhood friend settled in the country, to join them in founding CISA de Venezuela. As Claudio Visani recalled:

> Roberto offered me a 10% participation in the business and told me that they would not do it without me. We started the factory with 17 workers. Those days were hard, since I went to the factory during the day, and I worked as a calculation engineer during the nights to support my family. A year later I quit my job, and with the unconditional support of my wife Eunice, I fully committed to the new venture.

In 1975, the original partners founded Inversora Lockey C.A., including Schlage (a US lock systems manufacturer) and Grupo Machado Zuluaga (a local steel producer), owning 5 per cent and 26 per cent of the venture, respectively, and equally distributing the remaining 69 per cent of the shares between CISA SpA and Claudio. With new partners and a new plant, Inversora Lockey went through updating the manufacturing processes, the introduction of novel products and own brands (Visalock), and the process of branching out into external markets in Latin America, the Caribbean, and the United States.

Frequent changes in Inversora Lockey's ownership composition accompanied the successful operation of the joint venture with CISA SpA. Within a few years, Schlage was purchased by the global industrial group Ingersoll-Rand. In the 1990s, Claudio Visani and CISA SpA repurchased the shares from the hands of Venezuelan partners, acquiring 95 per cent control over the company's capital. Concurrently, members of the second generation of the Visani family started to get involved in the business.

The friendly coexistence of Claudio and his Italian partners ended in 2005 when Ingersoll-Rand acquired CISA SpA. The Visani family maintained its operational and commercial control, but the informality that was so particular to the relationship among the founding partners evolved towards a more professional management style, which was crucial to interact with the new global partner. The harmonious relationship between Ingersoll-Rand and Inversora Lockey remained despite the Venezuelan economy's volatility, which had worsened since 2009, but two events took place between 2013 and 2015 that changed Lockey's ownership composition. First, Ingersoll-Rand's security accessories unit completed a spin-off, and became an independent company named Allegion. Second, this new partner company recorded a US$11.5 million exchange loss in repatriating its 2014 benefits from Lockey's operation in Venezuela, because of the Venezuelan Bolívar's devaluation against US dollars,[2] encouraging the partner to seek options to mitigate its risks.

In August 2015, the Visani family, led by Claudia, negotiated the purchase of the shares held by Allegion, in addition to a 35-year-long licensing agreement over the use of the brand CISA in Latin America. Recalling the days that preceded the agreement, Claudia commented:

> The five of us [Claudia, Andrés, Marila, Diana and Claudio] met at papa's house one Sunday, to discuss the purchase of Allegion's shares and they gave me the power to negotiate. I hired a valuation expert, and we reviewed the balance sheets and cash flows and had a clear target we wanted to achieve. However, on the day of the negotiation, my father surprised Andrés and me with a different proposal that had occurred to him at the last minute. I had to kick him under the table because he was damaging the negotiation strategy. In the end, we managed to buy their 56% at a third of the value they expected and paid it in instalments.

After 40 years, patriarch Visani's dream had come true: the family had full control over Inversora Lockey, with equal shareholding (25 per cent) of the second-generation members and new freedom to pursue Lockey's strategy.

THE VISANI FAMILY IN BUSINESS

The Visani family involvement and managerial control of the business increased with the direct participation of Claudio and his wife Eunice León's four children: Andrés, Marila, Diana, and Claudia.

The first-born son, Andrés, joined Inversora Lockey in the late 1980s, once he completed his degree in Industrial Engineering at Lehigh University and his Master of Business Administration. To better understand the manufacturing process and acquire first-hand experience on CISA technological know-how, Andrés also worked for over 15 months at CISA SpA, in Faenza, Italy. The combination of formal studies, managerial knowledge, and factory work allowed him to lead operations of Lockey's plant, strengthening the production process, developing his team technically, innovating in different lines of products, and introducing quality control procedures.

Marila as the second-born was a successful investment banker, and was not involved in the day-to-day management, but actively participated in all crucial decisions, first in family informal meetings and then as a member of the board of directors. She was considered "the financial mind" of the family. The third-born Diana was also a member of the board and she

---

managed directly the two commercialization companies that distributed Inversora Lockey products. Diana actively participated in marketing decisions and took care of launching new products and development of Lockey's brands.

As the youngest in the second-generation team, Claudia became involved with the family business in 1995 as a lawyer specializing in the fiscal and financial areas, which were critical in the relationship with Inversora Lockey's several national and international partners. Claudia had the freedom to improve different management activities that allowed for documenting organizational processes, creating a simpler sales model, implementing SAP (a brand for enterprise resource planning software), formalizing the trademark registrations at an international level, and introducing marketing activities.

PASSING ON THE BATON

In 2007, Claudio, by then 80, decided to formalize the succession by designating Claudia as Inversora Lockey's CEO, and Andrés as Chief Operating Officer and Vice Chairman of the board. Commenting on this process, Claudio said:

> Succession has been very simple, my daughter Claudia is a lawyer, my son Andrés is an engineer who graduated from the University of Pennsylvania and trained in CISA factory in Italy … he fully understands the business and I feel we did well in transferring the knowledge. We have had some collisions but on little things … The technical part is well on track, our people are well trained and prepared with the mentality of keeping order and planning carefully. Andrés had to fight with the people here, but he was ready. Claudia has learned a lot working in law firms … now she takes care of the firm.

Commenting on her role as CEO, Claudia often repeated:

> I know a woman in charge of a company that makes locks may look a bit strange because we are used to seeing ourselves in more feminine settings. But this is what I and my sisters have been prepared for: taking over the business. We are multitasking, we do many things at the same time. In this situation, women have come forward without fearing the challenges we face daily.

Besides, she always thought of her mother Eunice, who had been a tremendous role model. She supported Claudio in becoming an entrepreneur, raised their four children, and waited for the firm to settle down before developing her professional career as an expert criminal lawyer. She held important positions in the Venezuelan public sphere and became the director of postgraduate studies in Criminal Law at the Central University of Venezuela.

Claudia and Andrés worked side by side putting their professional competencies in their respective areas and focused on professionalizing the firm and optimizing the manufacturing processes. They felt empowered but, at the same time, they knew that their father was always there. As Claudia commented:

> My dad is tireless ... he started retiring in 2007 when formally I assumed the role of CEO. However, it is very difficult for him not to get involved in day-to-day decisions. He is the one who built everything and knows every part of the business, but things are changing. Now he comes to the plant every day, spends a few hours watching how things work ... he is a constant presence ...

On the other hand, Claudio felt confident he had put the business in the right hands and remarked:

> Once I retired from the administration of the company, I let my children do what they have to do. What I want to say is that since I gave my children the company, I did not want to get involved, to say what had to be done, for a very simple reason, because I think they should make the decisions and I see that they grew with the company. I do not participate in the decision making of the company. Now it is in the hands of my daughter Claudia and my son Andrés.

THIRD GENERATION INVOLVEMENT

By 2019, Inversora Lockey included three generations of the Visani family (see Figure 11.1). The second and third generations were directly involved in the daily management of the family business, while Claudio, aged 93, kept visiting Inversora Lockey's facilities regularly, more out of habit than for managerial purposes.

Nine of the third-generation members aged between 17 and 34 were included at different levels, and three of them were envisioned as possible successors at the top management level. Juan Andrés Visani and Arnaldo José Issa were Inversora Lockey's eCommerce Manager and International Sales Manager, respectively, while Ana Luisa Visani acted as a Product and Industrial Sales Manager for Visalock C.A., a company that dealt with the distribution of Inversora Lockey's products.

Following the involvement of the third generation in the business, some tensions appeared in terms of their participation in the decision-making process and how to open new spaces for them to gain experience and responsibility. There was a tacit agreement among the second-generation siblings and the founder that had worked well for years, as Claudia commented:

> As a family, we made all the decisions together, the five of us, my siblings, and my father. Sometimes we are like a chicken coop, everyone wants to say their point of view and we can go on for hours in great discussions.

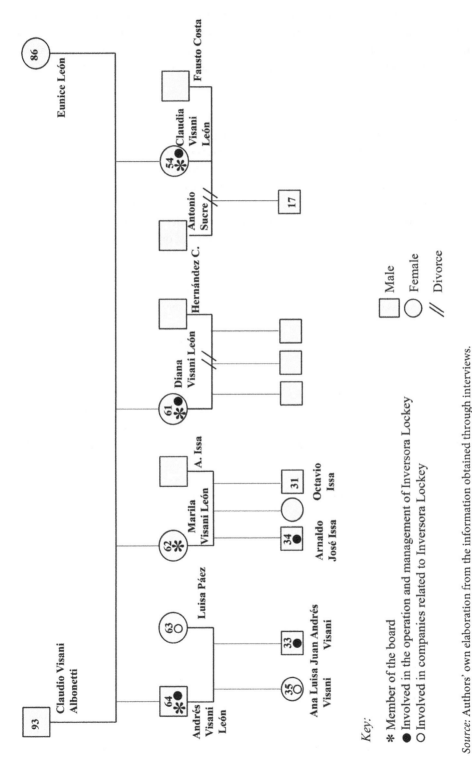

Key:

* Member of the board

● Involved in the operation and management of Inversora Lockey

○ Involved in companies related to Inversora Lockey

☐ Male

○ Female

// Divorce

Source: Authors' own elaboration from the information obtained through interviews.

Figure 11.1 Genogram of the Visani family

Succession also appeared again as a central issue in family discussions and evidenced different points of view on how to face the process in the future. However, they did not reach any formal agreement, and there were clear differences between second- and third-generation family members. On the one hand, Andrés seemed comfortable with managing it with his sisters, following their usual interaction:

> We have been talking about succession for eight years. We know that it is an important issue that concerns the company's survival. All the four siblings have had quite long conversations … although they have been informal conversations, the subject has been deeply dealt with. We have had meetings with lawyers and advisors, and we are aware of the challenges we are facing. Now, it is clear to us that for Inversora Lockey there are only two family members: my nephew and my son … What we are clear about is that the incorporation of these two family members should rely on their abilities. It will not be a hand-picked assignment, but they will progress up the career ladder based on their skills and considering what they can contribute to the company.

On the other hand, the Visani family's millennials seemed to push towards a more active role in decision making, as the third-generation member Arnaldo remarked:

> Every time we try to change things, they tell us "do what you have to", "show that you are doing what needs to be done". When we took a critical stance and called for a meeting they said no! Here we do things the other way around: you propose, and we decide. Regarding the family council, nothing has been concluded, despite our efforts taking it up to several advisers. If we ask Uncle Andrés about the succession plan, he would tell us that they [the four second-generation members] have talked about it … but we would like to be part of that plan because we manage several business lines and need to know what our strengths will be in the morrow.

An unexpected succession in the role of CEO, which could derive from Claudia's departure, could open a new discussion about the role of the third generation and their training and experience to assume positions of greater responsibility in the company.

LEADING IN A PERFECT STORM

During her years as Inversora Lockey's CEO, Claudia, supported by her sister Marila, had the opportunity to develop a set of financial structures that aimed at managing family-owned businesses and shared family assets. Both sisters promoted the development of a position to manage the family's inheritance, a sort of incipient family office, although lacking a formal protocol. At the same time, an ad hoc family council made way for a board of directors consisting only of the four second-generation members.

They also set up a holding company to effectively manage the portfolio of companies owned by the Visani family, which allowed them to adopt a shared vision on topics such as strategy, diversification, risk, profitability, taxation, and control, as well as consolidation and reporting of results. The organizational restructuring plan gave birth to the Lockey Group, formed by Inversora Lockey, Administradora Lockey (a financial and management firm), Tratamaq (a metalworking company for the manufacture of tools, parts, and pieces), and three companies in charge of Inversora Lockey's product distribution and marketing, namely (i) Distribuidora Visalock, (ii) Inversiones Okavango, and (iii) Inversiones Ok Tres.

Concurrently, the Venezuelan economy crashed, and the country faced the worst crisis in its recent history. By 2019, Venezuela went into a hyperinflation stage (with an inflation rate of over 9,000 per cent on an annual basis), and the economy suffered an unprecedented collapse, with a cumulative drop in gross domestic product per capita of –55 per cent in five years. As a result, the industrial sector worked with an idle capacity of more than 70 per cent, fuelling the unemployment growth. Over 60 per cent of Venezuelan households experienced "multidimensional poverty",[3] and more than five million Venezuelans left the country to "escape violence, insecurity, and threats as well as lack of food, medicine, and essential services".[4]

One of Lockey's main segments, the construction industry, was registering a ten-year contraction, with a dramatic loss of 93 per cent in revenue. As for the consumer markets, recession and inflation had annihilated the purchasing power to acquire durable goods but stimulated the need to protect and preserve personal properties from security threats. New product lines, such as a motorcycle security padlocks, were successfully launched to pursue these opportunities. However, overall Inversora Lockey's domestic revenues registered a fall of over 40 per cent in five years, with some lines, such as home security devices, plunging by 70 per cent. In addition, operation costs grew due to the need to maintain the one-year raw material inventory and support potential suppliers in the country. When referring to the challenges she had to face at the helm of her family business, Claudia commented:

> Venezuela is experiencing an economic crisis that hurts us all. Even if we are a recognized brand in security, we have been affected by the contraction of the market. The greatest challenge is, in the face of all limitations, to be more creative, engage better managers to obtain the raw materials and keep the company going. Migration is another factor that we must deal with. Indeed, many people have left, but it has also allowed us to engage new people with new ideas.

Fortunately, Inversora Lockey's international expansion, mostly following some of their key customers abroad, leveraging on life-long relationships and a competitive price–quality combination, partially compensated for the loss in revenues in Venezuela. Arnaldo, Marila's son and a key player in the consolidation of international operations, commented:

> We have a branch office in Colombia, and a distributor in the United States that does not sell massive numbers in that country but does resell the products in the Caribbean and Central America. We began to explore this business model in the mid-1990s and consol-

---

[3]   Encovi (2020). *Encuesta Nacional de Condiciones de Vida 2019–2020.* Retrieved 29 September 2021 from https://www.proyectoencovi.com/informe-interactivo-2019

[4]   Retrieved 29 September 2021 from https://www.unhcr.org/venezuela-emergency.html

idated it in 2005. Today, we take even more care of our markets abroad because they are critical for us to survive as a company. We are in Peru, Colombia, Panama, and on a large scale in the Dominican Republic, in addition to having small participation in Costa Rica and El Salvador.

A DIFFICULT CHOICE

As Claudia got ready to face her siblings in the board of directors meeting, she kept on weighing her future role in the business. She was also aware of her nephews' expectations, and her brother Andrés's view on preparing the "boys" to take care of the business in the future. She remembered her nephew Arnaldo's words:

> The family exerts a lot of influence over the company ... I think that no manager here thinks about becoming a vice president, ever, because there is a strong line within these three generations: my grandfather passed it down directly to Uncle Andrés, while Juan Andrés and I have been on the radar for the past 8 years ... However good or bad, that's how the business has been run so far.

Her sisters had been of great support. Marila was central to governance and organization restructuring, while Diana focused on the distribution and marketing firms of the group. Without a doubt, the Visani women were educated to play a productive role beyond the household. This aspect was always reinforced by their father, Claudio, who groomed his daughters from an early age in the family business.

Claudia could always insist on keeping her position and handle the business from Mexico, but she feared that a detachment from the Venezuelan context and the day-to-day family informal interaction could cripple her capacity to keep all things under control. She could travel frequently, but that could represent a high stake for her marriage and family.

In the end, it seemed that all was about family commitment and emotions, as she thought:

> All this is the product of my dad's work, and we all end up falling in love with it. This is his legacy and he entrusted me to preserve it.

Many questions stayed in Claudia's mind stepping into the boardroom: Should she become a distant CEO? Could she delegate some responsibilities to professional managers? How should she choose between her own family and the Visanis? Was the family ready for a new succession process? Who would be the more suitable CEO successor? What would be the role of the third-generation members?

LEARNING NOTES

Case synopsis

Inversora Lockey C.A. was a Venezuelan family firm focused on manufacturing and marketing security goods and services. It was founded in 1975 by Claudio Visani, as a joint venture with his friends and owners of CISA Group in Italy, whose shares were acquired by Ingersoll-Rand in the United States later in 2005. After four decades of growth and professionalization of the business, in 2015, the family (who owned 46 per cent of shares) took the risk of buying out the international technological partner, by then Allegion, and acquired full control of the company, thereby reinforcing their governance structures and strengthening their internationalization strategy.

The founder had retired from managerial responsibilities, the second-generation members stepped in as the top management, while the third generation entered the company in the middle management level. The leadership transition allowed Claudia Visani, the founder's daughter, to become the company's CEO. Along with her brother Andrés Visani and her sisters Marila and Diana Visani, the sibling team navigated the family business in a very hostile business environment.

Claudia faced many challenges, including professionalizing the firm, restructuring the family business group, and providing for a basic family wealth management structure.

In 2019, during the worst economic crisis registered in Venezuela, Claudia's husband, a successful multinational executive, was transferred to Mexico. This raised the dilemma for Claudia to give up her leadership role or to look for other options that could sustain her commitment to the family business while maintaining a necessary balance with her personal life.

Learning objectives

Inversora Lockey C.A. and the Visani family demonstrated the dilemmas faced by a family business and an entrepreneurial family evolving in an intertwined manner to preserve the business and the family legacy, while coping with a hostile environment.

Learners should be able to:

- Understand the overlapping business and family systems and their interrelations in investment, strategy, and succession decisions.
- Analyse the succession process in a family company as well as the difficulties that can arise and the importance of preparation for leadership succession.
- Evaluate the importance of family and business governance structures and the role that they play.
- Understand the role of women leadership in family businesses and the difficulties inherent in this role.

Discussion questions

1. What were Claudia's main dilemmas? What should she consider preparing for the board meeting? Why?
2. What options were available to Claudia? What were their advantages and disadvantages?
3. What were Inversora Lockey's strengths and weaknesses with respect to installing a new succession process?
4. Who should make the final decision? Should it be the board of directors? Should they also consider the voice of the third generation?

Epilogue

The Visanis did not have a formally settled succession plan, as they relied mainly on the close relationship between the siblings as a mechanism for generating consensus and decision making. Therefore, they did not have a specific strategy allowing them to deal with any unforeseen events related to the current organization leaders (i.e., death, serious accidents, kidnappings, unexpected and prolonged illnesses, among others). Any change or crisis was managed in an ad hoc manner by the family, as happened in the situation proposed in this case.

Suggested readings

Chrisman, J.J., Chua, J.H., and Sharma, P. (1998). Important attributes of successors in family businesses: An exploratory study. *Family Business Review, 11*(1), 19–34. https://doi.org/10.1111/j.1741–6248.1998.00019.x

Hoy, F., and Sharma, P. (2010). *Entrepreneurial family firms.* New York: Pearson Prentice Hall.

Sharma, P., Blunden, R., Michael-Tsabari, N., and Algarin, J.O.R. (2013). Analyzing family business cases: Tools and techniques. *Case Research Journal, 33*(2), 1–20.

PART III
UNCONVENTIONAL WISDOM IN UNUSUAL TIMES

12
"Should I stay or should I go?": Filipe de Botton's dilemma

Alexandre Dias da Cunha[1] and Remedios Hernández-Linares

SURFING THE BRAINWAVES OF FAMILY GOVERNANCE

As the sun set slowly to his right, Filipe de Botton slowed his car and pulled into the gas station to buy a refreshment and fill the tank. "There must be a big swell hitting soon," Filipe said to himself, noticing the unusual number of surfers in the rest area. Nazaré, a tiny fishing town on the Atlantic coast north of Lisbon, had come a long way from the sleepy days of sardines drying in the sun to big wave surfing and world fame. But Filipe's mind quickly circled back to the thoughts that had kept him busy since leaving Mesa Ceramics an hour and a half ago.

The 62-year-old entrepreneur really enjoyed the car trips between Lisbon and Estarreja, which he undertook every couple of weeks to visit the Mesa Ceramics factory. He preferred these trips to the intensive plane travelling that he endured in his days as CEO of Logoplaste, the packaging company that he took over from his father and led very successfully for many years. Mesa was one of the entrepreneurial ventures he and his family were developing through Nikky, a vehicle functioning as both the Botton venture capital firm and family office. He always changed his cell phone to flight mode and seized those moments to think about the challenges ahead that he and his family would have to face in Logoplaste, and in the entrepreneurial ventures that they were developing through Nikky. What role should each family member play in the coming years? How should they best coordinate their individual contributions and learn to work as a sibling team to preserve the entrepreneurial legacy? What did he want for himself? He knew quite well that he had achieved a lot, but he also had so many ideas about what could still be done! Should he speed up his own succession process, or should he stay at the head? On this Thursday afternoon in mid-September 2020, he was feeling especially contemplative.

---

[1] Corresponding author.

Certain details in the case have been disguised. The case is developed solely as the basis for class discussion. Cases are not intended to serve as endorsements, sources of primary data, or illustrations of effective or ineffective management.

BOTTON FAMILY HISTORY

Marcel de Botton, Logoplaste's founder, was born in Brazil in 1925, and that same year moved to France with his parents. But in 1940 the troops of the Third Reich broke through the French defensive lines and Paris was occupied by Hitler's army. Shortly thereafter the family moved to Portugal. There, Marcel married Huguette (who passed away in 2019), and they had three children, Isabel, Filipe, and Cristina, each now with their own family (see Figure 12.1 for the family tree). In their youth Isabel and Cristina worked for some time at Logoplaste, but eventually they separated from the business and at present Filipe was the only second-generation member of the Botton family who continued to be involved.

Filipe was born in 1958 in Lisbon, Portugal, and graduated in Business from the Universidade Católica Portuguesa. Ever since he was a boy and when he was not in class, he had helped his father in the factory. Even from 1981 to the early 1990s, as he became a successful businessman outside the family business, he always remained connected to Logoplaste, working hand in hand there with his father. Through their combined efforts, Marcel and Filipe made Logoplaste successful and created a thriving legacy for the Botton family. Filipe married Rita, a physician, in 1982. Rita and Filipe had three children.

THE FAMILY LEGACY'S ORIGIN: LOGOPLASTE

In 1956 Marcel de Botton, an immigrant in a country living under a dictatorial regime, created a small company dedicated to the marketing of pharmaceutical packaging. Sometime later he founded, together with his wife and a group of investors, the Titan Plastics Factory, one of the largest Portuguese plastic factories in the greater Lisbon area. But, in 1974, with the Carnation Revolution,[2] plant workers took over management decisions and Titan became unmanageable. Marcel decided to start over, and created Logoplaste, meaning knowledge (*logos* in Greek) of plastic.

However, the political situation remained unchanged, which prompted Marcel to think of an ingenious way of adapting. To avoid labour unions, the company needed to have a workforce

---

[2]   25 April 1974, a bloodless left-wing military coup in Lisbon, known as the Carnation Revolution, ended one of Europe's longest dictatorship, and led the way for the restoration of democracy after a transitional period known as *Processo Revolucionário Em Curso* (PREC). This period, which lasted from April 1974 to November 1975, was characterized by social turmoil and power disputes between left- and right-wing political forces. Popular movements flourished. Many of the old elites were removed and workers gained access to political decision-making, but also to higher education and better living conditions in general. The PREC also included nationalization of enterprises and banks. See Baumgarten, B. (2017). The children of the Carnation Revolution? Connections between Portugal's anti-austerity movement and the revolutionary period 1974/1975. *Social Movement Studies*, 16(1), 51–63. doi: 10.1080/14742837.2016.1239195.

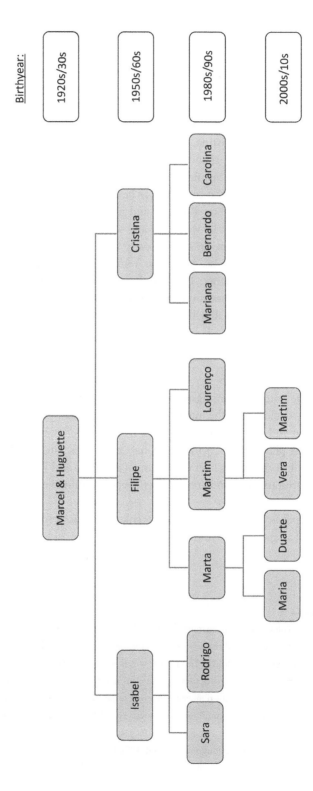

Figure 12.1   The Botton family

Birthyear:

1920s/30s

1950s/60s

1980s/90s

2000s/10s

numbering fewer than 50.[3] Marcel therefore installed small factories situated within his clients' premises.

While Logoplaste's competitors serviced multiple clients from a central plant, which allowed them to take advantage of scale benefits and to diversify client risk, Marcel based his business's expansion on offering just-in-time delivery and supply-chain integration, pioneering "in-house manufacturing in Europe, with its hole-in-the-wall concept".[4] This concept, linked to values such as demand for high standards and the search for continuous perfection, spurred Logoplaste's rapid expansion. The business never ceased to grow under Marcel's leadership. By the early 1990s, Logoplaste was a very successful company, dominating the Portuguese market. This success brought a new challenge, however.

THE SECOND GENERATION TOOK CHARGE OF THE BUSINESS IN AN UNUSUAL WAY

Logoplaste's success in Portugal meant that the company had no choice but to expand internationally if it was to continue growing. But Marcel, the founder that had led its expansion within the Portuguese market, was a man with scant studies. Filipe, however, was a family member with university studies, very involved in Logoplaste from a young age, and with a broad and successful professional trajectory. Indeed, between 1981 and 1992 Filipe was the representative for Portugal of several European banks, as well as a founding shareholder of a private bank and a wealth management company, now part of large financial institutions. Filipe not only had much more training than his father, but also had become a successful entrepreneur outside the family firm, which led Marcel to think that Filipe was the right person to face the new challenge: the company's internationalization. Thus, in 1991, 15 years after Logoplaste's birth, Marcel invited his son to lead the company, give continuity to the family firm and boost its international expansion.

In that same year, Filipe and his friend Alexandre Relvas, who since 1979 had been partners, sold their ventures – at the same time that Alexandre was invited to join the Portuguese government, as Secretary of State for Tourism. Thus, it was a good moment to face a new challenge. But Filipe had two sisters, Isabel and Cristina. Although only one was involved in Logoplaste at that moment, both owned a part of the shares. To fully dedicate himself to Logoplaste, Filipe wanted to be in control and to avoid putting the family's harmony at risk. The three siblings worked out and agreed on a deal by which Filipe invested the earnings obtained with the sale of his businesses to buy the company from his father and sisters. Marcel stayed on as Chairman (Honorary Chairman after 2017), which helped to overcome the challenges of this first generational changeover and avoid family tensions. Thus, Filipe became 100 per cent owner of Logoplaste, whose turnover was around €10 million in 1991.

---

3   Retrieved 30 January 2021 from https://www.logoplaste.com/about/our-founder/

4   Alcacer, J., and Leitão, J. (2013). *Logoplaste: Global growing challenges*. Harvard Business School Case 9–711–411, December 2010 (revised February 2013).

OPENING THE BUSINESS LEADERSHIP TO NON-FAMILY MEMBERS: A SUCCESSFUL CO-LEADERSHIP

After acquiring all of the Logoplaste shares Filipe started to win new clients outside Portugal. Nevertheless, despite a successful internationalization process, when his friend Alexandre Relvas stepped down from the Portuguese government in 1996 Filipe invited him to join Logoplaste as co-leader and minority investor. Since then, they had always worked as if they were 50/50 per cent partners in all their ventures. Over the next 20 years, focusing on excellence in both product delivery and customer service, the two partners further advanced Logoplaste's internationalization.

A KEY DECISION: TO KEEP GROWING OR STAY IN CONTROL

In 2015 Filipe faced a defining moment: a new expansion phase lay ahead, requiring heavy investments of about €350 million, of which €100 million had to be provided by Logoplaste. Since neither he nor Alexandre were in a position to invest such an amount of money, they had to decide between maintaining the company's control or boost its growth at the cost of giving up control. Making this decision was very tough, because, in Filipe's words, at the end of 2015, they "hesitated between to go or not to go ... which is very interesting because it is a process between reason and emotion, when you are the owner of the pitch and of the ball and you accept to share ...".

After careful consideration, they decided to open up Logoplaste's capital, and the company embarked on a beauty contest with different private-equity firms. Many investors showed their interest in participating, and three of them accepted to buy 40 per cent of the capital. But the partners also received a proposal to buy 60 per cent of the capital, which involved a significant increase in the implied valuation of Logoplaste and in the total amount of the transaction. This was the first motive that led Filipe and Alexandre to think about the proposal. But there was also a family reason, as Filipe knew that if they kept 60 per cent of the equity, he would burden his children with the obligation to closely manage and follow Logoplaste, while he kept 40 per cent of the business, they would continue to have weight in the company and in what was happening in the business. Filipe had to decide between maintaining control or growing, on the one hand, and between "forcing" his children to follow and manage Logoplaste, or take pressure off them, on the other. Finally, and after some sleepless nights, he and Alexandre decided that, according to his words: "The fact that we maintain 40% of the company ... gives us the best of both worlds – it is an important position vis-à-vis other shareholders, but it doesn't force us to be in management."

Thus, in 2016 Logoplaste completed a partnership agreement with Carlyle Europe Partners IV, a European buyout fund, which now held a 60 per cent stake in Logoplaste, while Nikky retained the remaining 40 per cent (89 per cent of Nikky was owned by Filipe and his children, while the remaining 11 per cent was owned by Alexandre). The deal with Carlyle implied that the Botton family would no longer have the majority of the firm but established that Filipe was named Chairman of the Board (stepping down from the CEO position), while Alexandre became non-executive board member, and a new outside/non-family CEO was hired. As a consequence, Logoplaste was no longer a pure family business. However, the willingness to sell part of the company's ownership did not imply his emotional disengagement from the business created by his father. Indeed, it was Filipe's clear intention that the Botton family continue to pursue its role in the governance structure of Logoplaste. In addition, although in his role as Chairman, Filipe did not have executive duties, he still was the family's leader within the company, as well as the reference person for the main customers such as L'Oréal, Procter & Gamble, and others all over the world, because Logoplaste had based its expansion on close and long-term relationships with its clients, who greatly favoured the continuity of the firm.

When Filipe bought Logoplaste in 1991 it was a small Portuguese firm, but Logoplaste had evolved into a global company. According to its *Sustainability Report 2019*,[5] by 2018 it owned 63 plants located in 16 countries across three continents and employed 2,361 workers. Having produced 11 billion units in 2018, Logoplaste achieved sales above €500 million.[6] And although the Botton family no longer held the majority of Logloplaste, it continued to be an enterprising family, which had led it to create Nikky.

NIKKY: A VEHICLE AT THE SERVICE OF THE FAMILY LEGACY

While Logoplaste grew and became an international company, Filipe had more recently started other ventures on the side and under a common holding firm: Nikky, which became something of a mix between a family office and a venture capital firm. The most important of these ventures were CadIn (a non-profit, to help children with disabilities),[7] Santini (a 50/50 joint venture with another family firm – the leading premium/niche ice-cream producer in Portugal),[8] LACS (a co-working space venture),[9] Carsol Fruit (a blueberry production venture),[10] and Mesacer (a ceramics venture).[11]

Filipe and Rita's three children had developed different levels of involvement in the family's businesses:

- Marta worked for three years in outside companies in Portugal and Spain and then in Logoplaste for 12 years, before going on a maternity break and then returning to become non-executive director of Logoplaste and general manager of Nikky.

---

[5] Retrieved 30 January 2021 from https://www.logoplaste.com/media/2564/logoplaste_sustainability_report_2019_eng.pdf

[6] Retrieved 30 January 2021 from https://www.logoplaste.com/careers/

[7] Retrieved 30 January 2021 from https://www.cadin.net/home-cadin-in-english

[8] Retrieved 30 January 2021 from https://www.santini.pt/

[9] Retrieved 30 January 2021 from https://www.lacs.pt/en/

[10] Retrieved 30 January 2021 from https://www.carsolfruit.cl/en/

[11] Retrieved 30 January 2021 from https://www.mesa-ceramics.com/en/

- Martim started working at the Santini joint venture, before deciding to work outside the family ventures because he wanted to have a more personal entrepreneurial experience. In 2018, he launched a home delivery company, allowing him to join Nikky at any point in the future.
- Lourenço "didn't like to be all day sitting at a desk". Nevertheless, his will to join the family enterprise was strong, and his commercial skills were valuable. He was working for Carsol Fruit, which allowed him to be in the countryside often and interact with the company's international customers – large European retailers.

PREPARING FOR THE NEXT LEG OF THE RELAY

Although Filipe felt that his retirement moment had not yet arrived, he believed that he had transferred to his children all the values they needed to relieve him when he retired. For example, Filipe was always stricter with his children than with others, since "they have to work harder because they have to give the example". He also tried to stimulate the same spirit of demand for high standards in them that he had learned from his father, because Filipe was convinced that such spirit made the difference. To him, exigency and persistence were values strongly related to their cultural framing. For this same reason, he believed that all three generations had a strong entrepreneurial spirit: "Entrepreneurship is taught and learned, it is not a genetic predisposition." To live in the middle of a business environment naturally led to having that spirit. Filipe's main concern was to set up a family governance system and to develop the areas of Nikky that were still in the early stage of business maturity. With the purpose of setting up family governance rules, the five blood family members (Filipe, Rita, and their three children) started to meet regularly. Filipe led the discussions, but he was careful to let the next generation figure out what they wanted and how they wanted to engage with each other. They seemed to agree that Marta would be the one to represent the family within Logoplaste, who was a non-executive member of the Board, and that a productive interaction between the second and third generation still mattered for Logoplaste, as it contributed to a feeling of security among the company's workforce and stakeholders.

During these family governance meetings, Filipe sought to promote the discussion about all topics, especially about the more controversial issues because "it's the healthy thing to do ... it is the only way to solve problems, to avoid people having unresolved issues. And with my children, we don't have unresolved issues."

Filipe was trying to capitalize on his life experience to help his children establish the family governance rules. He wanted his children to reflect about all alternatives, but also to understand that "simpler is better" because no contract would reflect everything that might happen. In addition, he tried to instil a spirit of consensus-seeking in his descendants, because he firmly believed that the dialogue needed to find true consensus would yield the best decisions.

Furthermore, Filipe reckoned that it would be harder for his children to succeed him than it had been for him to succeed his father, even if the recent change of focus (from Logoplaste to Nikky) had helped the Botton family to embrace these challenges, to seek alignments, and to develop common entrepreneurial goals.

On the other hand, Filipe believed that having one's children decide whether the older generation was still fit or not would be a heavy burden that they should not have to bear. Neither did he believe in establishing a cut-off date or age limit for leaving the family business. He considered that age should not be the defining factor because different people would age differently, and because any contingency might occur before the established retirement age. For him, the key to determine the moment of his retirement was his own capabilities. He was considering setting up a process by which the evaluation of the right moment for his succession to take place would be placed in the hands of a trusted outside entity (something like a "committee of the wise"). But whom should he trust? In any event, he did not think that he should retire immediately, because his children were not yet ready. While the moment had not yet arrived, he wanted to have the pleasure to work on the family legacy for some time.

A NEW AND UNEXPECTED CHALLENGE: THE COVID-19 PANDEMIC

Early in 2020 the COVID-19 pandemic led Filipe to face new challenges. In business terms, the biggest challenge for the Botton family had been communication. Virtual online meetings brought people together, but they lacked certain elements, such as non-verbal communication, and required making an investment in increased efforts, to compensate and make sure communication stayed fluid. Another challenge was to adapt to the lockdown impositions in all the geographies in which Logoplaste was present.

However, the pandemic had slowed some of the processes engaged by the family in terms of governance and succession, as the priorities had shifted towards the more urgent tasks that arose with the pandemic, in terms of the businesses and of the solidarity and philanthropy projects. For example, Logoplaste donated free meals and plastic containers to hospitals fighting COVID-19 and responded to an appeal by a local mayor to start a programme to supply meals to poor citizens of Arroios, a borough in Lisbon; and Santini offered free ice-cream to health workers at a hospital close to the factory.

In family terms, Filipe thought that getting involved in helping those who had been adversely affected by the pandemic had created an opportunity for increased bonding. In addition, in his view the importance of helping others, no matter if they were close to the family or not, had become much more evident through the COVID-19 crisis.

AN ICE-CREAM AND SOME DOUBTS...

Totally absorbed in these contemplations, Filipe hardly noticed how he shifted into reverse, to park the car in the driveway of the Nikky building. It was only when Lourenço came out to greet him, holding a Santini ice-cream cone in his hand, that his mind switched to "here and now". "Would you like some? Pomegranate and raspberry... it's delicious!"

Later that night, before turning off the light when leaving the office, Filipe thought that in his sixties, he still felt as fit as ever, and reminded himself of the Latin saying *nemo iudex in causa sua*: no one is ever a good judge in his own cause! Should he speed up his own succession process, just as Marcel did 25 years ago? It seemed to him that his three children were doing an outstanding job at carrying on the legacy of family entrepreneurship, but were they ready yet? While he certainly did not have the answers, Filipe knew that these were the right questions.

LEARNING NOTES

Case synopsis

In 1991 Filipe de Botton, a successful businessman outside the family firm, joined Logoplaste, an innovative plastics packaging company founded by his father, Marcel de Botton, 15 years earlier. Since then, Filipe had led the internationalization process of Logoplaste, which became a global company, while he had had to face dilemmas such as opening up (or not) the leadership of the family business to non-family members, maintaining family control, or grow. In addition, Filipe had started other ventures under a holding firm, Nikky, which was a mix between a family office and a venture capital firm and had made the Botton family evolve from being the owner of a family firm (Logoplaste) to becoming an enterprising family, involved in businesses as different as ice-cream and ceramics. It was September 2020, and while Filipe's retirement moment had yet to arrive, he enjoyed working on the family legacy. With his main concern of setting up a family governance system and developing the areas of Nikky that were still in the early stage of business maturity, Filipe wondered how he could make his "retirement" more seamless to his enterprising family.

Learning objectives

The case shows the challenges faced by Filipe de Botton during the process of a family enterprise (Logoplaste) evolving into a non-family enterprise, and his concerns about preserving the family legacy. The case describes the first succession in Logoplaste's leadership and ownership, the challenges and dilemmas faced by Filipe de Botton since he bought Logoplaste from his father and sisters, and the preparation of the generational relay, sustaining the family legacy.

This case serves the following learning goals:

- To recognize different ways to transfer a family business from one generation to another. Specifically, learners will learn how a firm may be transferred from parents to their children through an intra-family succession in both ownership and leadership. In addition, they will understand how an entrepreneurial family faces and prepares the transfer of a business (Logoplaste) that is no longer a family business but in which they seek to maintain the family's important position without the obligation of the future management of the company falling on the successors' shoulders. In addition, learners will understand the difference between the preparation process of a classic family business succession and the preparation process of the succession in a business family.
- To understand the importance of timing for a successful succession. According to Filipe, timing for his retirement was one of his main concerns, and often led to wondering about how much longer he should stay at the top or what would be the best moment to retire.
- To understand the importance of implementing family governance, in order to guarantee the enterprising family's future and to preserve the family legacy. This case

will help learners understand that the preceding and succeeding generations must work together to plan for a successful generational change, and that this preparation requires a frank and honest communication between different members and generations of the family that allows them to discuss all topics (including those controversial ones) for the establishment of family governance rules.

• This case promotes discussion about how to create transgenerational value for families beyond the core firm. Additionally, the case leads to reflection about how to transfer the business from one generation to the next and how to prepare the family governance to preserve the family legacy.

Discussion questions

1. What were the key factors in the successful transfer of Logoplaste from the first generation to the second one in the Botton family?
2. What were the main differences and similarities between how Filipe de Botton assumed the leadership and ownership of the family firm (Logoplaste) and how he was planning to transfer his businesses from the second to the third generation?
3. How will you evaluate Filipe's decision to change the focus from Logoplaste to Nikky?

Epilogue

Filipe had been working, together with his wife and children, to create the future governance rules for the family assets. Together, they were defining the guidelines, processes, and structures, in terms of governance, for the third and fourth generations of the family enterprise founded by Marcel and Huguette de Botton, at the same time as they were growing and strengthening the Nikky ventures.

Suggested readings

Dou, J., Su, E., Li, S., and Holt, D. (2021). Transgenerational entrepreneurship in entrepreneurial families: What is explicitly learned and what is successfully transferred? *Entrepreneurship and Regional Development, 33*(5-6), 427-441. doi: 10.1080/08985626.2020.1727090

Goldberg, S.D., and Wooldridge, B. (1993). Self-confidence and managerial autonomy: Successor characteristics critical to succession in family firms. *Family Business Review, 6*(1), 55–73. doi:10.1111/j.1741–6248.1993.00055.x

Habbershon, T., Nordqvist, M., and Zellweger, T. (2010). Transgenerational entrepreneurship. In M. Nordqvist and T. Zellweger (eds), *Transgenerational entrepreneurship: Exploring growth and performance in family firms across generations* (pp. 1–38). Cheltenham, UK and Northampton, MA, USA: Edward Elgar.

13
Can I retire? An early successor's dilemma

Dalal Alrubaishi[1]

After ten years of being the CEO of Salma Holdings, Faisal Al-Salm had nothing more to give to the business. He wanted to pursue his dream of starting a new career and building his own legacy, two things that were denied to him when he was suddenly obliged to run the family business. However, his father and siblings demanded that he continue in the family business. In a culture valuing family loyalty and parental respect, Faisal found himself caught in the dilemma of having to choose either satisfying his family or following his dream.

BACKGROUND

On the flight back to Saudi Arabia, Faisal, who had just graduated with an electrical engineering degree from Canada, contemplated how his plans had changed because of his father's recent diagnosis of Parkinson's disease. Faisal had gone to Canada with dreams of pursuing a future career as an academic researcher in engineering, but his father's sudden illness made him feel obliged to take over the family business as the only fit successor, although he had three sisters and two brothers. The business was founded in 1977 by his father, Ahmad Al-Salm, as a general trading and contracting Limited Liability Company (LLC). Ahmad Al-Salm was the sole owner and managed the business alone for 32 years while his children were young. He simultaneously built wealth by investing in the real estate and equity markets.

Upon taking his position, Faisal learned that the business had no clear structure. It was scattered, operating in diverse industries, and based on the pursuit of market opportunities driven by his father's relationships and connections. These opportunities were without clear strategy or procedures. Equipped with education, a wide range of knowledge, and international exposure, Faisal developed a vision to transform the company's structure and ownership, instituting sound corporate governance to ensure the continuity of his family's business.

[1]   Corresponding author.

He spent considerable time reading and talking with others running family businesses and consultants to gain a better understanding of his family's business before proposing his plans to other family members.

Faisal had a strong relationship with his father based on trust and empowerment; according to Faisal, "My father is supporting me 100%, if I told him let's jump from the bridge he would say go!" Faisal's father gave him full authority to transform the company's organizational and ownership structure. His plan was also supported by his siblings; their support led to the establishment of Salma Holdings (closed joint stock) in 2012, a family company owned by the second generation. The company timeline is presented in Table 13.1.

Table 13.1 Timeline of the Salma Holdings

1977	Company founded by the father.
2009	Eldest son came back from college and took over the business.
2012	• Company's legal form changed from an LLC to holdings (closed joint stock). • Ownership structure changed from sole owner (father) to shares among the siblings as per Sharia law. • Corporate bylaws established. • Eldest son became the CEO.

Although the siblings had some disputes over some governance policies and procedures during the transition period, Faisal handled these by maintaining a policy of transparency and a culture of open communication. Family unity and cohesion was a priority for Faisal, who wanted to preserve his father's legacy and protect the family reputation. Timing contributed to the transformation's success, as the family structure was still in the early stages of development. The business's transformation resulted in a higher growth rate and better performance.

NEW STRUCTURE AND OWNERSHIP

Faisal turned the different activities his father was working in into separate subsidiaries under a holding umbrella. This resulted in a new holdings company owning subsidiaries in a diversified investment portfolio that spanned different industries, including automotive, real estate, and healthcare (see Figure 13.1).

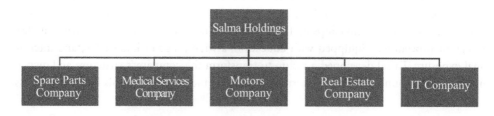

Figure 13.1   Structure of the Salma Holdings

Faisal was the CEO of the holdings company, his sister was the chairman of the board, and a brother and another sister managed two subsidiaries. Support activities, such as finance, accounting, IT, maintenance, design, logistics, and warehousing, were provided by the holdings. The holdings established service-level agreements (SLA) with their subsidiaries to ensure productivity and efficiency; this new structure helped scale the business and reduce operating costs. Faisal and his siblings owned the new holdings company. Background information for Faisal's siblings is given in Table 13.2.

Table 13.2 Background of Faisal Al-Salm's siblings

Birth Order	Gender	Age	Educational Background	Marital Status	Number of Children	Position in the Family Business
1	Sister	43	Bachelor of Arts (BA) Masters of Arts and Social Sciences	Married	1 daughter	GM of subsidiary
2	Sister	40	Business Administration (BBA and MBA)	Married	3 sons	Chairwoman
3	Sister	37	Bachelor of Nutrition	Married	1 son	None
4	Faisal	34	B.Eng.-Electrical Engineering EMBA	Married	1 daughter	CEO
5	Brother	31	Business Administration	Married	0	Board Member GM of subsidiary
6	Brother	29	Bachelor's degree in Law	Single	0	Board member/secretary Legal advisor

His father suggested that Faisal should have a higher ownership percentage since he was the business's leader. However, Faisal had witnessed conflicts within his uncle's family business that originated from the favouritism his uncle showed his eldest son by granting him a higher ownership percentage than the other siblings. Therefore, Faisal refused his father's offer and ensured that the new ownership structure was fair and agreed upon by all of the family members. The shares were divided among the siblings as inheritance under Sharia law[2] ("to the male, a portion equal to that of two females", Holy Quran, 4:11). This decision was made after discussions with consenting family members as well as consulting specialists in Sharia law. Such an ownership structure guaranteed fair distribution of shares and minimized conflicts among the siblings. However, Faisal's mother was excluded from the ownership structure based on his father's wish to keep the in-laws from having any influence on the company. Furthermore, while Faisal's father did not own any shares, he came to the office daily to oversee the work, as he was still viewed as the patriarchal head of the family and the business.

---

[2]   Sharia law (Islamic law) is the common law within the religion of Islam that guides Muslim people in their daily life. Sharia law is derived from the Quran (words of Allah) and Sunnah (the deeds, sayings, and silent approval of the prophet Muhammad (peace be upon him (PBUH))). The legal system of Saudi Arabia is based on Sharia law.

The Saudi culture is family-oriented and shaped by Islamic values. The kinship principle is prevalent, and the family is considered a core pillar of society. Family loyalty, trust, and respect are prioritized above self-interest. Islamic teachings support respect for one's elders and obedience to one's parents, and these practices are highly regarded within Saudi culture.

GENERATIONAL DIFFERENCES

His father was 72 years old when Faisal took over the business at the age of 24. This considerable age gap between the two men reinforced the cultural value of elderly and parental respect. The 48-year difference in age came with differences in vision, mission, and goals. Nevertheless, Faisal managed to navigate these differences and transform the business. Moreover, differences in education, family structure, and social environment between the two generations affected aspects of the business's operations, including investment decisions and the importance of policies and procedures for future leadership and ownership transition.

The father had run the business without a vision or clear structure; rather, he worked each day with the intent to make good money and be good to people. Faisal commented:

> My father is more of an investor than an operational [leader]. He didn't build a company, he invested with the right people, and invested a lot based on merit and good relationships and not on business plans and forecast. Today, we have a structured approach, we have risk appetite, we have certain sectors we want to be in.

Personality differences between the two generations also played a role in leadership style. Faisal was a planner with an active approach to succession planning, whereas his father, in his old age, was emotional and passive in handling family issues. As Faisal explained, "Because of my father's health situation, he is very passive ... My advice to anyone still in the business is to be active; nothing ruins a business like a passive patriarch! A passive patriarch can kill a business."

Nevertheless, Faisal's father gave Faisal full authority to transform the business structure and ownership. Faisal held his father in high regard and admired the way his father built his wealth; he retained the company name and family values in the new structure. This harmonious relationship between the two made the transition smooth and successful. Having seen the positive effect of this transition in terms of growth rate and high performance, his father and siblings were reluctant to let Faisal go.

The social and economic changes that occurred in the country over time also contributed to the changes in the business's structure and operations. Saudi Arabia is a young country undergoing significant development in its economy, society, and human capital; this development is due to the country's Vision 2030. Due to these changes, the younger generations have a different perspective on running businesses than that of their elders. Faisal believed that policies and procedures must be implemented, investment decisions should be based on analysis and research, and forecasts and long-term strategies need to be formulated to ensure continuity. Although Faisal appreciated his father's way of conducting business, his father's methods did not accord with the current complicated and competitive market, let alone with the expansion of the family and inclusion of the second generation in the business.

FAISAL'S SUCCESSION PLANNING

Differences between the father and son were obvious in the ways each handled or planned to handle the succession of the family business. Taking over the family business out of necessity made Faisal plan for succession at an early age. To prevent such a sudden succession from happening again, Faisal started planning for the next leadership succession at the age of 27, and, in cooperation with the other family members, he formulated the corporate bylaws. The bylaws stated that the CEO would serve five-year terms, not exceeding ten years in a row.

Such a bylaw was considered a necessity because the pool of potential successors was now larger, as his brothers had come back from college and started their careers. Faisal was the advocate of this specific bylaw to avoid any "negative competitiveness in the family". As Faisal commented, "We didn't want the kind of approach where I will always be the CEO because I am older!" However, this bylaw did not seem to be taken seriously by the family. Faisal brought up the issue of leadership transition when he was approaching the end of his five-year tenure after establishing the bylaws, but the idea was dismissed by his siblings. They considered Faisal to be the most capable person to handle the family business and wanted him to stay in his position for another five years.

FAMILY RELATIONSHIP AND COMMUNICATION

Communication within Faisal's family was open and transparent in all aspects of the business. Faisal encouraged family members to speak up and express their concerns in terms of ownership; he strongly believed that frank communication was the key to a successful transfer of leadership. Although such discussions are sensitive in family businesses and may lead to conflicts, Faisal saw them as an essential part of family businesses.

> What we did is we [had] open dialogue … we talked about death, we talked about scenarios [such as] what if you get a divorce, what if you do that … that was the key. When we did that, we were able to come up with a plan. The only problem with family businesses today is that they do not communicate. And it is a very awkward conversation, it is a very, very awkward conversation, and it will lead to conflict! But controlled conflict now instead of later.

This open communication within the family compelled Faisal to explicitly state his wish to pursue his own dreams to his father and siblings. While they did understand his wishes, they believed that his potential successor was not yet ready, and that it was best if Faisal stayed in the position longer. In a culture emphasizing the values of family loyalty and parental obedience, Faisal's wishes to move out of the business were put on hold.

THE DREAM

Faisal planned to explore his career opportunities and build a legacy of his own after handing the business over to his middle brother. Withholding the transfer of the CEO position to the next leader was seen by Faisal as a negative practice.

> A very dangerous thing in business [is that] the smallest shareholder could ruin the company. The smallest shareholder can bring it down! Maybe he can't bring it down through regulation, but he will bring it down through spirit … If it is time to transfer [power], it should not be fought, and it should not be a surprise honestly, it should be something you openly talk about.

While Faisal was serious about stepping down, his family did not take his intentions seriously. His decision was not triggered by age, as he was 33 years old, but by the amount of stress his work brought him and his desire to pursue his personal dreams away from the family business.

> On the stress … honestly, 10 years in this job, I think it's [like] 20 years somewhere else! The stress of being in a diversified business takes a toll on your brain … [The] second factor is: what am I doing for my own career? My CV looks like this kid came to cover [for] his father and he is a senior [executive] from day one … I have never worked under anyone. People think it has a spark of course, but I want to report to someone, and be penalized for not coming in on time or not meeting a deadline. I mean it is counterintuitive, but I would love to! I don't want to stay as CEO of a family business where I don't have anything else to give … I structured the company, and that is what I am good at, but [when it] comes to operations, I might not be the best [choice].

After more than ten years of being the CEO, Faisal reached his goal of restructuring the business and establishing clear corporate governance. Although the family wanted him to stay longer in the CEO position, he had prepared his middle brother to take over. He had nothing more to contribute to the business and wanted to pursue his dream of starting a new career and building his own legacy, two things that he was deprived of when he suddenly had to lead the family business. However, the sense of responsibility, pressure, and family expectations caused a real dilemma for Faisal: should he stay or should he leave?

LEARNING NOTES

Case synopsis

Salma Holdings was founded in 1977 as a general trading and contracting company. The founder ran the business alone for 32 years before his eldest son, Faisal Al-Salm, came back from college in 2009 and joined the business out of necessity at the age of 24, as the only eligible successor after his father's illness. Equipped with education, wide knowledge, and international exposure, Faisal came with a vision to transform the company structure, ownership, and operations to ensure the continuity of his family business. This transformation resulted in higher growth and better performance. Generational differences in education, personality, family structure, and social environment between the two generations have affected aspects of the operation of the business, including policies and procedures for leadership and ownership transition in the future. After ten years of being the CEO, Faisal saw that he had nothing more to give to the business and he wanted to pursue his dream of starting a new career and building his own legacy, two things that he sacrificed when he was obliged to suddenly run the family business. However, the founder and family demanded him to continue in the family business.

Learning objectives

The case highlights the generational differences in management style between Faisal and his father. When Faisal took over the business out of obligation, he changed the company form and ownership structure to ensure the continuity of the family business, an issue that the father had not acted upon. Having a strong and respectful relationship with his father as well as establishing open communication among his siblings contributed to his success in transforming the company. The case also introduces the dilemma of a young, ambitious, and successful successor choosing between whether to continue leading his family businesses or pursue his dream career.

The case discussants should be able to establish:

- Differences in management style between generations.
- The importance of establishing clear policies and procedures for leadership and ownership transition.
- The value of accomplishing a balanced and open communication between family members.
- The dilemma of the successor future.

Discussion questions

1. Assess the management styles of the father and Faisal.
2. What are the most critical factors affecting the differences in the management style of the two?
3. What are the factors contributing to Faisal's success in transforming his father's company structure, ownership, and operations?
4. From your point of view, what is the next step for Faisal, shall he stay or shall he leave? Why?

Epilogue

During the COVID-19 pandemic, businesses around the world suffered due to the disturbance of supply chains caused by lockdowns and health and safety restrictions. However, some businesses flourished by seeking new opportunities that came with the pandemic, such as those in the technology and healthcare sectors. For Salma Holdings, the pandemic had a positive effect on the business. The pandemic increased Faisal's confidence in his changes to the family business and assured him that the company was ready to move to the next level. During the pandemic, Faisal focused on developing human capital, something that had been overlooked in previous years. Having developed entrepreneurial skills by leading the family business, Faisal took advantage of the pandemic by pursuing the opportunity to recruit a high-profile human resource director who had lost her job during the pandemic. Thus, during the period of uncertain employment, he had the opportunity to capture talent to which he did not have access prior to the pandemic. Accordingly, he rebuilt the company's human resource department, giving it a strategic rather than a supporting function by providing training programmes to build workforce competencies and skills. As such, the business development never stopped, and Faisal will always have something new to add to the business. Moreover, leadership transfer during such a global pandemic is not a strategic choice for the company.

Suggested readings

Sreih, J.F., Lussier, R.N., and Sonfield, M.C. (2019). Differences in management styles, levels of profitability, and performance across generations, and the development of the Family Business Success Model. *Journal of Organizational Change Management, 32*(1), 32–50. https://doi.org/10.1108/JOCM-01–2018–0030

Zellweger, T., Sieger, P., and Halter, F. (2011). Should I stay or should I go? Career choice intentions of students with family business background. *Journal of Business Venturing, 26*(5), 521–36. https://doi.org/10.1016/j.jbusvent.2010.04.001

14
Which family prevails during divorce and succession? The Wagner Avila case[1]

Luis Díaz-Matajira[2] and Stefano Wagner

During an online meeting with other employees on the development of the new website, Stefano Wagner continued to wonder whether he should accept the proposal of his father, Petter Wagner, to work full time for the family business, the Wagner Avila Store. Although he had been offered this position a long time ago, the fact that it had been a month since he graduated from business school and was looking for job opportunities made his father's offer more serious and urgent. The decision had to be made in a week's time, before 1 July when the call for new employees would be closed.

As a third-generation member, Stefano had recently been working informally for his father's company, specifically, in developing the e-commerce plan. Despite this informal engagement affording him a deeper understanding of the company's operations and organizational climate, there were still many crucial aspects which he had to consider. For Stefano to make an informed decision, he had to further research the company's positioning, the hardware industry which they were in, and family background, among other aspects.

COMPANY AND INDUSTRY OVERVIEW

The Wagner Avila family owned Avila Wagner Ltd, a company that ran and managed both the "Argentina" and the "Buenos Aires" Hardware Stores in Pasto, a city in southern Colombia. While the business began in 1971, these two family-owned hardware stores had grown impressively in recent years. They benefited from a booming sector providing basic inputs for the country's economic development. According to the National Federation of Merchants, this

---

[1]   Research Assistant, Ana Jimenez, contributed to this project.

[2]   Corresponding author.

Certain details in the case have been disguised. The case is developed solely as the basis for class discussion. Cases are not intended to serve as endorsements, sources of primary data, or illustrations of effective or ineffective management.

sector represented 2.5 per cent of the country's GDP in 2017. In Latin America, the Colombian hardware sector was one of the largest, with more than 40,000 commercial establishments and moving around 18 billion pesos annually. In 2018, both Wagner Avila's businesses were ranked 136 and 130 in the list of the 500 largest companies in the sector.

The growth mentioned above meant that the company required many employees and much land. At the beginning of 2020, the family business had three stores with a total of 7,000 square metres built, as well as 80 permanent employees and 40 additional temporary staff working on the construction of a brand-new warehouse to add to the business.

FAMILY BACKGROUND AND HISTORY

The first crucial aspect which crossed Stefano's mind was his family history and the way in which the business was organized. It all started when his grandfather, Don José Ávila, who worked with the Hormaza family in a hardware store in Popayán, was offered to occupy a new establishment in the city of Pasto. To begin with, José owned only 20 per cent of the store. A few months later, given the Hormaza family's lack of interest in the great efforts required to take the supplies from Popayán to the new establishment in Pasto, José and his wife Doña Nelly Vélez were sold the remaining 80 per cent of the business, and the family moved to Pasto with their three children: Juan, María del Pilar, and María Fernanda Avila (see Figure 14.1 for the genogram).

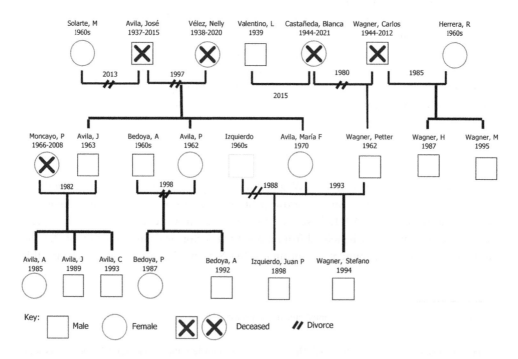

Figure 14.1   The Wagner Avila family genogram

In 1971, Nelly and José agreed to sell their house to invest the money in their new business, the Argentina Hardware Store. This gave rise to tension arising between the two due to the financial difficulties it created. In 1997, José and Nelly got divorced, as José began a new relationship with his friend Marta Solarte. The children were stunned by the news and decided to leave their father alone in the business as they did not want to work alongside Marta. They had worked in the family business since their teenage years, and they struggled to decide what to do next. The youngest, María Fernanda, together with her husband Petter Wagner, decided to start the Buenos Aires Hardware Store under the legal entity of Avila Wagner Ltd. The couple used their knowledge of the hardware industry to implement this new venture, which competed directly with José and became a major rival to the Argentina Hardware Store – which had been run by José, his new wife Marta, and their daughter until his death in 2015 – for many years.

CORPORATE STRUCTURE AND OWNERSHIP

At the time of his death in 2015, José's business, José Ávila Díaz Ltd, included three main stores, which had to be distributed among his heirs (his four children and Marta). This made the legal succession a long and difficult process. It took over three years of lawsuits and family conflicts, especially as Juan, María del Pilar, and María Fernanda, felt Argentina was part of their own legacy, effort, and sacrifices. They felt betrayed by their father. To end the lawsuits and keep working, they all decided to take different pathways as follows:

- The Hypermarket shop – the largest of all with around 15,000 square metres – would belong to Marta and their daughter.
- Argentina in downtown Pasto – the first and most well-known local hardware store – would belong to María Fernanda and María del Pilar.
- Las Lunas Argentina – the smallest store – would belong to Juan.

José's second marriage changed the succession process. The separation of all his heirs was mainly due to their different levels of emotional commitment, which meant that the governance and management practices of each store would vary. The properties remained separate and were controlled by different people with different values.

- In the Hypermarket shop, the family members of José's second marriage decided to delegate the administrative tasks and develop their professional careers in other areas.
- In Las Lunas Argentina, Juan managed and made all the corporate decisions.
- Argentina in downtown Pasto had two leaders, María Fernanda and María del Pilar, who generated cohesion between the companies and families, seeking to make decisions for long-term benefits.

SUCCESSION LEGACY

With all of this in mind, Stefano pondered on how José's death in 2015 evinced the lack of succession planning: one of the second-generation branches decided to create its company in the same sector as the original Argentina Hardware Store. Even though this led to a number of mishaps and arguments among family members, Avila Wagners did not at the time have a succession plan. Although the plan would foster the entrepreneurial spirit of the next generation by motivating them to develop decision-making skills and the knowledge to boost the company, it was true that the generational shock between the second generation and their children impeded this.

This generational shock was reflected in how some of the second- or third-generation family members were not participating, or they did not share the same values as the founders, running the risk of lack of trust in their capacities to own and manage the company. Stefano did not have to look too far to find an example. His own brother Juan Pablo, who joined and left the organization several times due to problems with his father, finally chose an external career, in which he felt his skills were better utilized. In Petter's words, "He came with a millennial mentality, thinking that he could take the reins at once. He tried to tell me how to do things, but I know how they should be done because I consider my experience to be very valuable."

Although Stefano believed this was a fixed mindset attitude which could prevent organizational regeneration and made it impossible for new ideas to be developed within the company, he also understood how his parents, Petter and María Fernanda, and his grandparents, José and Nelly, gave up much of their lives to build this legacy and did not want to lose control of their companies. They finally found a management team who could run the hardware stores properly and get rid of people who did not have the right experience such as the younger generations.

A NEW GENERATION'S PERSPECTIVE

Stefano noticed that the members of different generations' goals were not in alignment. The family discussed conflicting perspectives regarding the plans that had to be implemented to allow the organization to prosper. Each member proposed to develop his or her own entrepreneurial endeavour and they would have preferred to leave the family business rather than cause conflicts. Stefano was considering opening his own *Ferretería* (hardware store) like the one his parents opened after José's divorce, to avoid conflicts in case of potential divorce of his parents. While his parents and grandparents were concerned with maintaining the same values of providing excellent customer services with good prices and high-quality products, the younger generation were more concerned about renewing goals, rather than simply focusing on the existing legacy. They both believed that enhancing and adapting the existing objectives would boost the company's growth.

Despite these differences, the four members of Petter and María Fernanda's household agreed on the importance of developing a formal family council and on the successors participating in various areas of the organization, to understand and develop knowledge on how each duty should be performed. However, before doing so, they had to align the family members' different views: whoever wanted to join the business had to demonstrate deep critical skills and affective commitment. This was mostly due to the fear of incorrect decision making and, in the worst-case scenario, decisions being made based on a lack of commitment. As María

Fernanda stated, "By developing these capabilities, new generations can enter the organization to allow a greater diversity of ideas. Thus, generating a competitive advantage by exploiting the knowledge of those who have grown up in a more technological environment." If they were able to align the visions and values, they could take part in the decision making with proposals rather than impositions.

FAMILY COMMITMENT AND DYNAMICS

Another fundamental aspect was to prepare employees according to organizational values, so that they could support the hardware stores in case of the absence of a suitable leader. Besides, due to intense price wars among hardware stores, the company could not afford to hire expensive personnel, which meant that a consensus had to be reached to develop a strategy that helped to deal with issues such as death, accidents, or kidnappings, which were common in the region where the company operated. For these reasons, Stefano felt that he could have a great positive impact on the company, but that it could be undermined if his parents did not trust him enough to implement his plans. Although it was important to prepare the employees for the complex tasks performed at the hardware store, Stefano kept in mind that the family values were rooted in the business. This made the stores stand out against their competition, which is part of the reason why the family wanted to maintain ownership and control.

While continuing to consider the offer, Stefano remembered what his father always said: "You never know who could take over and it is even more difficult because as I have the experience, and I know what is right, but the new generation believes they do, so there is a generational shock." Despite his understanding of his parents' great concerns regarding the transition of leadership, he believed that the entry of the new generation and the family's joint work was the first step in transferring leadership and assets. Nevertheless, this would not be possible without having a retirement plan for his parents, which he believed they needed given their health and age.

ADAPTATIONS IMPOSED BY THE COVID-19 PANDEMIC

When the COVID-19 pandemic reached Colombia in March 2020, the government forced families to lock down their businesses. Sales decreased by up to 60 per cent in the first month, to which Petter, Chief Executive Officer of Avila Wagner Ltd, reacted calmly: "This is out of our control, so we have to be calm and take it easy." In the face of an extremely deadly disease, he was able to organize a crisis management plan by making the following initial decisions for the business:

- Provide emergency support to all their 120 employees. He managed the situation for his 80 permanent employees by extending vacation time and closing the construction site. The remaining 40 temporary employees were laid off.
- Enhance sales by phone and home-delivered products as well as implementing e-commerce, which meant that the website and online sales had to be enhanced.

- Begin negotiations with suppliers, focusing on Colombian and local ones, which were long-term allies.
- Develop and implement a bio-safety plan for the stores and delivery systems to resume operations once the government allowed it.
- Create a work area inside the company for Stefano to enter the company with a formal title to understand and manage small areas of the company.
- Delegate some of his major duties to his trusted employees, so that they could learn and incorporate the company's values.

STEFANO'S THOUGHTS ON SUCCESSION

With the above in mind, despite continuing to feel hesitant in terms of the decision to be made, Stefano stayed calm because he had a much better understanding of what influenced the processes within his father's company. Nonetheless, he grew uncertain about what to do, especially after understanding all of the complexities of the business model and the first generation's emotional attachment. He wanted to make an informed and conscious decision, which would provide the company with stability and his parents with peace of mind. Should he accept his father's offer? Stefano was simply not sure.

LEARNING NOTES

Case synopsis

The Wagner Avila family were the owners of Avila Wagner Ltd, a company that ran and managed Argentina and Buenos Aires Hardware Stores in the city of Pasto in the southern part of Colombia. At the beginning of 2020, the family business had 80 employees working on three stores with around 7,000 square metres built. They also had 40 additional temporary employees working on the construction of a brand-new warehouse in order to grow the business. Petter Wagner, his wife María Fernanda Avila, and his sister-in-law María Pilar Avila were the current shareholders. They developed the business from the one founded in 1971 by María and María's parents, Don José Ávila and Nelly Vélez. In March 2020, the COVID-19 crisis reached Colombia and the business and families were forced to lock down by the government. Petter, Chief Executive Officer, kept calm as he stated, "This is out of our control, so we have to be calm and take it easy in order to manage a better outcome." Petter, his wife María Fernanda, and their two sons, Juan Pablo and Stefano, took this opportunity to enjoy time together and had close conversations about succession. While Juan Pablo remained hesitant to join the business, he was helping out in the store with some minor duties. For Stefano, Petter's younger son, as he had just graduated from business school, Petter offered him a position in the business for him to gain working experience. However, Stefano was hesitant to accept the formal offer as he thought through his father's proposal. He looked at the prior family business succession and the family conflict that arose when in 1997 his grandfather José decided to divorce Doña Nelly and started a new marriage, without having any formal arrangements for the company. Should Stefano join the family business, which could be a breeding ground for conflicts?

Learning objectives

This case discusses the family and business governance implications of a family business that evolved from a single-family business to a dual family business due to the founder's divorce and his subsequent marriage. The family legacy and history of family conflicts created a low level of commitment in the next generation who, in a crisis, faced the challenge of joining the family business and began succession planning.

The case discussants should be able to learn:

- The importance of succession planning for family businesses.
- The importance of having a family protocol and agreements in place in case of a crisis.
- The family evolution (divorce and new marriage) as well as other crises in the path of succession.

Discussion questions

1. How can family dynamics lead to a different path of succession?
2. Should Stefano join the family business? Why?
3. What other advice would you offer to Stefano? How can he ensure the continuity of the business?
4. How can the older generation instil emotional value of the legacy business in their heirs?

Epilogue

Stefano decided to join the family business and to develop e-commerce, while running the business as his father, Petter Wagner, was sick at home due to COVID-19. The family was meeting and developing a new family agreement and succession plan.

Suggested readings

De Massis, A., Chua, J.H., and Chrisman, J.J. (2008). Factors preventing intra-family succession. *Family Business Review*, 21(2), 183–99. https://doi.org/10.1111/j.1741–6248.2008.00118.x

Lambrecht, J., and Lievens, J. (2008). Pruning the family tree: An unexplored path of the family business continuity and family harmony. *Family Business Review*, 21(4), 295–313. https://doi.org/10.1177/08944865080210040103

Sharma, P., and Irving, G. (2005). Four bases of family business successor commitment: Antecedents and consequences. *Entrepreneurship Theory and Practice*, 29(1), 13–33. https://doi.org/10.1111/j.1540–6520.2005.00067.x

15

"Chemical reaction": choosing a successor in a mosaic family

Elena Rozhdestvenskaya[1]

> *Business is not only about money,*
> *but a product in which you need to invest.*
>
> *–Vadim Pankratov, Founder, Vesta*

Vadim Pankratov, together with his third wife Anna Larina, were getting ready to celebrate Vadim's 75th birthday. It was a perfect occasion to gather all relatives, children, and grandchildren. They were apprehensive about the grandchildren coming from the side of Vadim's son, Michael Pankratov. They did not come to the house often. Vadim and Anna were not like many retirees: they were at the helm of Vesta LLC, which had been in operation in Russia for 30 years, and they had not officially decided how the company would be managed in the future. Vadim devoted his whole life to the business; even his repeated marriages grew out of workplace romances. Succession was a topic of heated debate, and several second-generation members of the family were involved in various positions in Vesta. Potential successors had different experiences, and Vadim and Anna could not reach a consensus on who could be a better candidate to continue the entrepreneurship in the first generation and manage the complex family dynamics involving histories of multiple divorces.

THE HISTORY OF VESTA AND THE PANKRATOV FAMILY

Amid the transition from the socialist economy into a market-based one in Russia, Vesta was founded to produce equipment and chemicals for chemical and galvanic processes in 1991. This was a period of tumult. Parts of the country were breaking away and connections between the former Soviet republics were broken. Many projects in electronics production were curtailed or closed altogether, and research and production institutes were closed, including the leading state enterprise where Vadim was the Chief Executive Officer (CEO). Vadim, with

---

[1]   Corresponding author.

Certain details in the case have been disguised. The case is developed solely as the basis for class discussion. Cases are not intended to serve as endorsements, sources of primary data, or illustrations of effective or ineffective management.

a PhD in Chemistry and the experience of running a state-owned enterprise, decided his best option was to become an entrepreneur. His decision proved to be a long-term investment. Vadim created his own venture and invested almost everything in the business. He did not even have his own home, which he had left to his ex-wife, and simply slept on a mattress in the office. From the first product brewed in a bath at home, Vadim's business evolved quickly, and Vesta opened its first factory. He was able to employ his family and colleagues from the state-owned enterprise he previously ran. The ownership of Vesta was split between Vadim (67 per cent) and Anna (33 per cent), who served as the CEO and the Deputy General Director, respectively. Anna's eldest daughter, Vera Bunin (40), was also engaged as the Commercial Director.

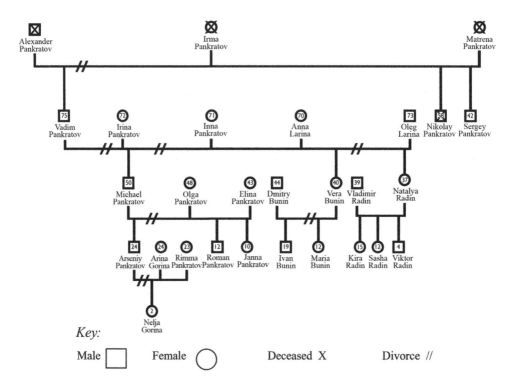

Figure 15.1   Genogram of the Pankratov family

Vadim came from a family that survived a divorce, but he kept in touch with his father, Alexander Pankratov, and his new family (see Figure 15.1 for the genogram). Because of his frequent contact with his half-brothers, Nikolay and Sergey Pankratov, Vadim grew a sense of responsibility for them and took care of them after his father passed away. At the same time, his mother, Irma Pankratov, supported him in getting a high-quality technical education in a big Russian city. He even had a former maid of honour of the royal court as his English tutor. The foreign language skill helped him build business relationships with overseas partners. Vadim was married three times and was divorced twice. His son Michael (50) from his first marriage was brought up physically distant from him. Michael later moved to the city to stay closer to Vadim. Given this proximity, he started participating in the business.

Vadim's third wife, Anna (70), a chemist with vast production experience in one of the former republics of the Soviet Union, also worked in the company. She had a lot of practical knowledge and regional production connections. Vadim and Anna had a long professional and collegial relationship. As their personal relationship blossomed, Anna and her daughters from the previous marriage were relocated from the former republics to the city where Vesta was located. Gradually, Vesta grew to be a place for engaging members of both Vadim and Anna's families.

The technological development of Vesta started with Vadim's business ideas and efforts, and Anna joined him later. The couple were able to preserve and build upon what had been achieved earlier – technological patents, chemical technologies of solutions and electrolytes, and construction of equipment to produce new materials. Almost 30 years' work resulted in developing a complete cycle of chemical processes for manufacture of electronics. The company employed about 70 highly qualified specialists in different fields such as chemists, designers, and programmers. Stabilization of business processes, on the one hand, and the need for integrating numerous relatives into the enterprise, on the other hand, set a difficult task for Vadim and Anna. Being technologists and owners of a profit-oriented business, they demanded knowledge, skills, and abilities. But as patrons of a diverse family clan, they were both interested in ensuring that their relatives had a successful life and a job that offered income and status.

WORKING TOGETHER AS A FAMILY

Vadim appreciated his responsibilities as the patron of a large family. He attracted his half-brothers, Nikolay and Sergey, with jobs and assistance in moving from the provincial area to the big city where Vesta was located. Their upbringing and socialization took place in the provincial city, and their background was significantly less sophisticated than that of Vadim. The attempts to involve his half-brothers were seen to be less successful. Sergey overestimated the strength of their family ties and relied on his connection to Vadim to keep his job safe. Eventually, Vadim had to make a difficult decision to fire Sergey. Vadim commented:

> With Sergey, it was the simplest problem as he did not meet the job requirements. He was a former chief engineer with good education, which seemed to be sufficient. So, I invited him [to join the business]. But his work did not meet the requirements of the position that was given to him. In probably less than a year, that situation cost us our family relationship. Now we practically do not communicate at all.

Another half-brother, Nikolay, died suddenly. Vadim said, "And with the other brother Nikolay, everything was perfect! He continued working; we started organizing a private enterprise [a subsidiary of Vesta] in his city. But it all suddenly ended with his death."

At the same time, Anna was very interested in the participation of her daughters and sons-in-law in Vesta. But her hope for a united family clan was not without disappointments. Anna commented:

> … to lead such a big team, one must have the knowledge. Don't just come, sit on a chair, and admire yourself! People see it immediately. They either accept or do not accept the leader. We tried to do this with my eldest daughter Vera's husband. We thought that he would help, so we appointed him as Deputy General Director for the production. But people did not come to him or resolve issues with him because they saw that he wasn't the right person to resolve issues. That's why we had to fire him by our own hands.

On the dismissal of Vera's husband, Vadim said, "I fired him. And a year later, they got divorced. They had two children, one was in the fourth grade, and the other was in the third year at the institute, at the Department of Electrochemistry, at my suggestion." According to Vadim, Anna's youngest daughter Natalya Radin (37) had also worked in Vesta but she did not get along with Vera and left to create a successful independent company. Natalya's success outside of Vesta demonstrated that her departure from Vesta was not associated with her incompetence but the competitive relationship between Vera and herself. Anna said, "Natalya cannot be taken out of her own business. She won't even go, and she doesn't pretend she would."

A DUEL IN ABSENTIA?

Thirty years after Vesta's establishment and in his mid-70s, Vadim had not yet decided on a successor to the CEO position. Yet he explicated his ideology of doing business, which emphasized production professionalism (namely knowledge, skills, experience, and reputation). He strongly believed that his successor should embrace this ideology:

> It is important to develop, to explore; the business is not only about money, but about a product that is needed, that is useful. And if there is one, then the money comes. Therefore, my business ideology is not only about money. For the continuity to happen, the next generation must get this idea as well.

Perhaps Vadim's most intense succession effort was associated with Michael, who made repeated attempts to work with his father (when Michael was 28, 35, and 38 years old). The two keen successors, Michael and Vera, were in equally symmetrical positions as the firstborn heir of Vadim and Anna, respectively. Vera's socialization and Anna's influence as a role model of a professionally working mother was more of a continuous process. In contrast, for Michael, Vadim's impact as a professionally employed father and the father–son communication had been a patchy process. In addition, Michael's education was far from Chemistry or Business Management. Vadim believed that non-core education and motivation to earn quick money was detrimental to business development and this stood in the way of Michael's path to becoming the successor. Michael's relationship problems with Vadim and Anna and the value differences between them had stalled him from serving as the next CEO. Vadim said with bitterness in his voice:

> If my son had been growing up beside me, he would have studied my profession, he would graduate from the same university; I would have taught him some organizational matters, it would be a successful ready-made business. Now, unfortunately, this is not the case because they all started with money first. The education was indirect.

Anna, however, mentioned:

> Vadim tried hard and wanted to involve his son, Michael. Well, after all, the man had to be the head of the enterprise! From this point of view, of course, a more advantageous position. Although we know that there were also examples of successful women in business, somehow traditionally, I would like a man to lead.

Anna's preference was closely aligned with the ambivalent gender climate in the Russian business community. On the one hand, women were ambitious and well educated; they could balance professional employment and family–partner and maternal roles; on the other hand, they shared gender stereotypes of male supremacy in society. Anna supported her husband in his rather strict assessment of his son:

> He involved his son since the 90s. He worked with him in the years 1995 and 1998, tried to work with him later too. But he realized that Michael did not have enough education … My husband offered to pay for his education, but Michael did not study ... he said he didn't need it; he had his own business and made money. He provided for his family and was successful.

Michael admitted that his experience of participation in his father's business was unfortunate:

> All the problems in our relationships and in the business were inherent in the upbringing. A business founder should not impose a type of activity but create opportunities. People do not become successors forcibly, only consciously. He can guide because one needs to be captivated and undergo some training. I had a completely different perception of reality with him; I didn't have the knowledge.

Michael allegorically described the difficulties of his relationship with his father, hinting at his dominance and lack of support, which he needed. His life perspective indicated subjective priorities: Michael had to earn money as he had an early marriage with a child. Later, he had his own trading business; he had taken the position as a businessman with his new family (second marriage) and his three children, one of whom was from his first marriage.

> It was easier to adapt to trade. My education was in shipbuilding, and this was the problem. I dreamed of building and using boats. But my father's production was chemical technology. I was not professionally prepared for this, and there was no time to retrain. I had several attempts to start working with my father and find a common coordinate system

with him, but those attempts were unsuccessful, and were stretched out in time. Plus, my father already had another family. We parted on a personal level and did not communicate for ten years … Everything is based on a family. Any problems can be solved if the family circle is clearly structured. Of course, divorce gets in the way. There should be family rules, and the notion of a "close relative" is vague.

After several attempts to enter his father's business, Michael had to step aside and started his own business related to the sale of product packaging.

VERA AS THE ONLY CANDIDATE?

Unlike Michael, Vera had a more comprehensive education, which helped her quickly adapt to the production process at Vesta. She graduated from Polytechnic University and got second education in Engineering and Economics; after that, she studied Marketing. Vera shared Vadim's ideology and understood the role of investment in modern production, the concept of "long money": "This is not the question of money now for sure, because the money couldn't be taken out of business. It is not easy to take it out! Over the past three years, we have completely changed the line of equipment." Like her younger sister Natalya thriving in a different business, Vera built her reputation combining professional employment and a family with children. She brought orders to Vesta and acted as the Commercial Director. She was the only one from the family circle who stayed at the top management position in Vesta.

Yet as a robust role model for Vera being a chemist and manager, Anna said evasively:

Nobody told her [Vera] about the succession yet, and it was not formalized that she would continue the business. No one even gave her such a promise. We see that we have not yet had another person who could drag such an enterprise ahead. And we do not consider it necessary to prepare her for this role … I think that the successor to the business does not necessarily have to be a technologist …We should have a team. I believe that the director should have a good team that will support them, and it should consist of a chief designer, a chief technologist, and a production manager. This team must ensure the process is correct …

Vadim did not make such statements. Indeed, he had quite a different perception:

We are already accustomed to doing business with our eldest daughter, being near, naturally, we look forward to the next generation. And they [other family members] know about it! And secondly, I gave Vera personally much of my power in the financial part, in relations with the outside world, in the internal organization, therefore – we watch, we help, we observe how she is growing up, and so we can move away with a clear conscience. But for now, I have to be close, to solve the main things myself, since the financial and other responsibilities remain with me.

SKIPPING GENERATION SUCCESSION A POSSIBILITY?

Some long-term factors of succession were laid down on the third generation. Both Michael and Vera tried to attract their children to Vesta. Michael's eldest son, Arseniy Pankratov (24), had his on-the-job practice at Vesta and wrote his master's thesis on Vesta's production processes, but he went back to work at Michael's packaging business afterwards. Hints of Vadim's ideology were also observed in other third-generation members of the family. Not only Arseniy's education but also the professional orientation of Vera's son, Ivan Bunin (19), became a subject of concern for Vadim:

> He [Ivan] was still at school, in the 10th grade, then he came to work for our company in summer. He liked Chemistry, and we gave him some tasks. That is, he saw it all, though he had a little idea of what it meant. Then I took him to the institute, to the department where I knew several people, they spoke to him. Therefore, he consciously enrolled at the Institute of Technology at the Department of Electrochemistry.

It seemed that Vera resolved the issue of professional orientation for her son more consistently than Michael. But given Michael's repeated attempts to enter his father's business, Arseniy's decision not to work at Vesta could hardly be considered final.

WHAT SHOULD VADIM AND ANNA DO NEXT?

Vadim knew that at the age of 75, further delaying the naming of the successor could be problematic and might impose a high risk to Vesta, his life creation. Looking at the faces of his children and grandchildren during his birthday celebration, he wondered what the chance was for Vesta to maintain a form of family entrepreneurship with continuity in family management and capital, especially when the clan was composed of families of different marriages. How should Anna and himself go about choosing the next CEO? Ultimately, should they choose between Vera and Michael or was there a third option? Vadim and Anna were a bit uncertain on what they should do next to secure a smooth leadership transition of this family fold.

LEARNING NOTES

Case synopsis

The Russian company Vesta LLC was founded by Vadim Pankratov, a man known for his technical innovation and academic background (PhD in Chemistry), in 1991. The company offered a full range of equipment and chemicals for chemical and galvanic processes in producing specific products. Vadim's third wife, Anna Larina, a chemist, joined the company later. The couple made repeated attempts to involve other relatives on both sides in the process of managing Vesta: two of Vadim's half-brothers (Nikolay and Sergey Pankratov), Anna's two daughters from her first marriage (Vera Bunin and Natalya Radin), Vera's husband, and Vadim's son from the first marriage (Michael Pankratov). In their 70s, the succession issue loomed larger, but Vadim and Anna struggled to name the successor. Who should they have on board as the next CEO? What factors should they consider in making this decision?

Learning objectives

The case examines succession challenges in a typical small and medium-sized family business based on technological production. The founder and his third wife were united by the company, but at the same time this brought two complex families with histories of divorce together. The case demonstrates the transition of a family enterprise, which widely involved the kinship network in the management process and attempted to select a single competent successor among the clan. It shows how immature attempts to engage clan members in the business could be costly, leading to relationship issues such as divorce, relationship cut-off, and even ruptures of family ties.

Through analysis of this case, learners should be able to:

- Appreciate the complexity of a family business when managed and owned by a clan composed of families of different marriages and with histories of multiple divorces.
- Understand the pros and cons of a highly heterogeneous family-in-business.
- Recognize the importance of the founder's ideology in the successor choice and how a technically based business may require specialized education and long-term investments in the next generation.
- Develop a set of criteria for successor choice and evaluate the appropriateness of the successors apparent based on this rubric.

Discussion questions

1. How did the structure of the Pankratov family influence the prospect of business continuity?
2. How did the education and other developments of potential successors matter in the successor choice? Were there any discrepancies between Vadim and Anna in terms of the qualities required?
3. Who should Vadim and Anna choose as the successor? Why? What should they do to ensure a smooth transition in power?

Epilogue

Vadim informally chose Vera as the successor. The successful integration of Vera as a representative of the second generation into the enterprise management process could be explained by several reasons: her strong motivation to continue her mother and stepfather's work, her technical education with subsequent marketing and managerial competencies, personal qualities, and good communication skills. At the same time, Vera was aware that her stepfather's social ties would greatly help her. Anna expressed hope that Vera could lean on the top management team to continue business growth.

Suggested readings

Campopiano, G., De Massis, A., Rinaldi, F.R., and Sciascia, S. (2017). Women's involvement in family firms: Progress and challenges for future research. *Journal of Family Business Strategy*, *8*(4), 200–12. https://doi.org/10.1016/j.jfbs.2017.09.001

Distelberg, B., and Sorenson, R.L. (2009). Updating systems concepts in family businesses: A focus on values, resource flows, and adaptability. *Family Business Review*, *22*(1), 65–81. https://doi.org/10.1177/0894486508329115

Lambrecht, J. (2005). Multigenerational transition in family businesses: A new explanatory model. *Family Business Review*, *18*(4), 267–82. https://doi.org/10.1111/j.1741–6248.2005.00048.x

16
Clease Auto: how a global pandemic allowed a family to maintain their family business legacy

Elizabeth Tetzlaff, Brittany Kraus and Albert E. James[1]

As John Clease walked across his car lot, he noticed the change in season. A myriad of orange and yellow hued leaves travelled playfully in the wind before landing on the windshields of the parked vehicles – autumn had arrived. Autumn brought with it the question of how to keep ahead of the lot and prepare for the coming winter. But that autumn was different. That fall, John was faced with a series of new questions.

It had been a year since John began seriously considering how he and his wife, Amy Clease, would retire and six months since the first COVID-19 lockdown. A lot had changed in 12 months. Over the past year, John had faced serious threats to the health and well-being of his family from the pandemic, along with the very real threat of defending his business against its impacts. Unpredictably, his dealership had not only survived but seemed to be surviving under the new normal of a socially distanced world and John was considering a new plan to sell the dealership to a group of employees. As John kicked at the leaves collecting around him, he knew he had many decisions to make about how best to achieve his and Amy's long-term goal of the family business transitioning from a business they owned to an asset that would ensure the security he wanted for himself, Amy, their sons, and their sons' families.

THE CLEASE FAMILY'S BUSINESS LEGACY

John was the latest in a long line of business owners in his family. His maternal grandparents were in business and, in 1970, John's parents started their own business. After years of working

[1]   Corresponding author.

as an auto mechanic in a dealership, John's father took the plunge and opened a business with his wife, an independent garage repairing vehicles. For 13 years, both parents worked together building a successful and profitable business. John's family had a tradition of building and selling their business, a tradition that became part of the family's legacy. John intended to follow this tradition as a means of providing long-term family prosperity, and in turn continue the family legacy.

In 1982, John went to university and pursued a degree in business with the goal of one day "retiring my mother", buying her out and continuing the business – thereby providing her with the secure post-retirement life he felt she deserved. A year later, in 1983, John was 19 and his father died suddenly, leaving his mother the sole owner of a business that lost 25 per cent of its business immediately after John's father passed away. His mother persevered and rebuilt the business. As John put it, "she was a good operator".

Like many children of business owners, John spent time working with his parents in the business, after school and during summer vacations doing odd jobs. It might have been during this time that John realized he had a passion for the challenges and opportunities of running a business. After all, John noted, "at the end of the day it [the business] is for my wife and I, for my family to enjoy a prosperous life".

JOHN JOINED AND CREATED A FAMILY BUSINESS

By 1990, John had completed his university education, worked in various roles at several companies, married Amy, saved enough money to buy a stake in his mother's business, and started working with his mother. Within two years, John had finalized his goal of retiring his mother by formalizing a payment plan that provided her with security and a healthy income from her stake in the business. John continued to grow the vehicle repair business and expand into selling pre-owned vehicles. By 2005, John and Amy were able to buy a local moribund new vehicle dealership and build it to a point where it consistently outperformed other dealerships of the same brand in much larger markets.

John had always been an owner who did not hesitate to make changes that could help the business operate better. Bringing on a General Manager (GM) from outside the dealership was one of these changes that not only impacted his goals for the business, but also affected those for his sons. The competence of this GM allowed John to step away from the business and enjoy his interests outside of it. It was also this GM who, as John put it, "straightened out" his sons by pointing out to the sons the "phenomenal opportunity they had" at the family's business. Peter Clease, the eldest, started working in the customer-facing side of the service department, and Robert Clease in sales. Moreover, John made it clear to his sons that their success in the business depended on them working harder than their peers and achieving higher results.

Under the tutelage of John and the non-family GM, Peter and Robert learned their roles, refined their skills, and achieved the success John had hoped they would when he thought about how best to set his sons up for long-term success and security. However, as the years progressed, John and his sons eventually recognized that the original hope that one or both of the sons would one day follow John's example and retire their parents was not on the cards. Robert had always talked about going into business for himself and by 2019 had left the extreme demands of sales to manage the vehicle cleaning and detailing department while simultaneously creating a property development company. Peter was by then where he wanted to be, the Assistant GM, the "numbers guy" in the management team, and had expressed no desire to run a business.

PREPARING FOR JOHN AND AMY'S NEXT LIFE STAGE

John was again at a crossroads, eight years older, closer to wanting to retire debt free and with the sense of security for himself and Amy and their sons' desires. Who would buy the business and take over the opportunity it presents? John was clear that it would not be one of his sons. When asked if one of his sons was to come to him with a big enough cheque would he sell to them, John's immediate response was: "That's not a possibility!"

Making money in a dealership had got harder and margins were always getting tighter. Manufacturer demands on dealers were also becoming more difficult and expensive to achieve. On top of all this were John's experiences with his peers in multiple industries, peers who had decided to go through a succession transitioning the business to their children only to watch the businesses fail: "This generation aren't able to put in the 30-year stressful career." John noted that the current state of the industry meant that stress levels were increasing, and it was more difficult to run a business profitably, which added a whole extra dimension of stress: "Um, but even if it was the same as it was 15 years ago, this generation would not be able to handle the stress that we had 15 years ago or 20 years ago." All added together, the high succession failure rate and the generational differences, John and Amy had come to realize that they would not feel comfortable with their security and their sons' well-being should the business be sold to them. Selling out to a faceless dealer group was now an infinitely more likely outcome.

Mid-March 2020, John and Amy were in the Southern United States enjoying golf, sunshine, and warm weather. Their peaceful days were interrupted by news from home that COVID-19 had been detected in their home province, the declaration of a state of emergency, and of a lockdown being imposed. The lockdown meant the immediate shutting down of most businesses and severe operational restrictions on all businesses allowed to remain open. In response, John and Amy immediately flew home to figure out how to manage the evolving situation.

Once home, John learned that the government had deemed dealerships *essential services*. This allowed John's business to remain open but under severe operational restrictions. John immediately switched from "working at the business to working in the business". What John found in the business was uncertainty about demand, pandemic fears, and questions about what kind of protocols would be needed to continue customer interactions, and how to manage costs with so many questions about how and if they could generate revenue. Fortunately, the government had quickly extended enhanced unemployment benefits. This enhancement freed John to, in good conscience, lay off 60 per cent of his staff, leaving only managers, including his sons, to run all the operations. John took on the role of receptionist, placing him at the "heartbeat of the operation". Amy came to work and helped to organize the needed processes and protocols as events developed.

Additionally, as a team John and his managers reacted and acted as things developed. Whenever a new implication of the pandemic surfaced, John and his team would come up with a response "on the fly in a little huddle" and put it into action. The result of this collaborative approach was record setting profitability for the dealership on a scale that placed John's business at the top for their region and across the country. When the lockdown and some of the associated restrictions eased, staff were brought back into the dealership, John moved from the receptionist desk, and things went almost back to normal despite some of the continued pandemic-related restrictions.

By August 2020, John had once again found some time to play golf and reflect on all the changes he had seen over the past five months and once more consider the future. Amy had spent a month helping him save the business and was now happily helping with the care of their first grandchild. Peter and Robert had been right there with John through the past five months, part of the team that huddled together coming up with needed solutions and making the solutions work. Robert was ready to move on with his business plans, preparing to break ground on his first property. Although, a year earlier, John was certain there was not a chance that either of his sons would be buying the business, he had become supportive of Peter's decision to join the employee group in talks with John to buy the business.

On that autumn day, as John reached for the door of the dealership, he wondered what it was that he needed to do next to ensure the retirement security he and Amy desired along with the future security and prosperity they wanted for their sons' families.

LEARNING NOTES

Case synopsis

This case is not only about a family and their business, but also about how families navigate ongoing changes, and associated challenges, facing them and their businesses. In this case, John is following the example set by his parents and grandparents, creating a business as a means of providing for his family and fulfilling his interests. Over the past seven years, John has started planning for his and Amy's retirement, thinking about his children's future, and considering what will happen to the business. During these seven years, John has witnessed his hopes of his dealership succeeding to the second generation dashed in the wake of the COVID-19 pandemic. By the end of the case, John is poised with an alternative option that will enable him to secure both his retirement and his sons' futures, while also being able to continue the family tradition of business ownership as a means of providing for themselves.

Learning objectives

This case provides learners with the opportunity to reinforce their understanding of the transgenerational nature of families and their entrepreneurial activities. The hope is that this case will also foster discussions around the issues of valuation of a business and transferring ownership. Moreover, the context of the case also provides learners with a chance to explore crisis management and the nature of available family resources. Overall, the case helps to inform discussions around succession, transgenerational entrepreneurship, and responses to crises – like a global pandemic.

Discussion questions

1. Consider John's approach to selling the business. Is his approach the best approach for providing the security that he and Amy desire? If so, why? If not, what would be an alternative?
   To help answer the question above, consider the following:
   a. What is the best way to set Peter up for success in the buying group?
   b. Would it be better for John and Amy's security if they sold to a dealer group?
   c. How does the hostile environment created by the pandemic impact selling the business?
2. How might John and Amy better help their sons to continue the family's legacy of owning and running a business to provide for their families?
   When answering the question above, consider the following:
   a. How might John and Amy fund new ventures involving next-generation family members?
   b. How does helping his sons continue the family legacy fit with John's goals?
3. Consider the benefits and costs of selling the family business. What are they? In addition, also consider what the benefits and costs are of having each generation start their own business(es) rather than proceeding with succession in the family business?

Epilogue

The story of John and his family's business is still ongoing. In the summer of 2021, the buying group, including Peter, had inked a seven-year deal to buy John and Amy out of the business. The deal allowed John to continue in a diminishing oversight capacity. By the end of the buyout Peter will be a majority owner and, as an added wrinkle, Robert will be a minority owner not involved in the business.

While he and Amy have yet to retire, John feels that they have learned many valuable lessons in their response to the 2020 global pandemic. These lessons, as articulated by John, will serve to strengthen the long-term health of the business and its ability to serve as a desired source of provision and security for John, Amy, and the younger generations of their family.

Suggested readings

Dana, L.P., Gurau, C., Light, I., and Muhammad, N. (2020). Family, community, and ethnic capital as entrepreneurial resources: Toward an integrated model. *Journal of Small Business Management, 58*(5), 1003–29. https://doi.org/10.1111/jsbm.12507

Le Breton-Miller, I., Miller, D., and Steier, L.P. (2004). Toward an integrative model of effective FOB succession. *Entrepreneurship Theory and Practice, 28*, 305–28. https://doi.org/10.1111/j.1540–6520.2011.00461.x

Matser, I., Bouma, J., and Veldhuizen, E. (2020). No hard feelings? Non-succeeding siblings and their perceptions of justice in family firms. *Journal of Family Business Management*. https://doi.org/10.1108/JFBM-09–2018–0048

17
The Ricci Durand family in the COVID-19 pandemic

Carmen Pachas Orihuela,[1] Antonio Martínez Valdez and César Cáceres Dagnino

In March 2020, the President of Peru had decided to keep the border closed as part of the measures to cope with the global COVID-19 pandemic. Worried for what could be the greatest crisis in the history of his family enterprise, Carlos Ricci Durand, Chief Executive Officer (CEO) of Chokekirao Travel, the tourism sector leader in the country, called for a family meeting.

On his way to the meeting, Carlos thought in distress about his collapsing company. He remembered in detail how his family had supported the company in the past by selling some assets but putting its estate at risk. Not being able to pay debts was making him very stressful and its effects were already evident. He was aware that he needed a new strategy for the survival of the company and keeping the family together. This would be the first challenge for the next generation in business governance in its consolidation process. He was not sure how the family enterprise should respond in such unpredictable times, and ultimately whether the business would be able to stay afloat while the sector was impacted by the pandemic.

THE START OF THE FAMILY LEGACY IN THE NATIONAL TURMOIL

Chokekirao Travel was created in 1973, and at the beginning it was only a company for issuing airline tickets. Martha Durand de Ricci was the one who had this business vision and started this undertaking with the assessment of tourism experts. Martha subsequently decided to start with receptive tourism providing services to tour operators in other markets and invited her husband, Carlos Miguel Ricci, to oversee the development of this new area. The company opened a branch office in the city of Cusco and kept on growing. In the 1980s, the workforce

---

[1]   Corresponding author.

Certain details in the case have been disguised. The case is developed solely as the basis for class discussion. Cases are not intended to serve as endorsements, sources of primary data, or illustrations of effective or ineffective management.

included almost 70 workers. The business was at its peak in 1985, even though Chokekirao Travel was still not the market leader.

The influx of tourists to Peru started decreasing in 1988, due to the atrocities of the terrorist group *Sendero Luminoso* (Shining Path) resulting in the deaths of thousands of persons with explosives, as well as car bomb attacks in several cities of the country, including the capital, Lima. Travelling was risky, and this was relayed to potential travellers from other countries. Besides, the roads and hospitality infrastructure started deteriorating and the airlines had to endure a critical stage.

In 1990 the Ricci Durand family faced a drastic business slowdown due to the sector's depression. Chokekirao Travel was left with only 15 workers and part of the family assets were lost with the sale of a real estate property in Cusco to keep the company afloat.

The capture of the leader of *Sendero Luminoso*, Abimael Guzmán, in 1992 marked the beginning of a time of peace in Peru and this stability favoured the promotion of investment and economic welfare. The government privatized the chain of state tourist hotels and adopted an open sky policy that made possible the arrival of the Chilean and Colombian airlines LAN and Avianca. Surviving the political and economic crisis of Peru in their first years allowed the Ricci Durand family to develop their full entrepreneurial spirit to build a successful family business, becoming a major tourist operator in the country.

THE EVOLVING FAMILY VENTURE

While the family expected some improvements in the business with these changes, the demand for national tourism dropped in 1998. The founders had to evaluate certain changes in the organizational structure. Some areas such as the issue of airline tickets were no longer of interest to the company because agency fees decreased from 15 per cent to 0 per cent due to online purchases.

Carlos, the eldest son, proposed to focus the business exclusively on inbound tourism due to its profitability. With the approval of the family members, the founding partners passed the control of the company to the second generation. Carlos became the CEO of Chokekirao Travel after his parents' retirement, and Martha and Carlos Miguel became directors. Miguel Ricci, their second son, decided to participate in the business as Chief Financial Officer (CFO), while Mariana Ricci, the youngest daughter, continued her school education.

The family enterprise had thin financial resources but had the great advantage of having a good reputation due to the high-quality service it provided and the credibility of the Ricci Durand family. As they faced keen competition in North American and European markets, they decided to focus on the Latin American market to generate more income.

As a development strategy, the Ricci Durand brothers divided their markets into two blocks in 2001. Miguel oversaw Mexico, Chile, and Argentina, while Carlos took care of Brazil, Colombia, and Spain. Those were the main markets at the time, and the results were outstanding. Both brothers travelled approximately 200 days per year and the strategy produced very good results. Sales revenue achieved their best points of US$45 million per year, approximately.

In 2014, the management of Chokekirao Travel was divided into two areas: one for Latin America and the other for the other countries. The first area would be supervised by Miguel and the second one by a professional manager. Two years later, Mariana joined the company and participated in projects with handicraft and local producer networks while she continued working on her master's degree in Sustainability and Environmental Management.

Carlos believed that there was no single leader in the family business:

> The formal organization structure has been defined, but to tell the truth, it is Miguel, my mother and myself who act jointly as the leader. Both Miguel and I have roles in the general management of the company and my mother consolidates our decisions because of her experience in tourism.

Regarding a succession plan, Carlos said, "Mariana would be the successor of our effort."

Chokekirao Travel started generating other entrepreneurial endeavours within the tourism value chain, such as being hotel operators in Cusco and Arequipa and moving into transportation services in their agency in Lima.

THE SIBLING TEAM IN ACTION

As the business continued to evolve, the second-generation members, Carlos, Miguel, and Mariana (see Figure 17.1 for the genogram of the family), grew into different roles in the business. Carlos, the CEO and the eldest son, joined the family enterprise in 1996 when he was 25 years old and was still studying Industrial Engineering. When he joined the company, he was already acquainted with the tourism sector, having previously worked there in his free time. His life project had always been to manage the company and to continue the legacy of his parents. He was the one who usually took the final decisions. He studied in the Program for Senior Management at PAD Business School.

Initially, Miguel, CFO, was not attracted by the family enterprise because he thought he had to travel regularly. He preferred to work as a manager in other companies not related to the family business. However, as time went by, he realized he could support the company management and utilize his know-how to strengthen the structure and communication of the organization, contributing to his family at the same time. He complemented his experience with the Entrepreneurs Program at PAD Business School.

Mariana, the youngest daughter, joined the company and started working part time in 2016. She studied humanities and worked in non-profit enterprises. The tourism sector was her choice after visiting a family hotel in Cusco, and subsequently she became interested in the welfare of the rural communities, especially those involved in handicrafts and producers. She realized she could contribute in this way to enhance the company value. She worked in the hotel until 2019 and travelled to France for her postgraduate studies in Sustainability and Environmental Management. Yet COVID-19 hit, and she returned to Peru in 2020. She had to face with her brothers the problems of the family enterprise in the pandemic period. She was a sensitive person who knew how to listen and understand the needs of others.

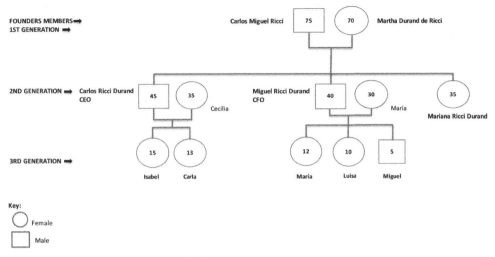

FOUNDERS MEMBERS ➡
1ST GENERATION ➡

Carlos Miguel Ricci | 75 | 70 | Martha Durand de Ricci

2ND GENERATION ➡ Carlos Ricci Durand
CEO
45 | 35
Cecilia

Miguel Ricci Durand
CFO
40 | 30
María

35
Mariana Ricci Durand

3RD GENERATION ➡
15 | 13
Isabel | Carla

12 | 10 | 5
María | Luisa | Miguel

Key:

◯ Female

☐ Male

Figure 17.1 The Ricci Durand family genogram

The two brothers and their sister complemented each other: Carlos was very passionate and managed the business; Miguel contributed with data regarding the operating reality of the company; Mariana provided an alternative perspective on the business towards creating social values. However, they had not faced any major crisis like their parents.

THE FAMILY BUSINESS IN THE COVID-19 PANDEMIC

On 11 March 2020, the World Health Organization classified COVID-19 as a pandemic. The President of Peru issued a series of provisions to safeguard the well-being of the population. The most radical measures were to bring to a standstill most of the economic activities and to close the borders. This rendered tourism in the country inactive and affected all the enterprises that made up the value chain.

To prevent businesses from going bankrupt due to the economic paralysis, the Peruvian Government provided measures to protect the companies. Among them was the one known as *Suspensión perfecta* (Perfect Suspension), which allowed employers and workers to immediately terminate labour relations in fortuitous situations or *force majeure*. Another measure that was issued to help companies with low liquidity was the *Plan Reactiva* (Reactivation Programme), a low-interest loan programme to cover short-term cash flow needs of the companies faced with the impact of the COVID-19 pandemic.

Carlos called for a family meeting to analyse the situation and make decisions. However, tension was growing. At the meeting of the Ricci Durand family and upon reading the organization reports, Miguel commented, "I think things as they are now will not last forever, and we will keep the company going." This optimistic way of seeing things found support in the experience gathered by the family in the previous social and economic crisis that Peru had undergone, and from which they had thrived successfully.

However, optimism was less with the arrival of the second wave of the pandemic that made the economic situation of the company more severe. The pandemic remained longer than expected, and there were focalized quarantines and curfews, so the tourists were afraid of travelling or not allowed to do so.

GROWING ANXIETY AS THE PANDEMIC CONTINUED

The Ricci Durand family had been quite united, and they had met every week in the past. The pandemic forced them to change this beautiful tradition. Carlos Miguel and Martha could only see their sons and grandchildren through virtual means or from the window of their apartment. The young people and children would show them posters, greeting them from the sidewalk. This measure, adopted to avoid contagion, affected them emotionally.

Carlos, Miguel, and Martha saw family unity as their legacy. But the growing anxiety in the family due to the pandemic seemed to take its toll on this unity. Carlos, the eldest son, expressed that while he was physically well, he was mentally distressed to see the company collapsing. The stress of not being able to pay the debts was affecting him.

Carlos and Miguel had been in contact with banks for financial restructuring. Carlos said, "It is important to persevere and to keep going." Carlos and Miguel proposed a *Suspensión perfecta* plan to reduce personnel to be consistent with the small number of operations. They were sure that they would depend more on technology in the future, which made them rethink what their employee profiles had to be to achieve a truly digital transformation of the organization.

Martha found it very difficult laying off the staff and not being able to continue helping the workers and their families. She believed that "workers are the heart of the company". Mariana was deeply worried because her brothers and parents had always been committed to their personnel, and this situation had affected all of them.

The situation was also difficult for Miguel because he had to dismiss people who had collaborated with him for a long time. However, he kept somehow optimistic as they were able to gather money through *Plan Reactiva* and provide their employees with severance pay. Those who continued to work were to be given all the means necessary to work remotely to take care of their well-being.

Over the past three years and since Mariana joined the company, the family was more conscious that every family enterprise was unique. It was a human development engine for the family members involved, and there was a strong desire to grow together, both personally and as a family.

Miguel believed that difficult times had made the family stronger to face adversity: "When changes take place in life, this necessity generates learning. This situation made us come closer together and endeavour to keep going ahead." Carlos valued everything they had done to keep the family happy and united since the beginning. He believed that the urgent task within the family business was to identify what was no longer relevant and to put it to the side, and that decisions to be made under the pressure of the crisis should not leave the business focus, a key success of the family.

Martha remembered the difficult years her family had to endure and thanked her children for what they had learned from that experience: "We have reinvented ourselves many times to be able to prevail as a company. Our family has many values, especially resilience and humility, which has been greatly positive for us and for our business. Without the family, the business is worthless, and every entrepreneur should know this."

DECISION IN THE FACE OF AN UNCERTAIN FUTURE

The tension in the family meetings was rising, and they knew they needed to agree on how the family enterprise should respond in such unpredictable times. Carlos and Miguel recognized they were in a stage of multiple personal, family, and managerial challenges. Risks had to be properly balanced, and decisions had to be made fast to win in the rapidly evolving COVID-19 environment.

Over time Carlos learned that investments should not be concentrated in the same sector and the family should secure cash flow to address different contingencies. Miguel agreed with him and added that to survive and thrive, they should review data and create scenarios to invest in other more profitable and diversified sectors. While both brothers were not sure of what decision was viable, Mariana stated with worry that it was the time to seek emergency help from external experts in how to respond to the uncertainty in this unprecedented turbulent time. Martha stayed positive and shared her entrepreneurial vision: "It is my belief that because of its relevance in Peru, the Government will further support the tourism sector, we are the promoters of an important source of income and jobs for the country."

Carlos listened attentively to all the worries of his family and thought that in the future, he had to generate innovative ideas for a market that would surge with a new style of competitiveness. At this time, however, in the absence of profit-generating activities, he knew he needed a new strategy. He repeatedly asked himself what the family should do to keep the enterprise going in this highly unpredictable pandemic, but he was a bit lost.

LEARNING NOTES

Case synopsis

Chokekirao Travel was founded by Martha Durand de Ricci in 1973, and her husband, Carlos Miguel Ricci, joined the company later. It started as a company for issuing airline tickets, and lately its activities focused on receptive tourism. The second generation of the family, Carlos, Miguel, and Mariana, managed the business, with Carlos, the eldest son of the Ricci Durand matrimony, the Chief Executive Officer. They had faced critical situations over the years such as terrorism at the end of the 1980s, but they had been able to keep the business afloat. The family enterprise had become stronger and generated other business undertakings within the sector's value chain, such as hotel operators in Cusco and Arequipa and the transportation agency in Lima.

On 11 March 2020, the World Health Organization declared the COVID-19 outbreak a global pandemic. Two days later, the President of Peru imposed extreme measures to prevent the spread of the virus. Most of the economic activities were stopped and the borders were closed. This rendered tourism in the country inactive and affected all the enterprises that made up the value chain. The family had to cope with unprecedented economic and financial scenarios.

Carlos felt distressed to see the company collapsing. He remembered clearly how his family had been able to keep the company afloat in the past. He knew that they needed to implement a new strategy for business survival, and to keep his family united. He had several questions in mind: How should they, as a family enterprise, respond in these unpredictable times? Could their business be kept afloat envisaging the issues faced by the industry?

Learning objectives

The case shows the challenges caused by the COVID-19 pandemic in a family enterprise in the tourism sector. Given that such scenarios were atypical and unprecedented, there was no guidance to manage this situation in a more effective manner. Leadership and resilience were the key to keeping the business afloat and the family united in the difficult time.

Learners should be able to recognize:

- The stamina needed in the family to guarantee business sustainability.
- The need for fast and precise decisions by the family members to adopt a new strategy.
- The importance of family unity in difficult times.

1. What were the main challenges the Ricci Durand family had to cope with during the pandemic? What did they do?
2. In such critical circumstances, should decision making be concentrated to facilitate the company's strategic process?
3. Should the enterprising family seek expert advice to help decide the future of the company?

Epilogue

The Ricci Durand family resumed operations within the limitations in place, and the company would continue to work under great uncertainties. "2021 has been the worst year in the tourism history of Peru. We cannot exceed 320,000 foreign tourists, which will present only 400 million dollars of foreign currency. We have to work hard to double the 2.5 million of national tourists that we have now," stated Carlos Canales, President of the National Chamber of Tourism (Canatur). According to his projections, tourism would recover in 2023, and the main challenge for the next government should be to accelerate the vaccination process, approve tax and financial benefits, provide labour flexibility, and facilitate the safe inbound flow of foreign tourism.

Suggested readings

Conz, E., Lamb, P.W., and De Massis, A. (2020). Practicing resilience in family firms: An investigation through phenomenography. *Journal of Family Business Strategy, 11*(2), 100355. doi:https://doi.org/10.1016/j.jfbs.2020.100355
Ferreiro, P., and Alcázar, M. (2001). *Gobierno de personas en la empresa.* Editorial PAD, Escuela de Dirección, Universidad de Piura, Lima.
Llano Cifuentes, C. (2004). *Humildad y liderazgo: necesita el empresario ser humilde?* Ediciones Ruz, IPADE, México.

PART IV
RISING-GENERATION LEADERSHIP IN ONGOING DISRUPTIONS

18
Pineola Nurseries: family business succession under fire

Steve Gaklis[1]

Becky Henley walked quietly into her father's office at Pineola Nurseries and noticed him praying and crying at his desk. It was not unusual to see her father praying at his desk, but Becky had never seen him cry before. It was April 2020, and Becky suddenly understood that the financial situation at her third-generation family business had turned from dire to desperate. Local banks had stopped lending, withdrawn credit lines, called all loans, and refused to deal any further with her father, Donald Henley. A bankruptcy filing at Pineola Nurseries seemed imminent. To make matters worse, Becky received news one month earlier that her beloved grandfather, Ray Henley, had contracted COVID-19 and in a weakened condition he was unlikely to survive. She desperately wanted to graduate college and then start her own nursery before her grandfather passed away, but she immediately questioned her plans and priorities as she walked out of her father's office.

At 19 years old and in her last semester at a local university, Becky thought about happier days visiting her grandfather's greenhouse range, walking the nursery fields with her father, and working vacations and summers at the family business, which presently comprised 1,600 acres of land, 200 employees, a sawmill, furniture factory, and one of the largest horticulture production nurseries in the eastern United States (US). Now, Becky contemplated leaving college, forgetting about her own nursery venture and entering her family firm to negotiate directly with banks and creditors to protect family, employees, as well as her father's and grandfather's reputation.

[1]   Corresponding author.

A HORTICULTURAL LEGACY

First generation, Ray Henley

First generation and Becky's grandfather, Ray, began his career as a brick mason but worked nights and weekends propagating native Mountain Laurel and Rhododendrons which were indigenous to the mountain region of North Carolina. His son, Donald, remembered, "My dad was also a brick mason by trade. That's what my father did for a living. So, whenever there wasn't enough shrubbery work, he worked as a mason."

In the 1970s and 1980s as many families fled major cities to purchase homes in surrounding suburbs in the US, there was a burgeoning market for horticultural landscape products like native Rhododendron and Mountain Laurel to plant around homes. In his greenhouses Ray hybridized Mountain Laurel and native Rhododendron for an expanding housing market and maturing green industry while providing an atmosphere for his son, Donald, and his grand-daughter, Becky, to learn and love to farm horticultural materials. Donald remembered, "I remember him carrying me on his shoulders into the field, you know. All the time when I was little ... I'd go with him to dig plants."

Ray was conservative and parsimonious in his religious views and in his finances believing debt financing only caused problems. He eschewed bank borrowing, believing banks were never there when you needed them and most often there when you did not. Donald remembered, "But [Ray] was always standard conservative – you know? If you went and bought something, he'd say well, you pay for it there and then. He carried no debt whatsoever."

With some hindsight Donald also recalled, "He told me to never get in debt over my head, which I wish I had listened to more than I did."

Second generation, Donald Henley

With a gift of 100 acres of farmland from his father, second-generation Donald started Pineola Nurseries in 1985. Over the next 30 years with guidance from his religious faith and his father's knowledge base, Donald aggressively expanded operations by increasing nursery production and continually buying land with bank financing to quickly become one of the largest and most respected horticultural growers on the east coast of the US. By the early 2000s the commercial horticultural industry, also known as the green industry, generated more than $100 billion in revenue of green goods from sales to homeowners, horticulturalists, and garden enthusiasts in the US. While it became one of the fastest growing segments of the nation's agricultural economy, it arguably remained an industry dominated by men, small family firms, and local contractors.

By 2017 Donald had increased land holdings at Pineola Nurseries with bank borrowing to 1,600 acres to satisfy what seemed to be ever increasing demand for horticultural products. Donald explained, "I felt like 'Well, if I'm going to ever expand, I'd better grab land, because it won't be there.'"

Feeling very confident and secure by 2017 with his success at Pineola Nurseries, Donald diversified operations by venturing into Christmas trees, a sawmill for cutting timber, and a furniture factory. Since he was a young man, crafting wood and making furniture with his uncle had always been a passion for Donald. Becky remembered, "Dad always loved wood-working, yes. His Uncle Carl was really into wood, and then Dad used to make things with Carl and that became a passion. That was always something he loved to do."

The furniture industry in the US had strong roots in western North Carolina where craftsmen and factories still produced some of the finest furniture in the world. The industry emerged after the US Civil War and overcame northern resentment to establish itself as an international force in furniture manufacturing.[2] The idea for a central marketplace emerged in the early 1900s, and the tradition continued in the International Home Furnishings Market. With a strong housing market across the US in the 1980s, 1990s, and early 2000s, outfitting every house with fine furniture and kitchen cabinets made in North Carolina became fashion-able and affordable.

Third generation, Becky Henley

Since she was old enough to walk, third-generation Becky remembered that her father, Donald, and grandfather, Ray, would take her into the fields to teach her how to farm. The three generations cherished their time together farming the fields. Becky remembered, "It's just something that I enjoyed. I got a lot of fulfilment out of growing plants and being outside … Being a farmer takes a lot of faith and I enjoyed that."

Becky repeatedly expressed admiration for both her father and grandfather. Both would imbue in her their individual passion for growing plants. Becky recalled, "Since I was a little girl, I spent my afternoons at my grandfather's greenhouse range and any other days when I could go far enough, I would go work with my dad."

In the fields Becky eagerly learned the tricks of the horticulture trade during vacation and many afternoons while she continued to study at a local university. She consistently ranked at the top of her class and early on considered graduating with a medical degree, but Becky mostly entertained thoughts of entrepreneurship with a business plan for her own nursery along with expansion of the family business. She recalled, "I took an entrepreneurship class and you had to create a business, and for that class, I created my own nursery. So, you know, it was always in the back of my head – 'Hey, I might like to do this!'"

Entrepreneurship intrigued Becky, and she focused her studies on new ventures and business start-ups, but during spring 2020 as COVID-19 ravaged many small businesses, her coursework and assignments quickly changed to reflect on the dire situation at her family firm. Becky commented, "Yeah, I mean I found myself taking strategic management and conflict management and management negotiations classes, and it was the real world for me."

---

[2]   Hall, C.R., Hodges, A.W., and Haydu, J.J. (2006). The economic impact of the green industry in the United States. *HortTechnology*, *16*(2), 345–53.

A SHOCK TO THE SYSTEM

In early 2020 the coronavirus pandemic emerged as an existential threat to the world economy especially among small businesses in the US, which closed at an astounding rate of 800 businesses per day.[3] A combination of fear and stay-at-home orders from local governments severely restricted sales at most small businesses across the US.[4] The knock-on effect restricted paying rent and paying employees despite the availability of $700 billion as part of the US Payment Protection Plan (PPP) for small businesses to pay employees. For many businesses it was not enough.

Fearing the worst, many garden centres and horticultural distribution centres cancelled their spring orders to horticultural growers out of caution or outright panic. Donald and Becky found themselves overextended with several large customers who dramatically reduced their spring orders for landscape material. At Pineola Nurseries COVID-19 had a combined effect of decimating sales, slowing shipping, slowing receivables, slowing cash for payroll, and frightening employees. Several key employees chose to leave operations at Pineola, creating additional difficulties for Donald and Becky during a very challenging spring shipping season when more than 500 tractor trailers would typically load horticultural material and leave their loading docks.

Although Donald had qualified for and dispersed more than $150,000 in PPP money from the government, he had also borrowed heavily from local banks over the years for all his venturing activities and existing businesses throughout the 2000s. Lending continued unabated with the purchase of the sawmill and furniture factory in 2017. Worse still, he continually intertwined his loans to support all his businesses. This was in direct violation of bank loan agreements. Becky recalled, "And he had intertwined finances of the sawmill with the nursery to try to keep them both operating, and that was a first-hand financial experience that I saw ... You cannot rob Peter to pay Paul, and that was a problem. It was a big problem."

COVID-19 was mostly to blame for difficulties at Pineola Nurseries in spring 2020, but Donald had exaggerated financials and intertwined operating capital to support all his businesses. His daughter, Becky, also recalled:

> He did borrow a lot of money, but if you look back at how the nursery grew ... it was quite honestly really an amazing and a beautiful thing, and I think he thought that he could do the same thing with the sawmill because he had already accomplished that with the nursery.

---

[3]   McKibbin, W., and Fernando, R. (2020). The economic impact of COVID-19. In R. Baldwin and B.W. di Mauro (eds), *Economics in the time of COVID-19* (pp. 45–51). London: CEPR Press.

[4]   Ibid.

A LEGACY IN CRISIS

A Chapter 11 bankruptcy protection loomed large for Pineola Nurseries, sawmill, and furniture factory as COVID-19, banks, and vendors closed in. Donald's successes, dreams, and debt quickly turned toxic in spring 2020, and banks which had eagerly negotiated with Donald 18 months before to expand existing nursery operations and restart a sawmill and furniture factory suddenly changed their tune as well as their asset valuation of his existing operations. Becky remembered, "It was mainly the banks didn't want to work with him, because at the time, it was a [crisis] and he couldn't get his loans refinanced."

By late spring 2020, banks began reducing their exposure to underperforming assets linked to real estate and housing like Pineola Nurseries with its nurseries, sawmill, and furniture factory. Banks relentlessly negotiated and renegotiated debt to asset requirements at Pineola for operating capital and additional lending.

In spring 2020, during peak shipping season, banks called in all loans extended to Pineola Nurseries. As a direct result, available cash to pay truckers, vendors, employees, and family dried up. With COVID-19 raging, banks closing in on his assets, operating cash unavailable, employees leaving, and his father, Ray, struggling with COVID and terminal colon cancer, Donald was at a breaking point and at his desk crying when Becky walked in. Becky recounted, "Remember the Bible story of the Good Samaritan? My dad was the guy in the road, and everyone walked by as he lay suffering!"

SUCCESSION UNDER FIRE

While managing the turmoil at Pineola Nurseries with her father and negotiating with local banks to maintain operating capital for daily operations, Becky also discovered that her paternal grandfather, Ray, had become gravely ill. The two men she admired most in her life – her father and grandfather – seemed to be hanging by a thread. In addition, she discovered her maternal grandparents had embarked on divorce proceedings. Becky recalled the plight of her father: "So, Dad had a lot on him, and he was trying to deal with taking care of his dad with all the emotions that go along with that ... At the same time, my other set of grandparents were getting a divorce."

These were difficult times for Becky, but she understood the need to decide whether to complete her education, start her own venture, and/or help save the family firm and what she considered to be her birthright – albeit a leaking ship. The challenges ahead including bankruptcy negotiation and venturing on her own seemed daunting, but Becky truly believed it was her duty to protect her father, her family, and her employees. She commented, "I was at work as much as I could, but I was also a full-time student, and I was aware that things were not easy for my family."

During her studies, Becky had written comprehensive business plans for several ventures in agriculture believing she might follow her dreams and start her own venture like her father and grandfather before her. Her professors praised her entrepreneurial acumen and ability to understand new business, while her father and grandfather encouraged her desire to one day have her own business. One of the business plans included details of a growing operation for contract futures on horticultural material. Since availability of horticultural materials was often scarce during extended economic boom periods, customers of Pineola Nurseries could secure inventory three to five years into the future and assure themselves inventory availability for sales. The business plan was sound in theory, but it required significant up-front invest-ment. Becky understood banks now held the key to not only the survival of Pineola Nurseries but also her future business plans. The bankruptcy filing would decide the fate of Pineola Nurseries and, to some degree, her fate as well. Debt financing was a necessarily evil; Becky knew first-hand the benefit and the pitfalls of borrowing too much or not borrowing at all. It was time for her to think hard and think creatively about future financing at Pineola Nurseries and possibly her own venture.

Despite plans to graduate from college at the top of her college class in late spring 2020, Becky looked towards the future with trepidation and some fear, but it was her firm, religious conviction that demanded family come first. She understood that her father was struggling personally and financially. She also understood that her grandfather was struggling physically. Becky and her family were juggling many struggles, but she managed to maintain focus on her studies, understanding education might be the best source for answers about new ven-tures, family business, bank negotiation, and strategy. Becky commented, "And so, instead of entrepreneurship I found myself studying and writing my papers on bankruptcy, strategic management, crisis management – things that applied to my life right then and there."

The urgency and gravity of the situation at Pineola Nurseries as well as the need to honour her grandfather pulled Becky in several directions.

BECKY'S OPTIONS

After the shock she received in her father's office watching him cry, the full weight of family circumstances consumed Becky. She returned to her college dorm room to console herself and contemplate what she should do next. There were urgent decisions to make in spring 2020, but there were as many questions as answers in her mind. She asked herself if she should leave college and make every effort to save her family, family business, and employees from bankruptcy? Should she graduate from college but walk away from the turmoil at Pineola Nurseries to start her own venture? Could she graduate college, manage the turmoil at Pineola Nurseries, and start her own venture? These were the questions Becky needed to answer and each included responsibilities and costs no 19-year-old college senior should face, but Becky understood it was her new reality. Over the past four months her dorm room had become a sanctuary for her to think and escape the reality that had engulfed her. Seeing her father crying in his office was certainly a shock, but seeing her grandfather deteriorate from COVID and incurable cancer was almost too much to bear. Though she had few answers, she clearly understood the urgent need to decide the immediate path of her future.

LEARNING NOTES

Case synopsis

After her senior year at a local North Carolina college Becky Henley planned to represent the third generation at Pineola Nurseries and lead her family business in horticulture to success. This case is not only a story about resiliency, but it is also a story about transgenerational entrepreneurship the hard way because upon graduation Becky also planned to start her own horticulture venture to work alongside her father and grandfather. However, in spring 2020 her plans quickly changed with COVID-19 raging, family business bankruptcy imminent, employees exiting, and her grandfather terminally ill with cancer and COVID. As a direct result, Becky contemplated leaving college, forgetting about her own nursery venture, and at 20 years old, entering her third-generation family firm to negotiate directly with courts, banks, and creditors to protect family, employees, and her father's reputation.

Learning objectives

This case will give learners a vivid example of succession under fire and transgenerational entrepreneurship the hard way. Becky is in many ways similar to most undergraduate students hoping to find their place in their family business. Many students might associate with Becky on multiple levels given her success at college and desire to start her own venture alongside a parent since transgenerational entrepreneurship is a key component of this study. Learners may also associate with the issues Becky must face given a family and family business in crisis. Transgenerational entrepreneurship is a key construct to discuss in this case, and learners might argue whether Becky should (1) make every attempt to save her family, her father, and her employees, (2) choose her own course and start her new venture, or (3) help save the family firm while starting her new venture. Consequently, learners might argue for agency and the need for Becky to act independently and make her own choice. Learners will understand there is tremendous pressure on Becky as a graduating college student, and they should discuss the gravity of her situation including a decision best for Becky and best for her family and family business.

Discussion questions

1. Recap and discuss Becky's options.
2. What would you have done if you were Becky? Why?
3. How should Becky communicate with banks now and in the future?
4. How do you think Becky should approach debt financing now and in the future?
5. Discuss how Becky managed her commitments to family and family business while being a student. Discuss her possible commitment to family and family business upon graduation.

Epilogue

While Becky worked diligently to finish her class work and graduate at the top of her class, she also took on the challenges facing Pineola Nurseries. She worked days, nights, and weekends with her father to fend off banks and keep key employees. She remembered:

> I mean, I can't count on one hand, the number of times I ever saw my dad cry, and I walked into his office (my dad prays a lot in his office), and he was praying and crying. And that's when I knew, this is what I'm going to do. This is what I must do!

To generate cash, she tightened credit lines to customers, introduced a factoring agent to ensure collection, extended vendor terms, and transferred Pineola key assets into her own name to start her own nursery venture. However, in January 2021 banks called all debt and forced Pineola Nurseries into bankruptcy protection. Becky also recalled:

> And I was a kid about to be straight out of college trying to figure out how a company was supposed to operate in [bankruptcy protection] ... and I had all this stuff going on at the same time as I was trying to start up something on my own.

Becky's new venture in horticulture purchased additional key assets liquidated by Pineola Nurseries in the winter of 2021, and her family continued the tradition of farming started by her grandfather. Further, Becky introduced innovative customer financing by promising inventory futures to customers having difficulty securing horticultural products year to year.

Unfortunately, Ray passed away from a combination of cancer and COVID in the fall of 2020, but Becky would honour his memory with her new venture in horticultural production and additional ventures in vegetable production and pumpkin propagation. At the time of this teaching case, Becky and her father continued to negotiate with banks while transferring Pineola assets into her own name and the business.

Suggested readings

Habbershon, T.G., and Williams, M.L. (1999). A resource-based framework for assessing the strategic advantages of family firms. *Family Business Review*, *12*(1), 1–25. https://doi.org/10.1111/j.1741-6248.1999.00001.x

Miller, D., and Le Breton-Miller, I. (2006). Family governance and firm performance: Agency, stewardship, and capabilities. *Family Business Review*, *19*(1), 73–87. https://doi.org/10.1111/j.1741-6248.2006.00063.x

Nordqvist, M., and Zellweger, T. (eds) (2010). *Transgenerational entrepreneurship: Exploring growth and performance in family firms across generations*. Cheltenham, UK and Northampton, MA, USA: Edward Elgar Publishing.

19

DC International: riding out of disruption as a third-generation successor

Marshall Jen,[1] Jeremy Cheng, Kevin Au and Kelly Xing Chen

It was not a tenure that Ronald Chan, a third-generation member of the family-owned DC International, had ever expected. *Dan Chee*, or bicycle, not only formed part of the company name but also supported three generations of the Chans. Ronald's return to his family's bicycle distributor and retailer was greeted by years of unforeseen waves of disruptions, from the globalized markets and supply chains to the social unrest in Hong Kong and the COVID-19 pandemic. DC International's sales had plunged by nearly 50 per cent in five years, and Ronald knew he had to come up with a new plan to secure the future of his 70-year-old family fold. While his father, Kenneth Chan, and his uncle, Stephen Chan, endorsed his aggressive plan to build a home-grown premium bicycle brand, he pondered how he could finance this revitalization project when the pandemic hit hard on the economy. Ronald saw interests from DC International's loyal clients to invest in this, but he was not totally sure how he might mitigate risks associated with the family reputation. He also wondered how he should position the new brand as the pandemic largely suppressed the high-end market but boosted the sales of the lower-end bicycles.

THE HUMBLE BEGINNING OF DC INTERNATIONAL

Ronald's grandfather, Shan Chan (hereinafter "Chan Sr"), fled to Hong Kong near the end of the Chinese Civil War in 1949. A village man, Chan Sr trusted no one but himself, and felt obliged to keep his family safe and united. "As the breadwinner of this family, my grandfather never ran away from his responsibilities," recalled Ronald. Driven by the survival instinct, Chan Sr would do anything he could to raise his six children (for genogram, see Figure 19.1).

---

[1]　Corresponding author.

Certain details in the case have been disguised. The case is developed solely as the basis for class discussion. Cases are not intended to serve as endorsements, sources of primary data, or illustrations of effective or ineffective management.

In 1950, he started a small workshop on a street corner in Yuen Long, a suburb of Hong Kong, where he offered bicycle repair services needed by commuters. This gave birth to DC International.

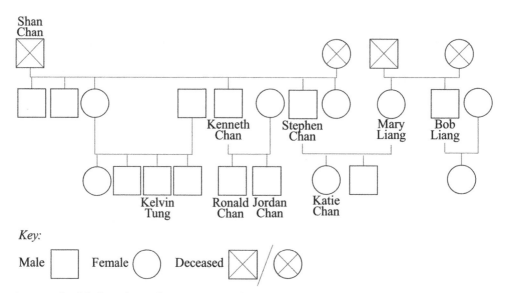

Note: Details of the branches without current involvement in ownership and/or management have been cropped for the sake of simplicity.

Figure 19.1   The Chan family genogram

Like other mom-and-pop shop in the early days, Chan Sr would ask his children to help out with the daily operations such as taking customer orders or fixing bicycles. In 1960, Chan Sr opened his first store and "hired" his wife and his children to work there. All his children had engaged with the business at one point in their life. Deprived of early education opportunities, Chan Sr always wanted his children to go to school. The wealth accumulated from the business enabled his children to complete middle or high schools, and this opened a window of opportunity for them to get decent jobs in the late 1960s to late 1970s. Gradually, his children left the store and started their own families. At the same time, Chan Sr's hair grew grey. Believing that he had completed his mission as a father, Chan Sr made plans to close the business. Yet his two sons, Kenneth and Stephen, had a very different idea.

THE BUSINESS BOOM IN THE SECOND GENERATION

The two brothers were true advocates of hard work. Even at a young age, their mother would comment, "You inherited your father's mentality of 'do do do and work work work'. That's why both of you couldn't wait to work once you graduated from middle school." By 1992, only Kenneth and Stephen remained at DC International to manage the business for Chan Sr. The brothers quit their jobs and worked full time at DC International, setting their strategy to import and sell European bicycles in Hong Kong.

Shortly after this game-changing decision, the business grew tremendously. From 1995 to 2013, DC International was always out of stock. The cycling business became a big hit in Hong Kong. On the one hand, between 1998 to 2010, athlete Kam-po Wong became the first Hong Kong World Champion of a UCI World Cup event and was most notable for winning triple gold medals in three Asian Games. On the other hand, the Hong Kong Government started to build a 60 km cycling network in the New Territories to encourage the sport and reduce pollution. Together, Kenneth and Stephen turned DC International into a sizeable operation. In their best year, DC International recorded a turnover of over HK$100 million (about US$13 million) and employed 40 staff.

DC International established itself as one of the leading cycling companies in Hong Kong, with a growing presence in mainland China and Macau. When Chan Sr passed away in 1996, the shares were allocated to each of the six children according to his will. However, the siblings believed that DC International would be best managed by Kenneth and Stephen in the absence of Chan Sr, and they agreed that the duo would each own half of the company while the other siblings inherited the properties and other valuables in the estate.

The switch of ownership gradually brought in new management structures, as well as widening engagement of other family members. Kenneth served as the Chief Executive Officer to oversee the retail business, while Stephen was Chief Operating Officer to manage the distribution. At the store front, Mandy Kwok, Kenneth's wife, oversaw the daily operations of the retail store. In China, Bob Liang, a brother-in-law of Stephen, acted as the General Manager and was the only authorized representative of DC International to negotiate deals there. Amid the cousins, Kelvin Tung, son of an elder sister of Kenneth, led the accounting team given his professional training in the area. However, Kelvin and his parents had no shares in the business. Katie Chan, Stephen Chan's daughter, tackled matters related to customs declaration with the government, and expressed no interest in taking over the company though. Ronald was responsible for business development and was the eldest among Kenneth and Stephen's offspring. Ronald's younger brother, Jordan, lived in Canada and was not involved in the business. Therefore, Ronald was seen as the successor in his generation.

LEADING UP TO THE ONGOING DISRUPTIONS

Indeed, Ronald was the only one who Kenneth and Stephen invited to serve as a key decision-maker of the company. When Ronald officially joined the family business in 2014, he had just earned his undergraduate degree in Economics from Simon Fraser University, Canada. Although Ronald returned home with a hint of reluctance, he was excited about the opportunity to apply his knowledge in economics and decision science to the family business, envisioning to bring DC International to new heights. Yet the task turned out to be difficult and at times frustrating to him:

> I think I have been roasted and rejected literally over 100 times by my father, for my ideas to help with different situations and for the ways I handled things … even for staying quiet, I got roasted because he felt that I was not contributing to help with the company's situation.

Coincidentally, Ronald returned in one of the most challenging eras of the business. By the end of 2013, DC International had marginally recovered from the after-effect of the 2008 Financial Crisis and the 2010 European Debt Crisis. Then in 2015, however, factory brands they dealt with went online and end consumers could get a substitute product 30 per cent less than the retail price in Hong Kong. His distribution clients were able to acquire stocks at a lower price than that offered by DC International. This put DC International in a very bizarre position as the exclusive regional retailer and wholesaler.

However, a particular incident inspired Ronald to reposition DC International in the market:

> A bicycle was brought for servicing, but when we tried to process the part that needed warranty repair from the factory, the factory was unable to trace the transaction of the product. It turned out that it was a stolen product! We had no choice but to deny all his warranty and repair, and the factory reported the case to the local police. The buyer then had to go through a police investigation.

Because of this incident, Ronald enforced an administration fee and announced a longer servicing time for those repairs that turned out to be emanating from the grey market. He also launched a "DC International approve" campaign so that Hong Kong cyclists felt confident about purchasing and selling second-hand bicycles locally. Ronald took this case as an opportunity to educate his customers on how to distinguish genuine products from parallel market products, and the risks of purchasing grey market products outside of an authorized dealership.

The challenges did not stop there. When bicycle sharing as part of the sharing economy hit Hong Kong in 2017, it affected the majority of rental and retail shops to which DC International distributed bicycles. Ronald treated their clients and the cycling community as if they were family. He bore no grudge for how his dealerships treated DC International by purchasing parallel products, and referred customers to shops that were struggling. In addition, he offered payment allowances and lowered the minimum order quantity for dealerships that needed a hand. DC International was able to stand tall, and became a highly respected player in the local cycling business community.

CHANGE OR DIE?

Over the years observing how DC International reacted to the ongoing crises, Ronald had gradually identified the reasons why the business remained relatively passive. One of the key issues was a lack of control over international bicycle supply. Ronald reflected on the potential loss in the future if the business continued to rely heavily on others' products. Not only did they have no control over consumers' demand for high-end bicycles, they also became rigid in supply quantities as there was an annual minimum purchasing order for every brand they signed into exclusively. The prior generation's focus on "perfecting the current operations" might hide the issue at hand. This drove Ronald to his grand vision: creating a home-grown premium brand under DC International. In his pitch to Kenneth and Stephen, the owners of DC International, he reuttered his grandfather's philosophy: "Don't you always tell me that Grandfather never depended on others to keep his family safe and we should bare this mentality of independency at heart? If this is the case, then does it not contradict with the business model we currently have?"

Almost immediately, they were all ears. They gave Ronald the opportunity to speak his thoughts. "It is time to plan for DC International's independence," continued Ronald. The seniors were engaged for hours tuning into the new vision. In the end, they agreed that DC International should set in place some crisis management for the sales drop, transform its management model by integrating decision science theories with stakeholders' experience, and empower the family business with control. Appointed as the Chief Business Officer, Ronald focused on building the first Hong Kong bicycle brand to compete in the World Series. Ronald already saw that he could leverage other world champion brands, selling them side by side with his home-grown one at the retail shop. The seniors and Ronald also discussed whether they should set this up as a division of DC International or as a spin-off, and they believed that the spin-off model would minimize risks to the mature operation of DC International and afford Ronald the necessary freedom. So, Ronald decided to establish a new company to sell home-grown bicycles and to seek funding for this company.

FUNDING AND REDIRECTING THE HOME-GROWN BRAND

Shortly after, in June 2019, however, came the protest triggered by the introduction of the Fugitive Offenders Ordinance amendment bill in Hong Kong. The riots smothered demand for high-end bicycles as no one wanted to put their bicycles at risk. The subsequent coronavirus pandemic abruptly stopped most social interactions and economic activities as it landed in Hong Kong in late January 2020. While it had a temporary effect on freezing the demand for all bicycle types, bicycle rides were considered a safer mean of travelling and the demand for lower-end bicycles increased. Yet DC International's stock could never meet the rising demand given the rupture of the global supply chain. The demand for the premium bicycles, however, remained stagnant. Seeing the disruption, Ronald hesitated and was not sure if he should stay with the premium brand strategy.

"This is also related to the cost of entry," explained Ronald. After a deep discussion with Kenneth and Stephen, the family wanted to retain a good buffer to prepare for the prolonged exposure of the pandemic. Even though they could allocate HK$2–3 million (about US$258,000–387,000) from their own pocket to support the initiative, it was only around 4–6 per cent of the required fund for manufacturing the first batch of 7,500 premium-brand bicycles, costing around HK$50 million (about US$6.45 million). On the contrary, producing a lower-end brand at a larger minimum lot size of 15,000 would only cost HK$13.6 million (about US$1.75 million), which could make the project more accessible to the spin-off. In either case, DC International would have to absorb the additional cost of logistics, storage, and marketing as the distributor and retailer of the new brand – which was HK$5.3 million (US$682,000) and HK$4.2 million (US$543,000) for the premium brand and the lower-end one, respectively.

Ronald explored various debt financing options such as the government's small and medium enterprise support scheme and bank loans, but he saw lengthy processes in securing any of these, especially as a spin-off lacking a track record. This brought Ronald to equity financing. All cycling enthusiasts knew DC International, which was one of the most qualified and had the most support to represent Hong Kong's high-end bicycle business. They were the sole distributor of many high-end road and mountain bicycle brands such as Colnago and Merida. A high-end model such as Colnago would cost an average of HK$60,000 (around US$7,740) and could go up to HK$120,000 (around US$15,480). Their most loyal clients were retired millionaires and wealthy millennials with an extravagant taste for hobbies, whom Ronald considered turning to for capital as silent partners:

In the old days, people would say "Business is done at a golf course". I don't play golf but I certainly wouldn't deny it if someone said, "Real businesses is done through cycling". Our customers are also members of exclusive clubs and active investors, especially the ones around the same age as my dad.

Sold to the dream of having a Hong Kong premium brand, a few long-term clients had already indicated their preliminary interest to invest. Ronald could hardly tell whether they would continue to support the venture if this were for the lower-end market. A lower-tier brand might also confuse DC International's existing clients, diluting their hard-earned reputation as a high-end bicycle retailer. Another quandary for Ronald was whether, even as a spin-off, failure of the project could put his family reputation at risk, driving a loss of trust of DC International's loyal clients. Ronald was at the crossroads, having to choose between the elite niche market or the general market while securing the necessary capital and preserving the family reputation. How could he balance all these and avoid dropping the balls in his hand?

LEARNING NOTES

Case synopsis

Founded by Shan Chan in 1950, DC International started from a humble beginning. Through the hard work of the second-generation leaders Kenneth and Stephen Chan, DC International grew to become one of the leading cycling companies in Hong Kong. However, the third-generation heir apparent, Ronald Chan, witnessed a sales tumble of nearly 50 per cent since he joined the family fold, and knew that he had to come up with a new plan to secure the future of this 70-year-old legacy. Ronald realized from the prior crises that their reliance on an external supply of bicycles made them less responsive in the ongoing waves of disruptions. Before the COVID-19 pandemic, he proposed that the family should create their home-grown premium bicycle brand, which would cost around HK$50 million (around US$6.45 million). While Ronald received initial support from Kenneth and Stephen, the family only planned to contribute about 4–6 per cent of the required fund for this spin-off project. The pandemic then landed on Hong Kong, suppressing the premium brand market yet boosting the lower-tier sales. Ronald wondered if he should change tack to a lower-end brand, but was uncertain about the response of the few loyal clients of DC International, who indicated their interest to invest in building Hong Kong's premium bicycle brand, and the potential dilution of DC International's hard-earned reputation. Ronald faced dilemmas in his branding and funding strategies for this new venture.

Learning objectives

The case discusses difficulties in accessing financial capital and other strategic challenges rising-generation leaders of small and medium-sized enterprises (SMEs) might face in launching a new venture and leveraging the capital and brand of the legacy business. The understanding is anchored in the evolving waves of internal and external disruptions that most family firms experience more intensively.

The case discussants should be able to establish:

- A key understanding of internal and external disruptors influencing family-owned SMEs, and how they may interact to take tolls on the firm's performance.
- How family business leaders can leverage the familiness, or the familial resource pool, to drive value-generating responses to disruptions of different natures. In addition to financial capital, the discussion should cover human capital (e.g., rising-generation education), intellectual capital (e.g., new management philosophy of the rising generation), social capital (e.g., the deeply nested relationship with other players in the supply chain), and spiritual capital (e.g., family reputation).
- Pros and cons of engaging loyal clients as silent investors for new ventures, considering the socioemotional needs of the owning family.

Discussion questions

1. What are the key internal and external disruptors of DC International?
2. Should Ronald approach the long-term customers to finance this project? Why?
3. If you were Ronald, would you go ahead with the home-grown premium brand or would you change to the manufacturing of the lower-tier brand in the pandemic?
4. How could Ronald minimize the risks of this new initiative for the family and the business?

Epilogue

Ronald chose to change tack to develop the lower-end brand first, which could sell better in the pandemic as well as capturing the local cycling market boom at a lower entry cost. He planned not to engage loyal customers as investors at this stage, to preserve the hard-earned family reputation and avoid generating conflicting brand identities to this core group of stakeholders. Ronald would like a greater degree of separation between the spin-off and DC International to avoid possible brand dilution as well as to make room for the premium brand if he could grow the seed capital from the sales of the lower-end bicycles.

Suggested readings

Au, K., and Kwan, H.K. (2009). Start-up capital and Chinese entrepreneurs: The role of family. *Entrepreneurship Theory and Practice*, *33*(4), 889–908. https://doi.org/10.1111/j.1540–6520. 2009.00331.x

Cheng, C.Y.J., Au, K., and Jen, M. (2021). Nurturing and financing transgenerational entrepreneurship. In H.-M. Chung and K. Au (eds), *Succession and innovation in Asia's small-and-medium-sized enterprises* (pp. 265–87). Singapore: Palgrave Macmillan.

Cohen, A., and Sharma, P. (2016). *Entrepreneurs in every generation: How successful family businesses develop their next leaders*. Oakland, CA: Berrett-Koehler.

20
Am I ready for this?

Andrea Santiago[1]

It was a quiet December morning. Patrick Morales wondered how he was doing as the president of BLPVMD CID Communications Inc. (CID): 2020 had been a tough year. Nine months earlier, the Philippines was placed under a nationwide lockdown, prohibiting the movement of people. The uncertainty surrounding the length of the lockdown as well as the impact of the COVID-19 pandemic resulted in the country's recession. Then, a few weeks into the lockdown, Patrick's father, Louie Morales, unexpectedly passed away after complications sustained from surgery. Overnight, Patrick found himself assuming the positions of president and chairman of CID.

While Patrick was being groomed to take over and everyone knew that he would eventually lead the public relations firm, the circumstances were unusual. There was little time to grieve as stakeholders who had lost their friend, mentor, colleague, and boss also had to deal with personal problems due to the global pandemic.

Preparing to release the government-mandated 13th month pay to employees, Patrick was pleased that the company survived 2020 without any manpower casualty. He was optimistic that 2021 would be better. He planned to call a general meeting in early January to discuss the plans for the year and the years to come. Yet, Patrick wondered if he was ready to do that. He was interested to make his own mark and grow the business so that his father's legacy would live on. "Remember, son, this business should not only outlive me. It should outlive you, as well."

LOUIE AND THE MAKINGS OF CID

CID morphed from Louie's earlier businesses. A creative individual with strong charisma, Louie established an advertising company, Image Dimensions, in the 1980s. Then in 1990, he realized that there was a strong need to address the public relations concerns of his clients. As

[1]   Corresponding author.
Certain details in the case have been disguised. The case is developed solely as the basis for class discussion. Cases are not intended to serve as endorsements, sources of primary data, or illustrations of effective or ineffective management.

a result, he created a public relations division within the firm. His small team of four included Larry Zurita.

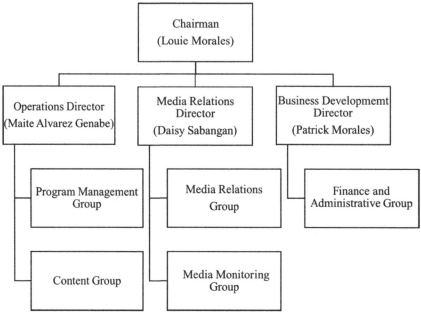

Source: From Patrick Morales.

Figure 20.1   CID organizational chart, 2013–20

In 1992, Louie spun-off the division and incorporated Corporate Image Dimensions together with Larry, among others. It was this entity that helped in the presidential campaign of former president Fidel V. Ramos. Louie and his firm continued to gain new clients, necessitating the formation of a media monitoring team. In 1994, CID was recognized as an affiliate of Ketchum, a global network of public relations consultants. The affiliation expanded the company's reach offshore.

As the pioneer in full serving communication services, CID began to win Anvil awards granted by the Public Relations Society of the Philippines during the period 1998–2006. While at its peak, Louie decided that Larry, who was designated managing director, should take more control over the business operations. Unfortunately, the business began to experience its first decline in revenues as competition became stiffer.

In 2009, Louie and Larry felt that the firm had to go back to basics, by focusing on content. The duo rebranded their firm as CID rather than its complete corporate name. With the shorter name came new logos and a new tagline – Equity with Integrity – reflective of the firm's values. The rebranding appeared to work as business picked up.

Tragedy, however, struck the communications firm. In 2012, Larry unexpectedly passed away, leaving Louie to take an active role in the business again. He reconstituted his team, this time bringing his son Patrick into the business (see Figure 20.1 for the organizational chart). Shortly thereafter, the new team members, Maite Genabe and Daisy Sabangan, who had been working in the company for years, were given shares of stock and became part of the board. The company changed its name to BLPVMD but retained its brand as CID.

THE ENTRY AND TRAINING OF PATRICK

Patrick was the youngest child of Louie and Lilia Morales. It was never in his plans to work with his father. After graduating from college, he chose to work in the sales department of multinational companies. It was his experience in these firms that shaped his work ethic.

When his father approached him to join him in the business, Patrick was recovering from a stroke. Thus, it was not difficult for him to decide to work with his father, having no job. Besides, three of his siblings were abroad and the one who remained in the country was not interested in the business.

Since 2012, Patrick began to shadow his father as business development director and concurrently as administrative head. He accompanied Louie during client meetings and learned how to negotiate. He attended board meetings and interacted with key directors. Since his father was no longer reporting to work daily, the employees were beginning to get used to Patrick being around, though they knew the final decision was always that of his father.

To help him understand the business better, particularly the financial aspects, Patrick enrolled in an executive master's in business administration programme. As part of his terminal report, he prepared a paper that would introduce the company to digital public relations.

After he graduated in 2019, Patrick felt his father did not think he was ready to assume the presidency even if internal and external stakeholders were just waiting for the announcement of his succession. He felt that his father was not confident he had gained a solid reputation as a public relations man. He had not yet generated his own clients. Even without a clear timetable, Patrick and the rest of the executives and staff knew that he would assume his father's position one day. He openly shared on one occasion, "I want to take over CID not just for me but for my father. I don't want anyone else running the business besides family because this company is my father's legacy, and I will do all I can to protect it."

PROPOSED DIGITAL PUBLIC RELATIONS

Patrick felt strongly that the business should offer digital public relations services. This would mean utilizing digital media to communicate about a company and engaging stakeholders in real time. To succeed, one would need staff who were familiar with the digital platforms.

However, Patrick's father did not see the urgency even when their competitors had already taken the lead. Louie had built the business from an original four-person team to a 20-person workforce. In 30 years, he developed deep relationships with clients and the media. Thus, his idea of public relations meant that communication had to be channelled through media personnel either through print, radio, or television. Besides, he believed that it was content that mattered and not the medium. "Content will always be strategic direction in communication," he once quipped.

Patrick agreed that content was essential. However, he continued to believe that the message would be lost if it was not read or heard. By utilizing digital media that the greater population were more attuned to, he thought there would be a greater chance that content would be read. Not only that. Unlike traditional tri-media (print, radio, television), which was unidirectional, social media platforms allowed for two-way communication. There were risks involved, and therefore Patrick believed a separate team would be needed to focus on digital public relation services. He envisioned he would be able to recover the salaries of the new team with revenues generated from the services. Unfortunately, Patrick was unable to implement his plan months after he finished his graduate studies.

IN HIS FATHER'S SHOES

On 16 March 2020, the whole country was brought to a standstill. People were asked to stay indoors, initially for a four-week period that was later extended by another two weeks. Patrick recalled how Louie fidgeted being at home. A natural extrovert who enjoyed the company of others, Louie had a difficult time accepting the situation. Left with nothing to do, he proceeded with prior intentions to have his kneecaps replaced. It was the aftermath of the surgery that led to his untimely demise.

As businesses were slowly being opened due to less stringent government regulations, Patrick found himself having to make decisions for the company. There were no new clients coming in, so he had to determine what to do with his staff who had all been home based but continued to receive full salaries. He reviewed the company's financials and realized the clients that had retained them still needed their services to communicate with their stakeholders. The retainer fees were sufficient to tide the company over, but this meant no salary movements and no performance bonuses.

To help his staff do their work in the office premises, he converted one of the rooms to living quarters so the employees could stay in the offices. Some employees felt this was a better alternative than being exposed to the virus during their otherwise daily commute. Besides, commuting was difficult since public transport should only be half-filled to maintain social distancing. This meant longer waiting times just to get a ride.

Other than that, 2020 remained a quiet year so no other major decisions had to be made. During the six months he had been president and chairman, Patrick relied on the expertise of his co-directors, Maite, the operations director, and Daisy, the media relations director. He was much younger than them and he often sought their advice. His operations director reminded him:

> To be successful in the P.R. industry a firm must have an exceptional reputation. This isn't given overnight it takes years to build the credibility firms need to be successful. The P.R. firm has to constantly guard its reputation because one wrong move or one mistake can cause the closure of a P.R. firm. It only takes one and it's all downhill from there.

PATRICK'S MANAGEMENT STYLE

Patrick recognized that his management style was different from that of his father. Louie was an authoritarian and used to getting his way. He was also paternalistic, and the staff looked upon him as a father figure. When he dropped by the office, he would find time to mingle with them.

On the other hand, Patrick considered himself a professional. He was certainly not the charismatic type. When his staff approached him for requests, he considered the merits and nothing else. He spent more time with his co-executive directors who he dealt with collegially.

MOVING FORWARD

Patrick was unsure if he could lead the company beyond 2020 but he knew he had to. He realized that the firm's long-term clients had been with them because they were confident his father was on top of their accounts. His father once told him:

> Our clients have stayed with us because they also became my friends. Take SM for example they have been our client for 30 years, but they value our relationship and service. Even though Tatang [the founder] has already passed Hans and Tessie [the children] still consider me as one of their business partners because their father has told them that they are in safe hands with us.

The SM Group accounts for 15 per cent of the business.

Patrick was optimistic that their clients would continue to trust CID under his leadership since he could bring in a fresh perspective as a millennial. He was also hopeful that the contacts his father established in the media industry would give him the same trust. He recalled his father's advice during their regular one-on-ones, "Relationships have to be built and nurtured. I have been friends with the media for a long time and, if I need something, it's always easy to call in a favour. They do the same and I never forget that. Do the same."

While contemplating what he could do to build on his father's legacy, Patrick remembered the implementation plan he prepared for the introduction of digital public relations services for the firm. Now that his father was gone, it may be an opportune time to put his implementation plan into motion. Perhaps, this was the mark he was looking for to ensure that he can further his father's legacy.

With that in mind, Patrick wondered if he should take a strategic move or remain tactical, at least for 2021. The strategic move would be to widen their services to include digital public relations. The tactical move would be to increase the client base and generate the resources needed to expand and to pay for salary adjustments and productivity incentives that the board had previously agreed to grant in 2020 but were unable to do so. As the previous head of administration, Patrick had proposed upgrades in compensation to keep on par with the bigger public relations agencies for talent retention.

Patrick mused, "increasing the client base would not be that easy though. As a result of the lockdowns and the uncertainties of the effectiveness of vaccines, companies were cautious about cash outlays. If stakeholder communications were needed, companies preferred to use their internal resources to drum up their own campaigns."

Preparing for the new year, Patrick began to miss his father. He always thought that when he assumed the presidency, his father would still be around to toss ideas around with. He has never felt so alone.

LEARNING NOTES

Case synopsis

Patrick Morales spent the last eight years preparing to take over the family's public relations firm. However, he lost his confidence when he inherited the business after his father's sudden death in mid-2020, at the height of lockdowns due to the global pandemic. Not only did he have to make executive decisions without his father to consult with, but he also had to do so at a time when the economy was at a low point. He was able to weather 2020 without manpower casualties but he was anxious about the coming years. He wondered if it was time to introduce a new service that he had worked on – digital public relations – or if he should focus on increasing the client base to generate resources needed to grow the firm and to pay for deferred salary increases and incentives. One thing he was sure of. He had to do well to honour his father's legacy.

Learning objectives

Succession planning increases the chances of a successful transition to the next business leader. However, there are instances where the best plans are unable to cover all the circumstances that could better prepare the successor.

After analysing the case, learners should be able to:

- Recognize the importance of succession planning.
- Explore the different paths to successor training.
- Understand the concept of family inertia.
- Accept that there will be unexpected challenges that successors may face.
- Consider the trade-offs between short-term viability versus long-term sustainability.

Discussion questions

1. Evaluate the succession path that Patrick underwent. Would you consider this to be sufficient to prepare Patrick to assume the leadership role and gain legitimacy from internal and external stakeholders? Are there things that his father should have done differently?
2. Explain the resistance of Louie to Patrick's proposal to introduce digital public relations services. Could Patrick have done something more to convince his father about the early implementation of his proposal?
3. Should Patrick focus his efforts on introducing digital services or should he spend more time increasing the firm's client base? Justify your response. How different would your response be if there was no pandemic?

Epilogue

In the months following, Patrick was able to introduce digital public relations services. The company was in the process of acquiring new contracts, with at least three pitches a week.

Patrick was hopeful that by the end of 2021, they would have closed at least three new clients on top of the targeted clients for traditional practice. His mother sat on the board as chairperson emeritus.

Suggested readings

Cater, J.J., and Justis, R. (2009). The development of successors from followers to leaders in small family firms: An exploratory study. *Family Business Review*, *22*(2), 109–24. https://doi.org/10.1177/0894486508327822

Miller, S. (2014). Developing next generation leaders in family business. *The Family Business Consulting Group*. Retrieved 10 January 2015 from https://www.thefbcg.com/resource/developing-next-generation-leaders-in-family-business/

PWC (2014). Bridging the gap: Handing over the family business to the next generation. *PWC*. Retrieved 10 January 2015 from https://www.pwc.com/gx/en/pwc-family-business-survey/next-gen/assets/nextgen-survey.pdf

21

Universal Cement Corporation: doing "one thing at a time" in the crisis of multiple needs?

Yi-Chun Lu,[1] You-Fong Wu and Hsi-Mei Chung

In July 2020, Chih-Sheng Hou, founder of UNEO Inc, was holding a series of virtual meetings with suppliers and clients from South Korea, Japan, and the United States. Based in Taiwan, Chih-Sheng knew that he had to secure prompt actions amid the supply chain and market disruptions due to the COVID-19 pandemic, although Taiwan had so far been able to keep stable control in the domestic market. For the engineers from UNEO, lockdowns in other countries resulted in delays in multiple projects, given the difficulty of performing equipment tests in clients' sites. Besides the crisis faced by UNEO, Chih-Sheng Hou needed to overcome more challenges since he was also the fourth-generation Chief Executive Officer (CEO) of Universal Cement Corporation (UCC), the parent company of UNEO. His younger brother, Jack Hou, was the Vice President of UCC. The two brothers were accountable to their shareholders, including relatives from the co-founding families of UCC and relatives of the Hous. The urgent task in leading this 60-year-old Taiwanese cement manufacturer was to deliver appropriate responses to the diminishing domestic demand of cement, the escalating expectation of corporate social responsibilities (CSR) from the local communities, and the strategic transformation for the future. With multiple goals needed to be fulfilled, the two brothers faced a dilemma as to how to best utilize their resources to achieve the greatest synergy. The family's approach to business had always followed their great-grandfather's adage of "one thing at a time", but the brothers wondered if the approach remained appropriate for the challenges they faced.

[1]   Corresponding author.

Certain details in the case have been disguised. The case is developed solely as the basis for class discussion. Cases are not intended to serve as endorsements, sources of primary data, or illustrations of effective or ineffective management.

HISTORY OF UNIVERSAL CEMENT CORPORATION

UCC was first founded by San-Lian Wu and Yu-Li Hou, the great-grandfather of Chih-Sheng, in September 1959. Cement manufacturing started in Taiwan during the Japanese colonial period spanning from 1915 to 1917. In 1954, the government deregulated the cement industry when Yu-Li was back from a business trip in Southeast Asia looking for opportunities in the cement industry. For this reason, Hou and Wu co-founded UCC and Tsun-Hsien Wu, the younger brother of San-Lian, was appointed as the first General Manager. The main products included cement, concrete, and drywall. As one of the top cement manufacturers in Taiwan, the company had been listed on the Taiwan Stock Exchange since 1971.

The Hou family had been active in Taiwanese business communities. Born in Tainan in 1900, Yu-Li was a highly successful businessman, helping establish various prestigious companies such as Tainan Spinning, Uni-President, and Prince Housing & Development Corporation, in cooperation with other well-known families such as the Wus and the Kaos. These families were all from adjacent locations in the Beimen District of Tainan in southern Taiwan. Along with their relatives and villagers in the neighbourhood, these families helped not only establish UCC, but also finance the creation of several companies in their communities. They were business partners, friends, and key leaders of what had been known as the "Tainan clan", a group of families that brought together their financial and human resources to build significant enterprises during a vigorous period of industrialization following the recovery of Taiwan from the Japanese colonization between 1895 and 1945. The firms of this clan were valued at over NTD 300 billion[2] (approximately US$10.7 billion), and they gradually developed a unique system of corporate governance to collectively oversee these ventures. With this unique system of cross-shareholding, major shareholders in a single firm of the Tainan clan could consist of members from multiple families, resulting in inevitable impediments whenever disagreement arose on critical business decisions.

DISCORDS IN THE THIRD GENERATION

The Hou family had played critical roles in both the ownership and management of UCC until 1989, when Yu-Li and his eldest son, Yong-Du Hou, died. Bo-Yi Hou, the eldest grandson of Yu-Li, was hence empowered to make decisions for the family. Knowing that he was unable to compete with the leaders from other founding families in terms of managerial experience at the age of 39, he decided that the Hou family would be a "happy shareholder" and would not be involved in the management of UCC. Serious family conflicts took place in 1989 and Bo-Yi decided that his two sons, Chih-Sheng and Jack, would move to Canada not only to stay away from the conflicts but also to receive a better education. His wife, Jin-Qian Su, flew to the new country with the two young boys, even though she could hardly speak English, noting "I speak no English. I study with my sons. If you come to our place, you can see that I sit in the middle

---

[2]   Retrieved 29 September 2021 from https://finance.ettoday.net/news/712523

of them, and we all read the dictionary." Bo-Yi did not forget his role as father and husband. Despite his busy schedule, he flew to Vancouver every two months, carrying with him books his two sons loved. He was never absent in important events in their life. Whenever they moved into a new house, studied in a new school, or performed on stage, Bo-Yi would try his best to be present. Jack said, "He will definitely show up in every critical moment."

In 2008, a critical change occurred. After seeing three straight years of financial losses, Bo-Yi decided it was time for the Hou family to be more than happy shareholders and become active in management. Yet other shareholders from the Tainan clan objected to the change of guards and refused to break the original tie. At that moment, Bo-Yi held 12.74 per cent and his two sons had 0.01 per cent and 0.02 per cent of UCC, respectively. To be in the driving seat, he spent NTD 4 billion (approximately US$120 million in 2008) to purchase shares from the open market. The two sons fought with their uncle and other relatives in the shareholders' meeting to gain the control. The discords among the co-founding families were unfortunate, but this gave the business a true rebirth with a stronger alignment of ownership and management. The two brothers of the fourth-generation management also inspired new hopes despite multifaceted challenges.

A DARKER GENERATIONAL CURSE IN THE MULTI-FAMILY BUSINESS?

Being a successor of the multi-family firm had never been Chih-Sheng's choice before 2008, especially when considering the family's history. In 2006, Chih-Sheng finished his PhD in Electronic Engineering at Massachusetts Institute of Technology when he was 24. He decided then that he would stay in the laboratories and keep working following his own passion. When back in Taiwan in 2007, he worked as an R&D manager in the Electronic and Optoelectronic System Laboratory in the Industrial Technology Research Institute for two years. In December 2008, however, he was summoned by his father to fight in the battle to take control of UCC. He knew that this was a call he could not decline as his father had never let them down over the years they were in Canada. His younger brother, Jack, was also requested to come home and join the fray immediately after he finished his master's degree in Eastern Asian Languages and Civilization at Harvard University.

The period was not without pain for the two brothers at the very beginning of their family business tenure. As the leader of the company, Chih-Sheng needed to clearly identify the core issues, which led to continuous losses of UCC. The cement industry had faced multiple challenges since 1993. The shrinking domestic market, the keen competition from mainland China, and the growing public concerns about the environment made the operation even more difficult. Within the multi-family firm, internal control and human resource management had shown room for aggressive improvements. Chih-Sheng and Jack needed to build their legitimacy and earn trust not only from their father, but also from the members of the Tainan clan. Jack described the period thus, "I felt very depressed in the first two years. I told my parents, but they told me I have to help myself. No one can truly help you."

Meanwhile, Chih-Sheng invested substantial resources in UNEO, a new venture he founded in 2010 to realize his research interest, tap into new opportunities in the technology field, and lead the group of UCC to a better future. UNEO was a pressure sensor company with the ability to design, manufacture, and implement system integration.[3] Their sensors could be applied in various fields, including consumer electronics, sports, medicals, wearable devices, and industrial equipment.[4] UNEO received the prestigious Gold Edison Award in 2015, in the category of material science for its flexible ultra-thin sensor. Beyond its role as an investment business of UCC, UNEO suggested the determination of Chih-Sheng to lead UCC into a different direction. UNEO was a rising star at this moment; however, it would need more investments from the group, which could be distributed as dividends or devoted to other projects.

RESHAPING UCC'S CSR EFFORTS

At the same time, concerns about CSR issues were competing for internal resources. High energy consumption made the cement industry synonymous with high greenhouse gas emissions. Since 1995, several scandals had raised concerns about environmental issues caused by the industry. Coupled with mounting environmental awareness, the government stipulated precautious measures, driving self-compliance and harsh restrictions on cement companies. Extant regulations included air and water pollution controls,[5] while dramatic new regulations were expected because of the global initiatives to reduce the climate change caused by the industry. For these reasons, major players in the cement industry kept increasing efforts on self-compliance, including the disclosure of CSR behaviours.

In the eyes of the public, UCC's CSR efforts seemed to lag behind those of its competitors. All major players except for UCC dedicated significant efforts to acquire certificates in quality control and management systems such as ISO 9000, 14001, and even the European Union's Restriction of Hazardous Substances (RoHS). Investments in equipment improvement were also made to make sure that the damage to the environment was limited in the manufacturing process. As well as pursuing reduced emissions and better CSR reputations, the other cement companies were seeking and finding new business opportunities such as lime-selling, tech-services, and bio-technological services.

Surprisingly, UCC had made little attempt to keep up with its main competitors. They only started disclosing CSR in 2016, five years after the practice began in the industry. And their only diversification effort was the creation of UNEO. Chih-Sheng and Jack needed to show that they were able to make the business profitable while ensuring effective responses to the needs of the larger stakeholder group.

---

[3]   Retrieved 29 September 2021 from https://www.uneotech.com/home.jsp?lang=en

[4]   ibid.

[5]   Regulated by Environmental Protection Administration with Environmental Analysis Organization Management Regulations. Retrieved 29 September 2021 from https://oaout.epa.gov.tw/law/EngLawContent.aspx?lan=E&id=250&kwStr=

THE CHALLENGES AHEAD

In the early months of 2020, the COVID-19 pandemic struck the whole world. Given UCC's focus on the local market, which was relatively stable because of the prompt and decisive actions Taiwan took to address the outbreak, the impact was minimal on the core cement business of UCC. The operations of its major clients from the construction industry remained stable. Although a few materials were imported from mainland China and their supply was somewhat disrupted, the chaos stopped soon after. That said, several long-term challenges, such as declining profitability, diminishing demand, and underdeveloped CSR strategies, were still on Chih-Sheng's work agenda.

Yet UNEO was facing a much more immediate challenge in the pandemic. Most of its suppliers were based in South Korea, Japan, and the United States, and several projects could not be launched because of the outbreak of the pandemic in these countries. As the products of UNEO were used in the equipment for factory quality assurance, the engineers had to travel to the client factories to help test the equipment, which was made impossible by the travel restrictions. Reaching breakeven in 2017 and being part of the supply chain of Apple Inc. in mid-2020, UNEO made tremendous success as a new company. To maintain its success, continued emphasis on R&D plus greater capital infusions from UCC or elsewhere were needed.

On 1 July 2020, a formal succession was announced in UCC. Chih-Sheng took the office of CEO in UCC, and Jack got a promotion from Vice President to Executive Vice President. Still, the shares of UCC were largely held in the hands of the co-founding families of the Tainan clan. Although most of them were not involved in managing the business, they kept a close eye on the financials, especially those who voted "no" when the Hou family took control of management of UCC in 2008. Chih-Sheng saw multiple goals needed to be fulfilled, in his roles as founder of UNEO and CEO of the legacy cement manufacturer. Chih-Sheng recalled the well-taught family adage by his great-grandfather, Yu-Li, which often provided guidance for family decision making: "one thing at a time." The adage reflected Yu-Li's wisdom from his tremendous success as a leading entrepreneur, but Chih-Sheng and Jack were not totally sure whether this would be the right strategy in this highly disruptive era.

LEARNING NOTES

Case synopsis

This case is based on Universal Cement Corporation (UCC), its wholly owned subsidiary of UNEO, and the fourth-generation leaders of the Hou family. Co-founded by the Hou and Wu families in 1960, UCC was a multi-family-owned, publicly traded cement manufacturer in Taiwan. Without intervening in corporate operations, the Hou family deliberately served only as a shareholder from 1989 to 2008. In 2008, the third generation of Hous took the management back and the fourth generation – Chih-Sheng and Jack Hou – started working in the family firm. Chih-Sheng, Chief Executive Officer of UCC and founder of UNEO, and his younger brother, Jack, Executive Vice President of the two firms, faced multiple challenges all at once. They needed to identify the core issues resulting in a serious loss in UCC, a 60-year-old family firm. Strategic transformation was also urgently needed for them to not only attain their legitimacy from shareholders, including descendants of the co-founding families of UCC and other relatives of the Hou family, but also secure the long-term sustainability of this family firm. In particular, its conduct of corporate social responsibilities (CSR) was seen as below par compared with its competitors. The relatively new venture of UNEO incorporated the research done by Chih-Sheng into the strategic transformation of UCC, stepping into the technology industry amid fierce competition. At the same time, UNEO needed continued investments from UCC to make it a real star. This case illustrates the difficulties faced by the two brothers in striking a balance of resource allocation between a 60-year-old traditional family firm and a ten-year-old rising star.

Learning objectives

The case draws the learners' attention to the importance of strategic renewal and implementation by next-generation leaders, especially in the setting of a multi-family firm. One of the biggest challenges family business leaders face is to ensure the long-term survivability of business while confronting emotionally charged events within the family, even more so when multiple families are involved in the business. Learners can explore how next-generation leaders should identify the drawbacks in current day-to-day activities and go beyond the operation routines to develop and renew strategies when the business faces multiple needs. The case also raises the need for executable approaches to implement the strategies.

After reading and analysing the case, learners will be able to:

- Understand the successor's curse and the difficulty in building legitimacy in a family business.
- Understand the way to develop new strategic directions while solving conflicts among family members in a family business.
- Learn the concept of strategic renewal and implementation and how they work in a family business.

Discussion questions

1. What are the pros and cons of engaging multiple families in UCC?
2. What are the goals of the Hou brothers? How should they prioritize them?
3. What will be the approach to execute the new strategic decisions in UCC?

Epilogue

A new era of UCC started amid the pandemic. In July 2020, Chih-Sheng, founder of UNEO, took the position of CEO of UCC. This indicated not only the importance of UNEO in the future of UCC, but also the formal succession from the third to the fourth generation in the Hou family. Although the pandemic had hugely impacted the business of UNEO, a prosperous future was still expected. The two brothers worked together and decided that strategic transformation was urgently needed and indispensable to the core business. Embracing the time-honoured creed of their predecessors, they believed that they should do only one thing at a time, slowly but firmly, and show a true commitment to make contributions to society, instead of simply following the popular conducts of CSR disclosures. "Put the resources to the key place, that's the true meaning of being responsible to the shareholders, employees, suppliers, clients, and of course, the public," said Jack.

Suggested readings

Chrisman, J.J., Madison, K., and Kim, T. (2021). A dynamic framework of noneconomic goals and inter-family agency complexities in multi-family firms. *Entrepreneurship Theory and Practice*, 45(4), 906–30. https://doi.org/10.1177/10422587211005775

Chung, H.M., and Au, K. (eds) (2021). *Succession and innovation in Asia's small-and-medium-sized enterprises*. Singapore: Palgrave Macmillan.

Ding, H.B., Chung, H.M., Yu, A., and Phan, P. (eds) (2021). *Innovation, growth, and succession in Asian family enterprises*. Cheltenham, UK and Northampton, MA, USA: Edward Elgar.

22
Conclusion: the lessons learned

Rodrigo Basco, Albert E. James, Nupur Pavan Bang, Andrea Calabrò, Jeremy Cheng, Luis Díaz-Matajira and Georges Samara

When we read books, we often rely on the conclusion to help us gain insights into what the authors' intended message of the book is. It is a way to establish a conversation with the authors and to confront ideas learned. As we thought about what our message should be it seemed appropriate that it should be about learning. After all, our Casebook's central aim is that cases based on real family businesses from around the world are a useful tool in educating, teaching, and training family business members. To this end, we, as editors, reflected on what we had learned from the cases we handled and how these insights might impact our future dealings with students, business families, and advisors. What follows are the lessons learned from the process of collecting, sorting, and packaging the family business stories presented in this Casebook.

Successful Transgenerational Entrepreneurship Practices (STEP) Project affiliates and collaborators engaged in developing this Casebook when the world was a different place than it is as we write these concluding thoughts. When data was collected there were no restrictions to mobility and physical social interactions. However, the COVID-19 pandemic interrupted that normal and swept our societies from their comfort zones towards a new normality. Recognizing that the pandemic represented a significant learning opportunity, we encouraged STEP Project affiliates and collaborators to return to their business families. The aim was to explore how the disruptions caused by the COVID-19 pandemic were affecting their business families and firms.

To our surprise, during a period that the economic and business press were calling "an unprecedentedly challenging time", the STEP Project affiliates and collaborators heard something else from the business families. Our interviewees, although they recognized very real health concerns, were less worried about their businesses. Business families were experiencing the pandemic as a new challenge in a long line of challenges to overcome.

Certainly, the global nature of societies' responses to the COVID-19 pandemic has led to an extraordinary period of history, but what the interviews highlighted was that the pandemic also triggered business family memories to display a common narrative to activate resilient behaviours. For years, decades, and centuries, business families have overcome external shocks – such as wars, revolutions, financial crises – and internal shocks – such as divorce, emotional crisis, loss of loved ones. Seen in this light, perhaps the COVID-19 pandemic was yet another crisis to be faced, endured, and with time, risen above.

Next, we summarize our experience as editors in five lessons we learned during the process of collecting interviews, organizing, and analysing data, and preparing and editing the case studies for this collection.

THE FIVE LESSONS LEARNED

- **Lesson I: Business families envisaged the COVID-19 pandemic as one more event in the sequence of events that are part of the collective family narrative**. The studied family businesses had already responded to revolution, occupations, unexpected deaths, family rivalry, and other family disruptions. We saw this in the Clease Auto case (Chapter 16), where the tradition of facing unexpected challenges was part of who they are as a business family – from the unexpected death of the father that pushed the current leader, John Clease, to join the family business to help his mother run the business, to the COVID-19 pandemic that sowed doubts in how to address the ongoing succession process to pass the firm from the second to the third generation. The Vesta case (Chapter 15) is an example of family businesses facing and overcoming external disruptions, in their case it was the collapse of the Soviet Union and its command economy. The Ricci Durand family case (Chapter 17) had faced critical situations over the years, such as the terrorism in Peru at the end of the 1980s, and their experience of growing stronger after their crises helped them build faith in responding to the COVID-19 pandemic. Perhaps an essential part of what makes family businesses uniquely prepared for our ever-changing world is the collective memory and knowledge held within the families. A good example of this is the Universal Cement Corporation (Chapter 21), where family members share, across generations, the family's moto of one problem at a time as a lesson learned and transmitted across generations.

- **Lesson II: In drawing upon the past to overcome the present, business families from around the globe each reacted in ways that were as diverse and individual as the families represented in our cases**. We know that businesses all faced various levels of lockdown, restrictions and constraints in their supply chains, and even their human resources were physically and psychologically affected by the pandemic. The actions and reactions reflected the unique nature of each family; much like the old proverb says: there are many paths up a mountain that lead to the same view (outcome). As in the case of Pineola Nurseries (Chapter 18), where the third-generation family member took upon herself the challenge to save the family's business when the current leaders were overwhelmed by how close to the precipice of bankruptcy the fallout from the pandemic-related shutdowns had brought the company. Taking a completely different approach to crisis, Inversora Lockey C.A. (Chapter 11) found the solution to facing their ongoing challenges in formalizing the governance of the Visani family. In this second lesson we were reminded of the heterogeneity of families in business that fires our imagination and makes our understanding, teaching, and consulting a fascinating area of scholarship.

- **Lesson III: Family firms are like a unique Pandora's box that when it is opened, all manner of problems, dilemmas, disputes, troubles, and obstacles are seen as never before, but HOPE plays an important role in their resilience.** We saw hope of transcending across generations, hope for shaping the future, hope of surviving the next crisis, and hope for reconciling family relationships. Hope, a feeling of desiring for something to happen, was the most valuable resource for all family firms we had the opportunity to embrace in the STEP Project Global Consortium as we developed this book. We learned that while all business families have their own problems resulting from external shocks or internal disturbances and their own resilient posture to interpret the past events, the future of the business family is built around hope. The case of Oleícola Jaén (Chapter 10) is a good example, focusing on olive oil tourism, AOVELAND was launched as a theme park where the family invested a lot of hope and enthusiasm by considering the importance of the park for their home community, and the sustainability of their business and industry. In the Etoffe Group case (Chapter 3), even though nothing concrete happened after the announcement of the succession plan, the next-generation leaders still saw hope from the small step the patriarch took. In the Sayla Company case (Chapter 5), despite all the stress and anxiety due to the sibling rivalry, the heir apparent kept his spirit and led the family via uncharted waters in the pandemic, even if he could choose an easier path for himself. Hoping to sustain the legacy left behind by his father, Patrick Morales of CID (Chapter 20) in the Philippines launched digital public relations services, a strategy initially rejected by his father, and injected new hope to the business. In each case there were examples of hope, the desire to achieve a yet unreached possible future, as the families endured and overcame past and present crises. After all, isn't involvement in owning a business as much an exercise in hope as it is in risk?

- **Lesson IV: Family firms were open to receive advice and recommendation from professionals to overcome difficult situations.** External help is an important pillar for family firms to take in, reflect upon, and identify possibilities from which to reinterpret traumatic situations as they occur. In the case of the Morillo-Ruiz family (Chapter 10), they used a family advisor to build a family governance system. Carmen Morillo-Ruiz summarized this idea as follows: "Someone from outside can see things more objectively without losing sight of what is really important, business continuity." In the Indian case (Chapter 4) we can observe the importance of an external advisor to incorporate/adjust internal changes to accelerate communications, improve decision making, or reduce conflicts. Rajesh Sheth – the second-generation Managing Director – brought in Nirmal Pandey, a family business consultant, to iron out the differences between Vipul Shah (a brother-in-law) and him. From the cases it seems that external advice is best heard when it comes from experts who combine expertise in their field with an understanding of the intersection of family and business. Having professionals with family business education and training is a pillar that complements family business survival.

- **Lesson V: Business families start developing their resilience behaviour via their participants' reactions to crises, traumas, and difficult situations by reliving the family history and reinforcing family values.** At the individual level, decision making seemed to always to start with the participants looking back to past events. As in the case of

Stefano Wagner (Chapter 14) who, after reliving his family's stories, decided to join his family's firm, and for Felipe de Botton (Chapter 12), who put into perspective his own family business experience to decide when and how to retire. In the case of the Schmidt family (Chapter 6), the third-generation members Marianne and Johannes decided to scrutinize what caused the severed relationship with their brother Paul and tried to learn from that experience to groom their children. Family business members turn to the past to develop narratives, which serve as inspiration for decision making, and to renew the family values across generations, which serve as a compass for decision making. We see this in the case of the Hoey family (Chapter 9) in how they found a way forward to overcomes the current crisis. At the group level, business families implement interpersonal mechanisms to develop collective resilient behaviour. Family dynamics require shared narratives to overcome frictions, make feelings explicit, and unlock frozen situations.

Shared narratives result in shared meanings which serve to unite family businesses through family leaders transferring their resilient behaviours to their firm by developing or activating governance, management mechanisms, and pivoting strategies. To counteract the effect of crises or traumas, family businesses develop governance mechanisms at family and firm level. In the case of Sjak van Noorden (Chapter 7), the family introduced several governance changes to twist the fate of the family firm from being sold and to maintain family harmony. Addressing governance gives a sense of maturity in a family business's transgenerational evolution. For the Faisal Al-Salm case (Chapter 13), the family understood the best approach for them was through management mechanisms, so they chose to rebuild the human resources of the family business by increasing the level of professionalization. In this and other cases where management mechanisms were addressed, it was clear that family leadership was important in identifying and implementing any managerial changes. Finally, in terms of pivoting strategies at firm level, resilient family firms attempt to align the business with its environment such as the case of Ronald Chan (Chapter 19), who shifted his initial plan to revitalize the firm with a premium brand product toward a lower-end brand because the COVID-19 pandemic affected the family firm consumers. Beyond the business strategy, successful business families are also able to internally pivot, in the relationship between the family and the business, when the circumstances change. As in the case of the Avendorp family (Chapter 8) who had to reconsider the best next-generation leader of the family firm because of a tragic family event. In all the examples the owning families had their own shared narratives and shared meanings from which they drew to understand the current crisis and overcome it.

The five learned general lessons must be interpreted in specific institutional and cultural contexts because context matters for specificities. The reader may think that all problems, troubles, and dilemmas of a Pandora's box are the same for all family firms and that it is possible to think that one-solution-fits-for-all family firms. However, this deductive reasoning is wrong. To illustrate why this is wrong, think about the feeling of happiness. Happiness is a feeling that embraces all of us, however what makes us happy could change from one culture to another. Even more, how we manifest the happiness varies across cultures. As we saw in the cases, for some family businesses happiness came in many guises. For some it lay in the ability to provide employment for extended family members, selling of the business, maintaining family traditions, and so on.

Family businesses and their members are embedded in multiple layers of contexts that may constrain or boost individual perceptions and reactions determining interpersonal relationships and organization mechanisms. A solution that fits for a business family in a particular time/space/context may not necessarily fit for another business family in a different time/space/context. For example, while the Sheth family in the Indian context (Chapter 4) split and distributed the family firm into three blocks to address the disruptive family dynamics, this successful solution would not be possible for Morillo-Ruiz family, the Spanish case (Chapter 10), where the third generation is planning to act as co-equal owners and leaders. This leads us to finalize our learning process with one premise: *"everything that we learned cannot be applied to your business families."* Recognizing this leads to what we consider the most important attribute of this case study book: *the opportunity to develop unique critical thinking skills.* In this sense, we expect that each of the compiled family business cases will help you, the learner, reflect on how other business families act and react to similar crises and traumas, expand your critical thinking skills to better interpret your business family, and be tolerant with the many solutions that similar problems can have. What are your learned lessons? We encourage you to take a piece of paper and write down your learned lessons with a short reflection. As part of our collective learning, we invite you to share with us and the rest of the learners your learned lessons (email your learned lesson to arpita@thestepproject.org or rodrigo@thestepproject.org), and we will place them on our web page and share with the STEP community.

INDEX

Printed and bound by CPI Group (UK) Ltd, Croydon, CR0 4YY

16/04/2025

14658496-0001